CHRISTIAN WISDOM
AND CHRISTIAN FORMATION

Christian Wisdom
and Christian Formation

THEOLOGY, PHILOSOPHY, AND
THE CATHOLIC COLLEGE STUDENT

EDITED BY
    J. Barry McGannon, S.J.
    Bernard J. Cooke, S.J.
    George P. Klubertanz, S.J.

with a FOREWORD by
    Edward B. Rooney, S.J.

SHEED AND WARD : : NEW YORK

FOREWORD

The current emphasis in every institution of higher learning in the United States is on intellectual excellence and academic achievement. "Education for excellence" has become a cliché in literate circles. Witness the number of educational conferences dedicated to this theme since Sputnik I was lofted into outer space. Honor courses have been multiplied, admission standards have been raised, course requirements have been sharpened, the curriculum has been revised. The intellect has indeed been enshrined on the campus pedestal. We live in a new "age of reason."

This is all to the good; for an emphasis that corrects an imbalance is healthy. There is no doubt but that "The House of Intellect" was to some extent in disrepair. It needed to be refurbished, refinished, perhaps remodeled. This has been done and done well. But there is a danger that this constant preoccupation with the intellect and unrelenting search for truth may lead to a dangerous myopia. Far from enriching the searcher, it may impoverish him. Man may come to limit his outlook on the world to what he can see, to the total neglect of the world of the spirit; he may so concentrate his attention on "what is" that he never looks beyond to a "why"; he may compress his vision of man to the intellect, failing to realize that man is made up of body and soul. He may forget that man has a will as well as a mind; that the will must be taught to embrace the good as the mind must see the truth; and that he must seek the truth, wherever it leads—even to God. And, knowing the truth, he must embrace the good even though it imposes moral obligations, both personal and social.

An unrelieved accent upon intellectuality to the neglect of personal and social morality, an insistence on intellectual freedom without moral restraints, is a hazardous policy to impose upon college students. Traditionally, church-related colleges have felt a definite commitment to the moral and spiritual development of their students. It may well be that in so doing they have made and are making their most distinctive contribution to American higher education. For in addition to their role as patrons and staunch defenders of the liberal arts training, the church-related colleges in the United States have historically, with the churches themselves, been the guardians of morality and the theological sources of mature spirituality. The nation as a whole, by the admission of detached observers, has profited from this influence. The decline of it is already causing a weakening in the moral fiber of the country and one hopefully looks for a new emphasis to bring into focus and balance once again the traditional values in which intellect and moral responsibility become partners in the collegiate enterprise. At least one group of colleges is making a renewed effort to keep a proper equilibrium in the pursuit of wisdom.

There are twenty-eight Jesuit colleges and universities in the United States. While each college has its own individuality, the institutional objectives of all have a common origin and a common goal. Like the leaders of all other American institutions of higher learning the presidents of Jesuit colleges are heartened with the stress on academic excellence, and they have seen to it that this stress also characterizes their own institutions. But because of their dual profession as religious and as educational leaders, they have perhaps been more alert to the necessity of seeing that the religious and moral training of their students keeps steady pace with their intellectual development. The curriculum of a Jesuit college, often applauded for its liberal arts content, includes scholastic philosophy and theology. These disciplines, even in their academic content, are particularly efficacious in their influence upon the moral, spiritual and religious life of the student. The problem is to make them more relevant and therefore more efficacious in the complex world of the sixties.

To help them attack this problem, the American Jesuit colleges and universities had the advantage, first of all, of common origins and goals; secondly, they had the advantage of an organization that could easily marshal forces most adequate for such an attack. Here surely was an instance where the Jesuit Educational Association and the unity and cooperation that are its basic purposes could be put to the best possible advantage. If it be true that philosophy and theology, authentic university disciplines in their own right, could best create the proper balance between mind and matter and could integrate the intellectual with the religious and moral training of university students, here was an opportunity to make certain that Jesuit colleges and universities were themselves achieving that balance and harmony in higher education which they claimed was one of their objectives. Moreover, by a concerted attack upon this problem they might exert a similar influence on the curricula of other higher educational institutions that sought similar goals.

From such considerations by the Conference of Presidents of Jesuit Colleges and Universities there grew the idea of the Loyola Workshop. Those who participated in the Workshop and those who have read the verbatim proceedings feel that it has created a new ferment in Jesuit colleges and universities to restore philosophy and theology to the places of honor that Newman would claim for them in a university curriculum.

This volume contains many of the papers presented at the Workshop. Interspersed with these papers is a series of essays meant to reflect the day-to-day discussions of the participants. Finally the volume records the Position Statements adopted by the Workshop on key topics which seemed to dominate the entire Workshop or which were immediate conclusions from it. In making these statements available to a wider public it is hoped that those who read will be inspired, or goaded, or provoked to mount their own attack on the crucial problem of how American colleges and universities may best serve to form not only the minds but also the hearts and the wills of their students. Lincoln once said, "This country cannot remain half-free and half-slave." If man's mind is free only to seek the truth that he can see and feel and measure, he is only half free. He will be wholly free only when he can go beyond into the realm of the spirit that will bring him to God.

> *Edward B. Rooney, S.J.*
> *President*
> *Jesuit Educational Association*

ACKNOWLEDGMENTS

The editorial committee extends sincere appreciation to the authors of the essays in this book, both to those who prepared essays originally for the Los Angeles Workshop and to those who wrote especially for this volume. We are grateful to the Jesuit Educational Association for permission to include here essays originally published as part of the Workshop Proceedings.

We wish to express very special thanks and gratitude to William Weiler, S.J., who was responsible for most of the detailed preparation of the manuscript for publication and was solely responsible for the preparation of the Index.

Our thanks go as well to Edward B. Rooney, S.J., President of the Jesuit Educational Association, to R. J. Henle, S.J., Director of the Workshop and Chairman of its Planning Committee, and to the members of the Conference of Presidents of Jesuit Colleges and Universities for their encouragement of this project.

BERNARD J. COOKE, S.J.
GEORGE P. KLUBERTANZ, S.J.
J. BARRY MCGANNON, S.J., *Chairman*

CONTENTS

CONTRIBUTORS

CARL J. BURLAGE, S.J. (Ph.D., Saint Louis), is Assistant Professor of Philosophy at Loyola University, Chicago, and Director of the Honors Program there.

W. NORRIS CLARKE, S.J. (Ph.D., Louvain), is Associate Professor of Philosophy at Fordham University and American Editor-in-Chief of the *International Philosophical Quarterly*.

BERNARD J. COOKE, S.J. (S.T.D., Institut Catholique de Paris), is Chairman of the Department of Theology at Marquette University and past president of the Society of Catholic College Teachers of Sacred Doctrine.

R. J. HENLE, S.J. (Ph.D., Toronto), is Professor of Philosophy, Academic Vice President, and Dean of the Graduate School at Saint Louis University. Past president of the Philosophy of Education Society, former editor of *The Modern Schoolman*, currently Secretary of the Executive Committee of the Council of Graduate Schools in the United States; he was Chairman of the Planning Committee and Director of the Jesuit Educational Association Los Angeles Workshop for which many of the essays appearing in this book were originally prepared.

HARRY R. KLOCKER, S.J. (Ph.D., Gregorian), is Chairman of the Department of Philosophy at Regis College, Denver, and author of *Thomism and Modern Thought*.

GEORGE P. KLUBERTANZ, S.J. (Ph.D., Toronto), is Professor of Philosophy and Dean of the College of Philosophy and Letters, Saint Louis University. Past president of the Metaphysical Society of America and of the American Philosophical Association, honorary member of the Société philosophique de Louvain, he is former editor of *The Modern Schoolman* and has authored several textbooks in metaphysics and the philosophy of man.

THEODORE MACKIN, S.J. (S.T.D., Gregorian), is Assistant Director of the Honors Division, and Chairman of the Department of Theology at the University of Santa Clara.

J. BARRY McGANNON, S.J. (Ph.D., Saint Louis), is Dean of the College of Arts and Sciences, Saint Louis University. He was Assistant to the Director of the Los Angeles Workshop.

JAMES V. McGLYNN, S.J. (Ph.D., Louvain), is Dean of the Graduate School at the University of Detroit, and former Chairman of the Department of Philosophy there.

VINCENT J. O'FLAHERTY, S.J. (S.T.D., Catholic University), is head of the Sodality Secretariat of the Missouri Province of the Jesuits. He was co-ordinator for a workshop on moral, religious, and spiritual formation held at Rockhurst College in August, 1963.

VINCENT T. O'KEEFE, S.J. (S.T.D., Gregorian), is President of Fordham University and former professor of theology at Woodstock College.

PATRICK H. RATTERMAN, S.J., is Dean of Men at Xavier University, past chairman of the Jesuit Conference of Student Personnel Administrators, and has been a member of the Executive Committee of the National Association of Student Personnel Administrators.

GERALD VAN ACKEREN, S.J. (S.T.D., Gregorian), is Associate Professor of Dogmatic Theology, Dean of the School of Divinity (St. Mary's College), Saint Louis University, Editor of *Theology Digest,* and Vice President of the Catholic Theological Society of America.

H. JAMES YAMAUCHI, S.J., is Chairman of the Department of Theology at Loyola University, New Orleans.

VICTOR R. YANITELLI, S.J. (Ph.D., Fordham), Director of Student Personnel at St. Peter's College, Jersey City, is President-Designate of the National Association of Student Personnel Administrators and will take office as President in 1964–65.

CHRISTIAN WISDOM
AND CHRISTIAN FORMATION

Part I

THE COLLEGE AND FORMATION

1

TOWARD THE EDUCATION
OF THE WHOLE MAN

J. Barry McGannon, S.J.

Most institutions of higher learning in America profess that their aim is the education of the whole man. Not education of intellect alone, but the development of character, personal integrity, moral fibre are aims expressly declared in statements of purpose. Such declarations of purpose are often more precise and explicit among private institutions, particularly church-related ones, than among many state institutions, which, it seems, do not feel as free about expressing this aim in their public statements.

The American colonial college was established to secure moral formation for its students in a Christian context, if not necessarily as the chief aim then certainly as an important one.[1] And surely the development of character has continued to be important generally in American colleges and universities.

Concern about the relevance of the Christian message in higher education and about the rise of secularism in American life has prompted periodic restatements of these aims and led to many studies on the subject.[2]

In our brief national history, education of the whole man has taken on a special meaning in many private colleges and universities. It has come to mean an education designed to instill a wisdom Christian in its orientation, and a quality of Christian formation, which it is hoped will manifest themselves in permanent habits of upright and virtuous action. Education of the whole man has never been the exclusive province of the academic disciplines, and certainly not of theology and philosophy. In addition to the academic disciplines, extra-instructional influences (such as: chapel services, religious emphasis weeks, retreats, social welfare programs, extra-curricular activities, etc.) have contributed significantly to this process of total education. Although required course sequences in philosophy and theology were original features of colonial colleges, today such required sequences are typically found only in church-related institutions, the theology sequence in most of them and the philosophy sequence only in schools under Catholic auspices.[3]

It is not surprising, then, that a group of Catholic colleges and universities should review and inquire into the nature and function of theology and philosophy as academic disciplines and how these disciplines relate to the moral, religious and spiritual formation of their students. Nor is it surprising that these Catholic institutions would want to share with American higher education ideas about their common concern for educating the whole man, and with other church-related education the findings of their common concern for instilling Christian wisdom and securing a Christian formation.

The twenty-eight American Jesuit colleges and universities participating in this study recognize that education dedicated to the development of mature human beings must take into account two interrelated factors: the milieu in which their graduates must live and the qualities which will best fit them not only to deal effectively with the world they will live in but suitably to change it.

Rapid and often unpredictable change is a characteristic note of our culture today.[4] How to meet this rapid change, adjust to it, even control it, is now a major challenge facing the college graduate. And no less a challenge faces today's educators: How to educate students not for mere survival but for leadership in an era of change? How to integrate the academic and the non-instructional aspects of student life to achieve a unified educational impact in the formation of tomorrow's leader?

Even if educators were content that their graduates be mere intelligent spectators of the drama of changes soon to come, it would be necessary to modify their educational approach to some extent. But if they expect their graduates to be shapers of this new world, molding into it the increasingly pertinent values of Christianity, then it is imperative that their students get the most effective possible formation, and in the mid-twentieth-century context.

What qualities need special development in the student of today? Michael J. Walsh, in an excellent analysis, lists three: commitment, tolerance, and flexibility.[5] By no means the exclusive possession of the educated, nor the prerogative of graduates of church-related institutions, such qualities nevertheless, when nurtured in a Christian milieu, should take on a meaning and interrelationship that is distinctive and capable of sustaining the graduates of these institutions in the kind of leadership they are expected to exercise. In the case of Catholic graduates of Catholic colleges and universities it is naturally to be expected that these qualities will take on a meaning still more specialized, though not necessarily more exclusive.

Church-related colleges and universities can, perhaps, best be described as "committed" institutions. Until recently a "bad" word in American education, "commitment" has become an accepted and an acceptable term. As committed institutions, church-related colleges and universities accept and present to their students the ideals and principles of the Judaeo-Christian tradition. They consciously present to their students a value system that runs through the humanistic experience of the race, that rests on God's revelation, that is refined in theology and philosophy, that, finally, is a basis for personal self-realization and personal action. They do not, therefore, accept the theory of "objectivity" that requires the scholar to be personally uncommitted and withdrawn. This nineteenth-century conception of "objectivity" appears now to be somewhat unreal and "naive."[6] Certainly partisanship and bias make scholarship impossible, but commitment, however strong, is not the same as a party membership, and when the commitment itself carries a sacral respect for truths, it simply reinforces the scholar's attitudes. Church-related institutions thus attempt to combine an objective pursuit of truth and understanding with the strongest personal commitment to the good. Humanly speaking, there lies here a tension between knowledge and action, between abstract consideration and concrete evaluation. But this is an inevitable tension in institutions which would form persons who are neither soliloquizing Hamlets nor unreflective actionists. If ever the world needed men of thought who were prepared to act and men of action who directed their action with knowledge and understanding, it needs them today. It is this difficult balance that church-related higher education seeks to form in its students.[7]

Three principal commitments should be strengthened in students today. For the Catholic student these are, of course, commitment to the Catholic Faith, commitment to the intellectual life and to intellectual excellence, and commitment to service of the community, both local and global.

Complementary to commitment is tolerance, the virtue that keeps the committed man, the man of zeal, from becoming a zealot. Genuine tolerance does not mean compromise, but rather a courageous commitment to one's values that neither fears contamination from contact with those of other commitments nor renders public discourse and cooperation ineffective through contentiousness or nervous quarreling.

The accelerated rate of change in the milieu in which the college graduate will move makes the quality of flexibility so important. More than a willingness to consider and test new ideas, flexibility involves the ability to adjust to new physical and spiritual situations, to radical revisions in one's environment. It implies a clear grasp of the distinction between the essential and accidental features of life that makes it possible to adhere to basic commitments despite revolutionary upheavals or cataclysmic alterations of accustomed ways of living.

It was this challenge to their students and themselves as instruments in their formation, along with the realization that educators must constantly re-examine their approaches in the light of goals to be achieved, that led the Presidents' Conference of the Jesuit Educational Association in January, 1960, to propose a workshop to explore these problems, especially in the subject-matter areas of philosophy and theology. Accordingly, a committee chaired by R. J. Henle (who was later to be the workshop director) began to lay plans for a workshop centered around this rather involved theme: the role of philosophy and theology as academic disciplines and their integration with the moral, religious, and spiritual life of the Jesuit college student.

Since this book is an outgrowth of that workshop, it will not be out of place here to review briefly the concept of the workshop and its conduct. Two years of careful planning preceded the workshop. This included studies and surveys involving the faculties of philosophy and theology and student personnel officers of the twenty-eight American Jesuit colleges and universities. The planning committee commissioned a number of papers, some to serve as general background papers, others to serve as the immediate basis for discussion during the workshop. These papers and three volumes of surveys and studies, totaling some two thousand pages in all, were distributed to the participants prior to the opening of the actual sessions.

In previous workshops of this type the isolation of different groups had prevented thorough and balanced discussion. So this meeting was structured to bring together representatives of various interest groups: presidents, deans, teachers of philosophy and of theology, student personnel officers, and regional directors of education. In the actual conduct of the workshop every sub-committee and every discussion section mirrored the diversity of the entire group. When the seventy-nine participants assembled at Loyola University in Los Angeles August 4-14, 1962, they came not as representatives of regions or institutions, but as experts in their own right, selected for their ability to contribute to the solution of problems of common concern to their own and to other American institutions of higher education. In consequence, the "position statements" (reprinted in large part in the Appendix) have as their authority the personal competence of the participants. The workshop was never intended to be a legislative body for Jesuit schools.

To make it possible to accomplish something precise within the limits of a workshop, the theme was devoted to the academic disciplines of philosophy and theology because these disciplines are a common and important core in the undergraduate programs of American Jesuit colleges and universities. This does not imply that humanistic studies and the social sciences are unimportant for the moral, religious and spiritual formation of the student. As a matter of fact, during the workshop it was constantly recognized that the humanistic and social disciplines particularly had an important relationship not only to philosophy and theology but to the total development of the student, and the hope was expressed that future workshops on this theme would involve the humanities. In the same way it was suggested that future workshops include laymen in the discussions.

Of the papers circulated prior to the Workshop and discussed either directly or indirectly during it, a number appeared to have a general relevance to the wider audience not only of Catholic, but also of other church-related, and indeed of all American, higher education. If such papers were published individually, the common theme would be lost. It was decided, therefore, that this book should be prepared as an outgrowth of, though not a report on, the workshop, a book which would preserve the common theme by the publication of selected papers and which would further amplify and unify that theme by the addition of specially commissioned essays. In this volume, then, are ten essays selected from the papers circulated prior to the workshop. Four other essays were prepared specially for this book. Chapter 13 is actually an extension of the work of the Los Angeles Workshop in that it derives its inspiration from a workshop on moral, religious and spiritual formation held at Rockhurst College in Kansas City in August, 1963. Chapters 7, 11, and 15 appear for the first time. It was felt that much of the value of the workshop would be lost if no consideration were given to the interchange of ideas which took place during the discussions and to the consequent rethinking of basic positions on the part of the participants. A summary of workshop discussions was out of the question in a book of this length, owing to the great diversity of opinions expressed and the rethinking that has gone on since the workshop. It seemed best, therefore, to choose three participants to present their own personal views in the light of their experiences at the workshop and in the light of their reflection on these ideas over the succeeding year. They were free, of course, to draw upon the discussions and on the "position statements" adopted by workshop participants. These three essays are, then, at once the fruit of the workshop and the personal views of their authors. A substantial portion of these "position statements" are included as an appendix to this volume.

Many of the chapters are followed by a short bibliography which is the personal selection of the author of the chapter. The items listed are not intended as a complete survey of relevant literature, but rather supplementary readings either by way of amplification or contrast to the ideas expressed in the chapter. A short general bibliography concludes the book.

The pluralism of ideas and attitudes toward academic disciplines and student formation within the Society of Jesus (Jesuits) has more than once been commented on. This pluralism has made it impossible to summarize all that was said at the workshop. It also explains why the workshop attempted no such impossible and thought-stifling task as that of legislating some kind of official "Jesuit position" on such complicated problems. Still less, therefore, can this volume, edited on the subjective judgment of the editorial committee, and containing the subjective reflections of experts a year after the conference, claim to be official in any way. It seeks rather to stimulate serious thought and discussion through the presentation of ideas which the editorial committee considers significant.

If there is much room for pluralism within one religious order of the Catholic Church, there is certainly much more within the Church at large. For example, Chapter 12 is an attempt to apply the principles of Jesuit spirituality to the formation of the college student. It does not imply that the spirituality distinctive of the Society of Jesus is the only way students can be formed. Rather it seeks to show, using Jesuit spirituality as an example, how the spirit distinctive of the members of one religious order can be applied to the formation of lay men and women between the ages of eighteen and twenty-two. Certainly the spiritualities of other religious orders can be applied to student formation in the same way, resulting in a formation which will be similar in fundamentals but different in emphasis. The focus in Chapter 12, as elsewhere is on the Catholic student, but the application extends as well to students of other religious persuasions.

What is said in this book, then, is more broadly applicable than merely to Catholic higher education. The problems here explored and the principles offered in solution are applicable to all education concerned with the education of the whole man, to all education which recognizes a responsibility extending beyond the merely academic and including the perfecting of the total person.

The problems are real. They affect all segments of American higher education. The explorations of these problems given here are based on a sincere quest for truth and the solutions offered are scarcely complete. But it is hoped that they will provide the foundation for further explorations and more complete solutions. In this quest all those are invited to join who are dedicated to educating the whole man.

Notes

1. Frederick Rudolph, *The American College and University: A History* (New York: Knopf, 1962), pp. 6 ff.
2. The Commission on Christian Higher Education of the Association of American Colleges issued "A Statement on Christian Higher Education," *Association of American Colleges Bulletin,* XLIII (1957), 503–505. The

Hazen Foundation has sponsored important studies on this topic, among them *Religious Perspectives in College Teaching* (New York: Ronald Press, 1952). See also *Religion in Education: An Annotated Bibliography*, compiled by Joseph Politella (Oneonta, New York: American Association of Colleges for Teacher Education, 1956). A recent book which treats, among other things, of the importance of theology in a complete education is Nathan Pusey's *The Age of the Scholar* (Cambridge: Belknap Press, Harvard, 1963). The Danforth Foundation, long interested and active in the area of church-related education, is presently (1964) conducting a comprehensive study of church-related colleges and universities, under the direction of the Danforth Commission on Church Colleges and Universities.

3. Rudolph, *op. cit.,* pp. 28–32.
4. Laurence J. McGinley, S.J., "The Challenge of Today's World to Our Graduates," *Final Report of the Workshop on the Role of Philosophy and Theology as Academic Disciplines and Their Integration with the Moral, Religious and Spiritual Life of the Jesuit College Student* (New York: Jesuit Educational Association, 1962), pp. 94–106.
5. Michael J. Walsh, S.J., "The Challenge to Our Colleges to Meet the Needs of Future Alumni," *Final Report,* pp. 108–114.
6. The word is used in this context by E. Harris Harbison in "History," *Religious Perspectives in College Teaching* (New York: Ronald Press, 1952), p. 6.
7. R. J. Henle, S.J., "The Centrality of Liberal Education and the Disciplines" (unpublished manuscript).

2

OBJECTIVES OF THE CATHOLIC LIBERAL ARTS COLLEGE

R. J. Henle, S.J

The ultimate goal of all Christian activity is the achievement of man's last end, his supernatural destiny and the glory of God. This end, however, does not specify or determine any specific activity. There is no activity which receives its being and its formal nature solely and simply from an ordination to man's last end. For example, even the nature of supernatural love is determined, at least partially, by the nature of man. The supernatural order presupposes the order of nature; and, in man, the direction to the end must take place by the incorporation and elevation of all that great variety of activities which constitute the life of man. All these activities display a specific diversity constituted by their own intrinsic natures and their own intrinsic finalities and, consequently, have a specific and intrinsic kind of goodness; they are values. When they are subsumed, therefore, under a supernatural end, they are subsumed according to what they are, as the values they are, perhaps indeed intrinsically elevated and transformed, but not annulled or destroyed. Grace does not destroy nature; the supernatural does not place a moratorium on the laws of nature and is not a simple denial of the order of natural goods.

No doubt the relationship of nature and the supernatural is a perennial theme for Christian speculation and continually poses, for Christian prudence, perplexing practical problems. Yet, one thing at least is clear: Christian prudence can make no adequate decision unless the activity which is being submitted to judgment is understood in its own nature. Moreover, when an activity is to be directed to man's supernatural end, it is *this* activity with its own intrinsic formalities and intrinsic finalities which must be so directed. There are indeed cases in which the supernatural end itself demands or justifies the renunciation of activities. Thus, the martyr embraces death; the monk chooses his vows. But the case is quite different when the supernatural goal is to be achieved through and in an activity; for in this case the perfecting of the activity itself, as such, is imposed and demanded by the very ordination to God. If, for example, a man, under the impulse of supernatural motives, chooses the vocation of a doctor, the obligations of competence and responsibility, according to the nature of medicine, become thereby not less but more binding.

In any case, it is clear that the formalities and finalities of subordinate activities cannot be simply deduced from the ultimate ordination to the last end and that the decisions of Christian prudence will depend, therefore, not only on a clear acceptance of the supernatural, but also, and without exception, on a clear understanding of and respect for the nature of the human activities involved.

In the problem which we are here facing, we have a case, not of rejection of natural goods or activities in view of a higher good but of the ordination to supernatural ends of the activities which make up the operation of a college. It is in and through collegiate activities that we intend and hope to achieve supernatural values and goals. If, then, we have, as Christians, committed ourselves to the achievement of supernatural purposes through collegiate activities (and I take this to be a settled commitment), the necessary practical judgments require a full and accurate understanding of collegiate activities. A retreat house, a hospital, a college are all different, though all three may be operated for the glory of God. It is not this end which differentiates them; and it would be absurd to operate, in virtue of this common end, a hospital along the lines of a college, or a college along the lines of a retreat house. To concretize the end, to embody and specify it, we must relate collegiate activities, according to their own intrinsic nature, to that end. Thus and only thus can the ultimate end become an operative and immanent finality.

The Nature of the American Catholic Liberal Arts College

It is obvious, therefore, that we must ask ourselves: What are collegiate activities? I should like to call attention here to a distinction which will be useful at several points in our discussion. You will have noticed that I am using the term "collegiate activities" to embrace all those activities which together make up the operation of a college. Now, these activities are, as a matter of fact, of different kinds—teaching, counseling, athletics, etc.— and the immediate intrinsic finality of each kind of activity is specific to it. It is, therefore, useful to distinguish the over-all finality of the college as an institution from the immediate finality of each kind of activity within it.

What, then, is the nature of a college, what is its intrinsic institutional character and finality? Perhaps such questions cannot be properly asked in regard to a college; for the concepts of nature, intrinsic form, and intrinsic finality properly apply to a being substantially constituted as such in nature. Man, for example, can be properly analyzed through these concepts; but a college is not a substantial entity and is not an entity given in and determined by nature.

As an institution the college—and I am now speaking specifically of the American liberal arts college—is a social creation. It is not totally determined by the nature of things, nor even by nature manipulated by man, as, for example, the electric dynamo or the atomic bomb is determined. No doubt, the college is determined to some extent by the nature of man and of knowledge, but its precise structure and function is the result also of human desires and decisions—carried certainly by social and cultural media—

social decisions indeed, but still open to reconsideration and to change. To some extent at least, the college has no final determinate form, no absolute and inviolable character, no ideal glowing in a Platonic heaven by which all struggling individual colleges are to be judged. Thus, for example, the American liberal arts college is a unique institution in the history of the West. I do not find any truly comparable institution either in past history or in contemporary Europe. The college, to some extent, is what we decide to make it, is what we want it to be. Once again, however, in making our decision we cannot ignore either the nature of things or the contingent human situation in which we find ourselves. Once the function of the college is socially determined, we can examine the activities required for that function, remembering, again, that these activities, because of their own nature, bring their own formal determination with them.

Let us then examine the actual nature of the college within our society.

Now, the college is part of our system of higher education; that is, of the American university system. By a social and cultural commitment, the university is, in our culture, the one institution that is formally dedicated to truth as such; that is, to intellectual knowledge, to its extension and development, to its preservation and communication. However necessary truth and knowledge may be in all other parts of culture, there is no other institution whose primary concern is the cultivation of truth and knowledge. The university's obligation to society is, therefore, its obligation to truth; or, its obligation to truth is its obligation to society. The college, as part of the university system, falls under this same commitment and carries this same obligation.

The activities of a college must be governed by the truth and must communicate truth. It cannot become an instrument of propaganda, a mere training-ground for partisans; its only prejudice is to favor the truth, and its training is in the light of truth. In its dedication to truth lies its right to independence from all vested interest and private purpose, from political parties, from statism as well as clericalism. From this dedication arises also the obligation of the professor not to make his position an opportunity for the enforced indoctrination of personal opinions and prejudices. The nature of the college as an institution established by a social commitment within our culture is partially specified by a dedication to knowledge and to truth. This is also a partial specification of its service to society as a social institution. But, though this dedication is established by social commitment, it follows, precisely because this dedication is to the *truth,* that the nature of knowledge and truth (*which is not dependent upon social decisions*) governs the activities of the college.

But the college is only one of the specifically different institutions which make up our system of higher education. Though dedicated to the truth, it is yet differentiated from other parts of the system by special objectives. It is not dedicated, like the technical or professional schools, to the training of competent practitioners or professional men, or, like the graduate school, to pure research and scholarship. By a social commitment, it is dedicated to the development of mature human beings. Its diploma does not pretend to certify that its graduate is an accountant or a doctor or an engineer; it presents its graduates to society as developed human beings. This is also the aim of primary and secondary education; what distinguishes the college is the level of maturity at which it operates and the dedication to truth under which it operates. Its aim is not indeed to achieve full maturity—for this is a lifelong process—but to establish human personality basically in its proper human self-possession and independence. This is the social commitment of the college as we find it in our society; and it is ratified in our time, indeed re-emphasized, by the expectations of students and parents, of the Church, and of society at large.

Again, though the college is established by a social commitment as an institution for the development of human beings, once so established it must be governed, in all its activities, by the truth about human nature; and *this* does not depend upon a social decision or consensus.

Thus we find the college dedicated to truth and to the development of human beings; it is both truth-centered and student-centered. Some would see in this twofold dedication an internal contradiction, but in fact there is no contradiction. For the development of human beings at a mature level and the basic establishment of human personality are achieved primarily through the acquisition of knowledge and truth; and, indeed, all the development of human beings must be guided by knowledge and truth. The two aims are not incompatible and, indeed, to a certain extent and in various ways, become in practice identical. Moreover, the college, under this double dedication, is, as a social institution, ordered to the service of society, both natural—the state and cultural society—and supernatural—the Church. But it is in and through the primary double dedication that this service is rendered.

The ideal of developing human beings does, of course, include a broader group of objectives than intellectual growth. When, however, we are speaking of the college, the central specification, the primary distinctive character, lies in its ordination to knowledge and truth. All development and all human growth involve moral goodness and supernatural virtue; on the other hand, a college education is not absolutely necessary to salvation or even high virtue. For those who do not want intellectual culture, many other means and agencies exist to aid the growth of human beings and the achievement of virtue. The college exists as an institution precisely to supply intellectual culture; this is its specific contribution and basic means to human development. Thus from another angle of consideration we find the college's dedication to truth and to human development resolved into a harmonious and intellectually specified unity.

The objective, therefore, of the Catholic liberal arts college is to achieve the glory of God by (1) developing human beings as such to maturity in and through a dedication to truth and intellectual culture and (2) thereby serving Society and the Church.

The Idea of Man

Obviously, the objective of developing mature human beings has no real meaning unless it subsumes an idea of human nature and an ideal of human development. The development to be fostered and the means to be selected depend upon the truth about human nature, knowledge of what it is and what it can and ought to be.

It is a matter of observation that men live and grow through an interaction with their environment. If all man's contacts with the reality surrounding him were sealed off, he would be unable to grow, indeed unable to exist. Man's nature demands reality at every level: food, light and air for physical life, a field of action, objects to know and to love. His development and growth are, therefore, conditioned by two interrelated factors: (1) his subjective potentialities and powers and (2) the realities over against which he stands and of which he is a related part.

If we look for what is previous and peculiar in man, we find it in those activities which make up his conscious life. Certainly the physical reality, activity, and development of man's body are part of his life; but all these have meaning for him only in so far as they undergird, make possible, and are dependent upon his conscious life. Certainly, too, we analyze man into substance, soul, faculties, and habits; but the nature and indeed the existence of all these we only discover through the activities of consciousness wherein likewise his being, as peculiarly human, develops and expands in act and in acquired habit. Without this conscious life, there is no possibility of personal development, of society, or of human happiness.

The activities of consciousness are immanent; they constitute an "inner" life and growth. And yet they are "intentional" and relational, relating men to reality. They are the ways in which man relates himself to his environment, to the universe, to other men, indeed to himself; through them he sets up an intercourse with all reality, through which alone he himself grows and, by taking unique possession of reality through knowledge and love, becomes more himself and, through grace finally, more than himself.

Philosophy and theology, as well as the main humanistic traditions of the West, have seen in man's ability to know and to love (essentially immanent relational activities) the highest and noblest level of man's life. And as soon as we recognize the nature of knowledge and love, we understand that no "geographical" limits can be placed around man's environment. By a stroke, the stroke of intelligence, his environment sweeps out to the limits of reality itself and becomes co-terminous with and inclusive of all things. The mere fact that he can conceive such a wholesale transcendence of limits displays radically the impossibility of delimiting his environment and enclosing the sweep of his knowledge and love. Hence his insatiable thirst for knowledge, his hunger for good and beauty and that high good which is the love of persons, human and divine.

Knowing and loving are indeed relational activities, but of their very nature they are immanent in consciousness and inseparable from self-awareness. They are fully possessed and fully realized only when held in conscious reflection, by which both the self and its objects are fully grasped. Only at this level of reflective realization are both the self and the whole of reality truly possessed, immanently indeed, yet as they really are. At this level then, a personal control of truth and a rational control of self which are essential to personal maturity appear; thus is human nature established in individual and personal self-possession; the personality is brought to actuality within consciousness. Thus also from the very nature of knowing and loving, an ideal of the perfection of knowing and loving arises; not only do we know things, but we know we know and we can know why we know; not only do we love and choose, we know we love and choose and can know why.

The relations set up between man and his environment are thus reduplicative; reality is fully possessed only in self-possession, which in turn is possible only through possession of the real.

It is within this context that responsibility and freedom, maturity and human perfection must be understood. Intelligence is not wholly intelligence in act until it is reflective intelligence; the pursuit of good is not wholly human or itself good until it is consciously and reflectively understood and directed.

This is the view of man to which the West has been traditionally committed and is still, though often unconsciously, committed. It is undoubtedly the view to which the Catholic educator is committed and which, therefore, must be a guiding ideal in Catholic liberal education. And Divine revelation has shown us that, from the supreme liberality of Love, God has set as the final term of man's growth and development the complete fulfillment of that hunger and thirst for reality which displays itself in knowing and loving. This term is, however, a trans-terrestrial good; yet not unrelated to present living, for it is precisely the goal of each human life as it is lived here.

From the standpoint of educational theory and truth, the growth of human beings must be continuously—and hence through college —a growth towards the supreme fulfillment, the vision of Truth itself. Moreover, this term—though it is supernatural—is not unnatural and, indeed, presupposes nature, and, ideally, the full development of nature. Just as grace perfects and does not destroy nature, so supernatural growth enters into, without violating, the proper development of nature. Man's life here is, therefore, not an idle and leisured expectancy of the Beatific Vision; he must live and grow within his total environment and so achieve the fullness of life.

So we come back to a detailed analysis of man's environment. Obviously, taken in the full sense, seen without limits, it transcends time and space and locates man within reality quite independently of the contingent circumstances of his immediate environment. Hence, the release from complete relativity, the common transcendence, the common ultimates which lace through the life of all men and are common elements of all human maturity and make possible human community. But though man lives and moves within this ultimate framework, which being the ultimate frame of reality must be also, in so far as possible, the frame of his conscious activities, he yet does find himself within a changing environment, defined by contingent events, the immediate culture within which he must live and act. Hence, though each individual must indeed possess himself in ultimate fashion by relating himself to the unchanging ultimates of all human existence and growth, as an individual he must grow, develop, and expand his personality, unleash his activity in relation to a society which embodies and determines the common elements of humanity in a defined and limited culture. To be a full human being he must indeed become a citizen of the universe, simply man; but to be a fully formed human individual he must find his individualized growth within his own time and his own culture; he must live in his own age and his own time, knowing its distinctive realization of human living and assuming its distinctive forms of responsibility. The medieval man, the renaissance man, the modern American man, however united in a common humanity and sharing the same ultimate transcendence, will, when fully educated, be specifically differentiated and must be differentiated, if each is to be, as fully as possible, a human person.

Human Development

In the light of this general idea of man, let us now make a schematic study of human development. Since it is the development, in the full sense, of man's conscious activities—which by nature are related to objects—we can consider it from the standpoint either of the subject related or of the objects of these relationships.

This distinction of viewpoint serves as a base for a distinction in educational theory, one which indeed is necessary; for man

grows not only in extending the reach and range of his relationships, but also, on the subjective side, by deepening and enriching
his capacities for wider and richer relationships. This is not to say,
of course, that the growth in capacities does or can take place
independently of the acquisition of objects.

Therefore, a fundamental objective of any education must be
the development of man's capacities for conscious living.

At this point we must borrow from the philosophy of man.
Several points may be summarized.

(1) We find that, within man's conscious life, activities of quite
different kinds are revealed. We distinguish on this immediate
evidence an order of sense (seeing, tasting, etc., imagining, etc.,
desiring, etc.) and an order of intellect (reasoning, knowing, etc.,
willing, deciding, etc.) and, within each order, we distinguish the
awareness of knowledge from the attitudes of appetition, etc.

(2) We find that these various activities, though distinguishable,
do not take place in isolation; they interweave in a pattern of
mutual dependence and mutual influence. Within this pattern we
can perceive certain relationships given with the very nature of the
activities, e.g., deciding is dependent upon knowledge, appetite
upon sense perception and imagination, etc. Moreover, we find,
in actual human experience, a certain confusion and disorder,
a certain struggle among these activities, which belie the basic
order of the pattern.

(3) Thus, when considered in their total reality and as existentially given, the activities of consciousness reveal the possibility
of a certain "rightness" of operation and interordering which,
though not a given fact, ought to be. Though conclusions often
enough rest on prejudice rather than arguments, though decisions
often enough are made in the heat of passion rather than in the
calm of reasonable consideration, we understand that a different
situation ought to exist.

(4) Thus an ideal is set for the educator which has a twofold
aspect—the development of rich capacity within each kind of

activity and the development of the right order, the rightness of integration among the whole group of activities.

Thus, the objective of developing mature human beings is seen to include the objective of developing man's capacities in all the varieties of conscious activities in right relationship to one another and to reality.

Human Knowledge

Let us look now at the knowledge side of the human activities. In the development of human culture, knowledge relationships have been refined into different approaches to reality, made possible partly by the nature of things themselves, partly by the specific character of man's knowing, and partly by the creativity and ingenuity of the human mind. I distinguish here five different approaches: the humanistic, the philosophical, the scientific, the theological, the mathematical. All of these arise indeed out of man's primitive encounter, in individual experience, with reality and out of his spontaneous questioning of that experience; but they are consciously refined, requiring, therefore, the development of capacities and habits—even artificial ones—and the conscious possession of techniques and methodologies.

As there is no room here for a full discussion of these, a brief characterizing description of each is necessary.

The humanistic approach is characterized by a certain concrete completeness. It deals with an object in its concrete reality without abstracting aspects or even elements; in a sense it reaches and sees reality in the round and in its living fullness. In its refined form— as in the portrayal of human life in drama—it exercises a subtle selectivity; but this selectivity results in a concrete emphasis rather than in an abstract universality. But the approach itself is likewise integral on the side of the subject; for while the humanistic approach includes the operation of intellect and will, it also includes emotion and imagination and whatever other factors analysis may reveal in man's conscious life. Thus it is concrete and non-abstractive; it is not purely intellectual but is a combined and integrated operation of all man's conscious activities. Thus, for example, when one reads a great play like *Hamlet* or *Macbeth* and observes human beings living in concrete and particularized situations and reacts to this play not by cold analysis or abstractive generalization but by a living sympathy that engages direct intellectual understanding, emotional sympathy, and undifferentiated conscious absorption, he is engaged in a humanistic activity. In this broad and loosely defined area, therefore, belong literature, the arts, and history (when it is not a "science").

The philosophical approach is distinguished from the humanistic, first of all, in that it is an activity of pure reflective intelligence working upon actual experience. There is, therefore, a kind of subjective abstraction which puts aside the influence and co-activity of emotion and will and makes of imagination a purely extrinsic instrumentality. The object is examined in so far as it is, in its own real nature, intelligible. Philosophy does not try to correlate or organize things in some extrinsic way, but to *understand* them as they are, in so far as this is possible to man's intellect. It deals, therefore, with reality as it is and drives towards understanding that reality as it is and so reaches out for ultimate real—not hypothetical, theoretical, or constructural—explanations of all reality.

Science, likewise, is a refined discipline of pure intelligence. However, it does not directly deal with the intelligible nature of things; it is concerned with the interrelation of facts, the organization of data only indirectly related to the real nature of things; it draws out generalizations of facts, elaborates constructural concepts and constructural theories. Its methodology opens the way for a vast intellectual effort of nature and an enormous application of knowledge to practical matters, but it does not drive through to the ultimate meaning of things or the ultimate real explanation of the world.

Theology differs from other disciplines in that its point of departure does not lie in experience but in revelation and that its basic data are not found by man but are truths accepted from God. The effort of human intelligence, using all its resources, to understand the facts of revelation gives rise to the discipline of theology. The elaboration of the data of Faith into a refined discipline may be carried out in two different ways. Understanding may be developed by using the insights and methods of the humanities (as in much Patristic theology) or by using the insights and conclusions of philosophy. In the latter case "scientific" or "scholastic" theology results; in the first case a humanistic type of theology is worked out.

Mathematics is also a discipline of pure intelligence, which, by an idealizing elaboration of experience, develops a purely intellectual world of intelligible entities which yet are applicable to physical problems in the real world.

All these disciplinary approaches to reality are developed, indeed, in function of man's basic powers; but they are formally different developments, each bringing a new and different dimension to man's intercourse with reality.

Consequently our objective of developing man's capacities in all the varieties of conscious activities is found to include the development of the basic habits of the great distinctive approaches to reality in the order of knowledge.

How are these approaches to be ordered? Since they are ways of knowing, specifically different knowledge habits, they can be interrelated only by someone who knows the ways in themselves and who understands them precisely as *kinds* of human knowledge. Thus, one must be able to evaluate, compare, and order these knowledges according to their nature as knowledge. This requires a philosophical theory of knowledge subsequent to and, at least partially, based on a personal experience of these ways of knowing.

Thus we must add to the statement of objectives just given: "and an understanding of the nature and interrelationships of these approaches."

Character and Virtue

We have already seen that the college, since it aims at the development of full human personalities and since it is established by social demand and commitment as a training institution for young people, must include in its aims the development of that side of personality defined as moral virtue or moral character (which, in a Catholic college, is subsumed under the ideal of the supernatural character). Now it is clear that character, virtue, and motivation are related to and in some sense dependent upon knowledge and reflective intelligence. It is a commonplace both of ordinary experience and of philosophy that knowledge must precede love; reflection, choice; right understanding, right action; and Faith, charity. Yet it is also true that loving and choosing, appreciating and valuing are not the same as, not reducible to or simply to be deduced from, knowledge and understanding. The mere possession of knowledge does not entail, as a necessary consequent fact, rightly ordered loves or rightly ordered actions. Virtue, therefore, as a personal and effective possession, cannot be taught, as can science or philosophy, history or literature. The development of character can be promoted by persuasion and exhortation, by example and counsel, by the guided opportunities for personal reflection, choice, and action. Even so, virtue remains an intensely personal and privileged possession. Character and virtue cannot, therefore, properly be the direct objective of the specifically academic activity of the college, of the classroom and lecture hall. Teaching of its nature results immediately in knowledge and understanding and the personal grasp of truth. Yet, the very teaching itself is not unrelated to the development of personal character. Increased understanding helps to heighten appreciation and a strengthening of the choice of good. Moreover, while the primary activity of the classroom is teaching, the total situation is larger; for a human being teaches human beings within a social setting. A pure intelligence does not go to school to personified mathematics; an individual human student learns mathematics from a human teacher. The impact of personality on personality, all the subtle influences of social association, are inevitable and indeed sharpened by the situation itself. Obviously, the effectiveness of this indirect influence on character will be a matter of degree, varying with the individual teacher, the sort of subject taught, the receptivity of the student, and the mode of teaching.

While the direct and immediate objective of teaching, imposed by the very nature of the teaching activity, is understanding and knowledge (a fundamental nature which must not be violated), the concrete teaching situation will also be controlled by the general objective of the college as an institution for the development of human beings, hence also for the development of virtue and moral and supernatural character.

Since the college as an institution aims at the full development of human personalities, its objective includes the development of moral virtue and supernatural character. However, since the immediate objective of the teaching (and, in general, academic) activities of the college is understanding, knowledge, and truth, the development of character can be an objective of *teaching* only secondarily and indirectly (1) through the intrinsic influence of knowledge on character, (2) through the incidental effects of the teaching situation. The college may and indeed should promote character development through other activities (e.g., religious counseling, retreats, etc.) directly ordered to virtue.

Mode of Teaching

If teaching is to be defined as communication of knowledge, the word communication must be carefully interpreted. For knowledge is not a commodity, chunks of which can be distributed to the students as their share and possession. Knowledge exists only within the activity of an individual mind; it is a highly personal product and a personal possession. The teacher induces rather than produces knowledge; he directs, guides, prepares—but learning is

the student's own activity. The teacher can skillfully set the
intellectual stage and manipulate the scenery and props, but
understanding depends on the intellectual vision and the intellectual activity of the student.

Moreover, knowledge has degrees of perfection. To possess
knowledge fully is to have a full intellectual insight into and understanding of the object considered; it is to have *true* knowledge
and to know that it is true and why it is true; it is to know with
certitude because the evidence is grasped and possessed. When
this sort of knowledge is reached, the perfection of knowledge is
achieved; the student has become independent of teacher and
books; he knows simply and without qualification.

At this level the student brings knowledge to perfection in
the possession of certitudinal truth.

In order to achieve this high possession, and, indeed, in and
through the very achieving of it, the student develops the capacities, the intellectual virtues, the attitudes, habits, methods, and
techniques which increase his capacities for understanding and
knowledge. The capacities of the student are deepened by the
very activities which bring them to full actualization; while, by the
deepening of capacities, fuller actualization becomes possible.

Now, whether one views this process of learning from the
standpoint of the development of capacities or from that of the
progressive conquest of reality through knowledge and understanding, it is this process which defines the proper objective and
the intrinsic nature of "teaching." Thus we define in general the
primary and indispensable purpose of the formal teaching activities
of the college.

The process of teaching may indeed be modified by the cross-
play of other legitimate aims. We may require that, in the concrete,
teaching activity be carried out in such a way as to promote virtue
and to allow the influence of mature and spiritual personalities full
play. But however important these aims may be, they must, in
the teaching situation, be secondary to, indeed, incidental to, the
primary activity of teaching. Certainly, considerations specific to

Christian culture, to particular vocations, and to contemporary needs and demands may help us select the areas in which truth is to be achieved and intelligence developed. But within these areas the teaching activities will aim, immediately and of themselves, not at piety but at knowledge and understanding, not at mere indoctrination of right answers but at the personal possession of truth, the ideal perfection of knowledge. To forget that this is the primary intrinsic end of teaching, to regard it as a mere occasion for producing pious Catholics, is to forget and ignore the proper nature of the truth and of man himself.

The sort of teaching here described as being teaching in the proper sense must be clearly distinguished from that sort—better perhaps called "training"—which aims at imparting certain bodies of knowledge or techniques in order to enable the student to perform some definite action. Thus to train a nurse to take a blood count, to train a man to run a complicated machine or to keep books or pull a tooth, requires the communication of certain kinds of knowledge. This sort of teaching or training does not aim at understanding or truth, it does not aim at the development of the human being in himself; the knowledge given, the mode of its communication, and the perfection of its possession are all dictated by the requirements of the desired practical action. Hence, it is not teaching properly so called; and, precisely, it is not liberal teaching.

The teaching activities of the college will be determined, therefore, by

(1) the primary and intrinsic reciprocal objective of, on the one hand, developing the full capacities of the student, and, on the other hand, bringing him to a personal possession of understanding and knowledge;

(2) the general intrinsic objective of the college as an institution (secondary objective of teaching activities)—to develop moral and supernatural character. This objective may indeed modify and influence the teaching activities of the college, but it cannot interfere with the intrinsic objective of teaching as such—much less substitute for it.

The primary and intrinsic objective which we have laid down for the teaching activities of the college is indeed a realistic objective but sets up an ideal for achievement. For it is difficult to attain its full perfection in any one field or in any one student, impossible to attain in all matters, even in all basic matters. In fact, such mastery of knowledge even in a single field remains the specific objective of graduate education, that mastery of which the doctorate is education's highest symbol; but even in graduate education it remains an ideal that is only partially reached.

Yet, it remains the absolute goal of intellectual development and of all good teaching. If it is impossible of attainment in all fields of learning in the college, we must as a second-best be content with a certain amount of partial knowledge, of indoctrination and acceptance of authority.

But partial knowledge is dangerous, and indoctrination and authority cannot be accepted by a mature mind unless there is a controlling personal grasp of fundamentals which in principle justify them. If the practical limitations of college make partial and authoritative knowledge inevitable, the demands of intellectual maturity make indispensable a personal grasp of an ultimate frame of reference.

This personal grasp is primarily to be attained in religion, philosophy, and the humanities. First, as we have seen, these knowledges are ontological in character; secondly, they touch ultimates of the most vital and universal significance for human life; thirdly, personal insights and understanding are possible, even for undergraduates, at certain points in all three.

Consequently, no course or sequence of courses should be considered as a substantive part of liberal education unless

(1) they are taught in such a way as *to aim primarily* at the twin goals of developing the capacities of the student and of bringing him to a personal possession of truth at its highest level;

(2) they are handled in the total concrete situation in such

a way as to promote, indirectly and in function of, dependent on the primary goal, the growth of personal character;

(3) as part of a curriculum or individual program, they make a specific and definite contribution to the total development of student capacities, to the areas selected for truth-mastery, and to the total pattern of integrated knowledge and ordered love.

Objectives in Subject-Matter Areas

We pointed out above that man's total relationship to his total environment could be viewed from the standpoint either of the subject related or of the objects of the relationships. To adopt the second viewpoint is to speak, in academic language, of subject-matter areas. Very briefly, the general objectives may be interpreted, within curriculum objectives, as follows:

(1) Those subject-matter areas should be included which, because of their nature, relate man to his ultimate environment and thereby reveal the ultimate meaning and explanation of human life and of reality. Here are areas common to all liberal education, quite independent of contingent and changing circumstances.

(2) Those areas should be selected which will make a personal experience of the great approaches to reality and will reveal the nature and interrelationship of these approaches. These areas are likewise common, in principle, to all liberal education but depend in detail upon the cultural maturity of the various disciplines.

(3) Those areas should be selected which will relate the student to his own immediate environment and so prepare him to understand, criticize, and live in the culture and times which are his own.

(4) Those subjects and aspects and parts of subjects should be selected which, because of their nature, or because of psychological reasons, or because of contingent circumstances, will make the strongest impact on the student and stimulate thereby the profoundest personal intellectual and humanistic development.

(5) Within the integrated pattern of subject-matters, while the objective of personal possession of truth and understanding should

always be maintained as an ideal, a realistic objective of developing personal insight at basic points should be carried out—at points, that is, such as are essential for a personal grasp of the ultimate frame of reference and such as are necessary for a critical acceptance of right authority and of knowledge and direction from competent authorities.

(Note: The most effective liberal courses are those which achieve multiple objectives. This is particularly possible in the humanities because of the concrete richness of the subject-matter and the full involvement of human powers required.)

APPENDIX I
THE FREE MAN

It is sometimes said that the object of liberal education is to produce the free man. Freedom viewed as an internal character of personal activity is grounded in the transcendental character of intellect and will as correlative to being with its intelligibility and its goodness. The possession of intelligence makes it possible for man to rise above the relativistic determinations of his physical and social environment and to judge, to love, and to choose in an absolute and objective way. Intelligence becomes operative for freedom through reflection; to extend the power and range of intelligence is to extend the range of both freedom and responsibility. The subjective conditions of freedom, making possible a direction of will under reflective intelligence, lies in the controlling right order of moral virtue. If passions are rampant, reflection is impossible and a man finds it impossible to make even those choices that he, ultimately, wants to make. The development of knowledge, of capacity for reflection and critical judgment, of virtue and character, is a development of the range of personal internal freedom, truly proper to human beings. Right use of freedom depends upon the possession of rightly ordered knowledge and rightly ordered loves. All of these fundamental developments have been included in the objectives outlined in this paper; and consequently personal freedom is, indeed, one aspect of the liberally educated man.

Nor does this clash with the Catholic insistence on authority; for the acceptance of right authority, whether in knowledge or action, requires a free human act. Only the free man can accept authority whether of a competent scientist, of the Church, or of legitimate government, in a way proper to a human and Christian personality. It is no part of the Christian ideal to produce the drilled response or the unthinking obedience of the automaton. Only a free man can yield Christian obedience. The liberally educated man will be a free man, but not one who rejects all authority; rather he will accept authority—but right authority rightly defined and delimited.

APPENDIX II
THE CRITICAL MIND

Prominent among objectives listed by educational theorists is that of developing a critical mind. The critical mind is one which habitually judges the truth and certitude, the probability or doubt, of propositions and proposals. It must be equipped with the habits, knowledge, and attitudes necessary to make sound judgment. Criticism is then a function of trained and reflective intelligence and operates under the ideal of truth and validity. The critical mind will be interpreted, therefore, according to a man's theory of knowledge, truth, and certitude. If one holds that truth and certitude are impossible, he will identify the critical mind with the skeptical mind. If one believes that all truth is relative, or that it can only be attained in natural science or within some other qualification, the critical mind will again be described differently. Since, in Christian thought, truth is indeed primary and a personal commitment to it requires personal certitude and, at least in the last analysis, adequate personal evidence, the critical mind is a necessary part of the ideally educated Christian. The requisites for the critical mind are all included in the general objectives laid out in this paper.

APPENDIX III
LIBERAL EDUCATION AND
PROFESSIONAL OR VOCATIONAL
TRAINING

Liberal education does not profess to train a man directly and immediately for a profession, a vocation, or a specialization. Yet, it is not impractical. Of course, it is held to be the best preparation for human living since its primary concern is the development of human beings precisely in regard to those matters most specific to human personality. By the same token, it becomes a matter of great practical importance, precisely in proportion as the pursuit for which the student is preparing is more intellectual and more distinctly human. In this same proportion it is possible to achieve liberal objectives and practical objectives in the same course. There are some subjects and courses which do not admit of liberalization; the teaching of typewriting, for example, cannot be made into a liberal subject. Many subjects, however, may be taught in a liberal manner and yet achieve a practical purpose; thus, engineering physics can be taught with a view to genuine scientific understanding while at the same time truly preparing (and perhaps in a better way) for professional work.

Courses, therefore, with a professional or avocational purpose may become a substantive part of liberal education, if they are made to conform to the requirements of liberal teaching outlined in this paper. In admitting such courses (as, for example, pre-medical courses) into the liberal curriculum, care must be taken to orientate them to the objectives of liberal education. A similar care should be exercised in advanced courses which are prerequisite for graduate work; the liberal arts college does not aim at producing professional scholars or specialists.

Other courses which do not admit of liberalization may indeed be added to the college curriculum, though they should not be considered as a substantive part of liberal education. In fact, with the increasing pressure of practical needs and the increasing num-

bers of college students, a wide variety of mixed curricula will
probably be necessary. Liberal education is always a matter of
degree; and, to a greater or lesser extent, it can and should be
worked into all collegiate and even professional and practical
curricula.

3

KNOWLEDGE AND ACTION

George P. Klubertanz, S.J.

One of the oldest controversies among philosophers is the relation between knowledge and action.[1] The view that "virtue is knowledge" is imputed to Plato with good reason, as well as its corollary, that virtue can be taught. Aristotle's position is that there is a difference between speculative and practical knowledge, that virtue is not knowledge even though knowledge is necessary for virtue, and that virtue cannot be taught by ordinary instruction.

There is a long Christian tradition that knowledge is not necessarily virtue. Beginning with our Blessed Lord's indictment of the scribes and Pharisees who sit on the chair of Moses, and His parable about the sower and the seed, and St. Paul's statements that science puffs up, and that the Romans who knew God were blameworthy in not worshipping Him, the Christian tradition distinguishes between the hearers and the doers of the Word. Tertullian and St. Peter Damian suggest that faith is somehow against reason; the *Imitation of Christ* registers its author's preference for those who feel compunction over those who can define it;[2] some writers approvingly report the Cynics' comment that people write books on humility and sign their names to them.

The relationship between knowledge and action is thus a speculative problem and a practical problem as well. And, as the sketchy historical references above indicate, these problems are serious and urgent. It would, therefore, be rash to try to solve these problems and settle the controversies. The most that a prudent man can attempt is to cast some light by careful analysis. Much could be done through a series of historical studies of the views of philosophers and leaders of men, and perhaps such studies should be undertaken. But our approach will attempt to be a direct analysis of personal experience and the reported experience of others; it will use techniques and distinctions derived from others, not so much according to their exact historical meaning as according to such meanings as will be most useful.

Let us then begin our own investigation by asking: What are the immediate springs of action? Rationalists would like to say that knowledge is the sole source. But experience goes in another direction: not only the traditions alluded to above but our own experience, with ourselves and with our students. In fact, the workshop for which this was written can pertinently be alleged as evidence that knowledge, taken generally, does not necessarily or always lead to action. On the other hand, it is clear that knowledge is a condition of human action as human. Surely anyone who makes a distinction between merely external conformity and interior voluntary acceptance is implicitly at least admitting that blind, unknowing action is not properly human. The proper principles of human action are thus knowledge and something else. We can also generically isolate this "something else": to be properly human an action must be voluntary as well as known. About the necessity of the voluntareity of human action there is little controversy and very few problems.

Our next question is then: Can any sort of knowledge be conjoined with will? Traditional discussions seem to leave this question unanswered, at least as far as any detailed response is concerned. In the scholastic tradition there is very little to be found. On the whole, one could gather the impression that any knowledge can be made practical, simply by answering the question, "How do I do this?" or "Is this the kind of thing I want?" That this approach is of no help can be seen from a reflection on the role that knowledge has for a knowing being.

Cognition is ultimately and intrinsically connected with action—

every form, we know, is followed by some inclination.[3] Indeed, there is a point of view from which action—some kind of action—is the very *raison d'être* of cognition; and that is the view of being as existing and good. To forget this relationship is seriously to misconceive the nature of knowledge.

It seems probable that the lower animals have a very limited cognitional activity; they can sense only the objects they are dealing with here and now. Higher animals have more ample powers, so that they sense many more objects than they need to contact in action; yet it is again probable that their imaginative life is very restricted. They are said to display curiosity, actively to seek out knowledge of things. But it seems probable that they do not exploit their abilities purely for the sake of knowing.

In man we find a remarkable proliferation of cognitive activity. Even at the very sense level, it is natural to man to seek to know for its own sake—to see, to hear, and so on, as much as possible—and to take pleasure in the act of knowing. So, too, at the level of imagination, it is both possible and enjoyable to engage in activity which is purely cognitive. The spontaneity and richness of imagination in man is a condition and foreshadowing of the marvelous versatility of his intellect. Intellectual knowledge is even more varied and more versatile; it is inexhaustible. It is evident that man knows many things which have no immediate bearing on action. Somewhat of a separation between cognition and action is even a condition of human freedom, as Bernard J. Lonergan, S.J., points out.[4] For this reason, ideas as such do not have the contrary qualities of good or bad in themselves.

Knowledge is intrinsically connected with action, yet not every act of knowledge is for the sake of action or leads to action. Are there then differences in the knowledge itself, or is any act of knowledge followed by any sort of action indifferently? The second alternative would be to make the sources of action ultimately irrational—a view that is at the opposite extreme from rationalism.

There is one sort of difference in knowledge which is due to the nature of the object known. There are objects which can only be known—*speculabilia*—and objects which can be known and acted upon—*operabilia*. The *speculabilia tantum* are objects which are necessarily what they are, concerning which man has only the function of knowing them. Granted that the ancients and medievals erred in thinking that the heavenly bodies and natural processes were merely *speculabilia*, the distinction is nevertheless valid in principle. Whatever necessarily and of itself is what it is cannot be subjected to human action. Does it follow that speculative knowledge is always and only of *speculabilia*, and that the knowledge of *operabilia* always leads to action?

The distinction is not quite that simple. For there is speculative knowledge of things which can be done, even of such things as directly pertain to human and moral action. We must distinguish knowledge into speculative and practical both in regard to object and to manner of knowing.[5] About necessary objects, knowledge is speculative both in object and in manner; and this must be so. But about operables, knowledge can be either speculative or practical—in manner.

A preliminary question is, "What are the speculative and practical manners of knowing?" In general, these two kinds of knowledge differ "in end"—speculative knowledge is for its own sake, practical knowledge is for the sake of action. This, however, cannot be an ultimate answer. For if the two kinds of knowledge differ in end, they differ in intention, and intention presupposes knowledge.

Most analyses of knowledge end here. They have pointed out a fact, but they have not given any reason for the fact. It might seem that we are still left with the original dilemma, simply moved back one stage; we must still choose between a sheer rationalism which deduces the action from the knowledge and a voluntarism which simply bases action on non-rational grounds.

We must beware here of misstating the problem. We are not presently concerned with establishing the fact or the nature of human freedom on the one hand, nor with the nature and source of obligation on the other. We assume that man is free, as far as

the first question is concerned; as for the second, it seems that
we must hold that obligations, even particular concrete obligations, can be known with rational certitude. And, if we want to
put our problem in its sharpest focus, we can ask, "How is it that
a man can know that some action is good and even necessary,
and yet not do it?" However, our problem actually is broader than
the knowledge of moral obligation.

The considerations we have been using till now have been more
epistemological and metaphysical. Knowledge can also be considered descriptively, as a psychological fact; and we can investigate
acts of knowledge as they are concretely performed. In this
description, we will look for such characteristics as will illuminate
our present problem.

We can begin with acts of conception or apprehension. Are
there different ways of apprehending which have a relation to
action? A qualitative difference can be found in this, that we apprehend some things merely abstractly, according to bare notions
which we may have of them, and other things we apprehend
concretely, as real. A useful terminology which we can apply
here is that of "notional" and "real" apprehension.[6] A notional
apprehension is of conceptions or notions; a real apprehension,
one of realities. But are not notions of real things, and are not
real things grasped in notions? This objection states a truth, but
it does not touch the point. Notions are often of real things, and
we may know that these things are real, but the knower does not
"realize" them, as one of our common expressions has it. In other
words, we can know notionally that something is real. The adjec-
tive *notional* qualifies our knowledge, not the object of that
knowledge merely. Therefore, a notional apprehension is a grasp
of notions or of realities in the abstract way in which notions are
found in our minds.

A notion is an intellectual apprehension, either of something
which is abstract in itself (like a mathematical object), or of something real according to an abstract intelligibility. Intelligibilities can
be abstract in several ways: they can be merely general; they can

be of some one aspect without the other perfections with which that aspect is joined in the thing; they can be immediately a grasp of some symbol of the thing (as is the case with verbal knowledge).

A real apprehension is an apprehension of a real thing according to its real way of being. The distinction between notional and real apprehension therefore does not bear directly on the metaphysical constitution of the real. The "real things" are those which are real *for us,* which belong to the same order of reality as we ourselves have, in whose reality our own reality is involved and which in turn are involved in our basic reality. Real apprehensions, therefore, are always of particulars, or individuals.

What is the difference, in the knower, between real and notional apprehension? A notional apprehension is one that takes place either without object-images, or at least with the barest bones of imagery. A real apprehension is one that takes place through "living images."

Some examples will be of help here. A schoolboy can understand—notionally, or abstractly—what a Vestal Virgin is, but he has a very minimal image of a Vestal Virgin marching in a procession along the Via Sacra. But a well-read and travelled man has an altogether different imagery. He knows what the Roman garments looked like, what the surroundings of the Via Sacra were, what the whole action meant to the Roman spectator, with whose feelings he finds himself in sympathy. He has a "living image," and so he really apprehends the Vestal Virgins. In a similar way, apprehension is real in an experimentalist, who personally handles the objects or at least the instruments he is studying; it is real in the philosopher, who studies things in their reality; but apprehension is notional in the grammarian, who deals with what others say about things and not with the things themselves. Apprehension is real in the economist, who knows the market, the use of money, the flow of goods and services; but apprehension is notional in a schoolboy translating, who has some understanding of what is said but may be wholly lacking in the experience of the things talked about. We can likewise analyze real apprehension in regard to many truths of faith, for example, the ones about our Blessed Lord and His Mother. (We can note, incidentally, that St. Ignatius's "application of the senses" and his "contemplations" intend to bring about such living images.) In all these cases, the reality which is being known is in itself directly sensible and therefore can be imagined as such.

The easiest illustrations of real apprehension are drawn from things which have their "reality for us" from the living image. Often, things which are directly perceived by us are really apprehended. It is true that perception is often not a very intense act, and that for many people what they imagine is more real than what they perceive. Indeed, perception can even seem unreal and shadowy. Hence, the emphasis is correctly put on the *image* rather than on sensation itself. True enough, all images are derived from sensations, but Hume is surely wrong in holding that sensations are always more vivid than images and that images always present themselves as less intense, like diminished, shadowy copies. A "real apprehension" in perception therefore would be one in which attention is directed to what we perceive, and which in an adult is reinforced by vivid and subject-related images.

Real and notional apprehension each have their own excellence and corresponding limitations. To apprehend notionally is to have breadth of mind, clarity, and organization, but to be shallow; to apprehend really is to be deep and firm, but to be narrow-minded and possibly in the wrong. Though these kinds of apprehension differ so much, they are not really inconsistent with each other; in fact, they can coexist in the same mind.

A related distinction is to be found in regard to judgment or assent: that between notional and real assent. This distinction is not simply identical with the preceding, nor with other distinctions of kinds of judgment. For clarity's sake, it is necessary to show what this distinction is not.

In the beginning of this paper, a distinction was made between speculative and practical knowledge, but both of these types can be held with either notional or real assent. The distinction between opinion and scientific knowledge is another well-known distinction, but it also does not coincide with the distinction between real and notional assent. Nor does this latter distinction pertain to the constitution of a science, and so is not helpful in discussions about what a science is or how conclusions are related to their premises. Finally, it is not like the well-known distinction of the kinds of certitude.

A notional assent is an assent to notions (as we have defined them above), whereas a real assent is an assent to real things. Each of these assents presupposes a corresponding kind of apprehension, yet it is more than an apprehension, for it is an assent, or judgment: an admission and assertion of the truth of what is said in the proposition which expresses it. Real assent is very much like "commitment" except that it is a more inclusive term. "Commitment" usually is taken to be an act of realization of values and a voluntary adherence to them as to the goals we are determined to seek. "Real assent" is thus the knowledge-component of "commitment," but it is also the assent given to truth in all orders where reality can be found and known as real for the knower. A simple real assent is often referred to as a belief—we "believe" the world is round, and so on.

Real assents are often enough given to the things which we immediately experience as real, to our concrete sensible surroundings when we apprehend them as real for us. Most people, indeed, when they are asked what they mean by "something real," will indicate immediate sensible reality as the primary instance. But often we do not attend to perceptual objects, so that our judgments are not directed to them. In such cases, real assents are commonly those we give to a proposition when we have a living image of the reality which is the object of that proposition. A notional assent, on the other hand, is one which we give to propositions which we understand abstractly, without object-images or at least with relatively abstract, selective, and schematic imagery.

We must be careful not to belittle abstract knowledge. Abstract knowledge is the only means we have of transcending the particular and of clearly distinguishing the true from the false. But in man these most desirable qualities of abstraction are accompanied by another consequence, that what can be known only abstractly is capable of being held with only notional assent.

The two modes of apprehending (that is, notional and real) do not change the nature of the assent itself, which remains the unconditional acceptance of the proposition. But they give it an external character corresponding to these modes. Real assent is keener, more intense, than notional. It is directed to things represented by distinct and vivid images. Real assent, however, is not necessarily true; an assent can be most real and in error. Notional assents are equally absolute and unconditional, but they are directed to notions expressed in abstract or general propositions.

Assents can be either simple or complex. A simple assent may be either a real assent or a notional one; a complex assent contains both a real and a notional assent.

So far we have dealt with apprehensions and assents to propositions where the objects are directly sensible in their own right and therefore also in themselves able to be the objects of the imagination. But not all objects are such; some things which we can know can be reached only by reasoning.

Reasoning, or inference, can be considered in a way similar to that which we have used in dealing with apprehension and assent. But the analysis of inference is more complex. Inference is a movement of the mind from one object (truth, notion, or thing) to another and implies a dependence of the second knowledge upon the preceding one or ones. There are two major varieties of inference: formal and non-formal.

Formal inference is much more familiar to those trained in the scholastic tradition; it is the inference with which logicians deal and which trained scientists practice in their acquisition and use of scientific knowledge. Formal inference is a work of deliberate reasoning, clearly laying out in intelligible fashion the connection between evidences and conclusions. Because of its clarity and explicitness, formal inference infallibly connects its conclusions with their premises. But of itself, formal inference is hypothetical. When we are using *only* formal inference, we are working with notions, so that the assents operative throughout the reasoning process are notional. Therefore, the real application of our conclusions is not immediately made—the conclusion as such is hypothetical: "If such and such, then so and so." Formal inference is not necessarily deductive and *a priori;* "fact-proofs" are also capable of being put down formally, and so too are the complex inferences of science, which are most accurately displayed by the techniques of modern (symbolic) logic.

Non-formal inference is any inference which does not rest exclusively on notions and their formal interrelationships. It is typical of the traditional approach to reasoning to think that the perfect mode of reasoning is one made in fully explicit logical form, and that all other reasoning can be brought into a formal structure and completely expressed by such a structure. This view, though widely held, does not seem to be correct. There is inference which cannot in principle be reduced to a formal explicit structure. Indeed, much of our ordinary reasoning is such.

For instance, the way in which we reach conclusions about most matters of daily life is extremely complex. Manifold evidences move us, and in many different ways. If you ask a farmer why he plants his corn at this time, he will propose a reason or two, which most likely will not be conclusive ones when considered in their formal relationships to the conclusion drawn. If you ask a man why he buys this suit of clothes, why he uses this tool in this way, you may or may not get a reason; but if you do, it also will seem a flimsy one. If the ordinary man were capable of adducing all his reasons and interested enough to do so, any one of the reasons taken singly probably would not be conclusive. And traditional logic says that a group of inconclusive reasons is no better than those reasons taken singly. True enough, probabilities accumulate and converge. This accumulation and convergence is not subject to rules; yet an experienced person judges unhesitatingly. Let me

offer as an example my knowledge that Missouri is bounded on
the north by Iowa. Any single piece of evidence that I can adduce
will not be an absolute proof. It is true that I have more than one
reason for saying this. Now, from the point of view of traditional
logic, I could indeed argue that the very accumulation and convergence of all the reasons is itself a new evidence distinct from the
individual evidences. Quite so—but whereas there are rules about
the individual pieces of evidence, what rules can be given to tell
that such a convergence is occurring? This situation is much like
the one we meet in induction:[7] we say commonly that a constant
conjunction must be observed "in a *sufficient* number of instances."
But nobody can tell us in the abstract what a sufficient number is.
One who has experience in a particular subject matter can tell us
what concretely is a sufficient number. Accumulation and convergence of probabilities is a similar thing; this convergence can
be known in the concrete, but it cannot be reduced to rules. A
procedure which cannot be reduced to rules is not a formal inference. For this reason at least, one can say that not all inference
can be reduced to simply formal evidence.

There are several kinds of non-formal inference. First—and
lowest in the scale—is "natural inference." A natural inference
is one that takes place, as it were, naturally, that is, without any
art or deliberation ("unconsciously"), and moves from *one thing*
to *another*. It is, as it were, forced on a man by the exigencies of
living and the conditions of action. Thus, the natural realism of
ordinary people is partly a natural inference. Similarly, the same
people's conviction that there is a God is a natural inference.
Natural inference, because it is entirely non-reflective, is easily
confused with human faith or with prejudice, and obviously is not
capable of defending itself or clarifying any difficulties that might
arise. There is no reason, however, why it cannot reach conclusions
which are true.

A second kind of non-formal inference is sometimes called
"informal inference" (par excellence). Informal inference is the
reflective stage of non-formal inference; therefore, it involves some

GEORGE P. KLUBERTANZ, S.J. 49

notional apprehensions. Though it keeps in touch with experience
and living images, informal inference looks at the evidence as
evidence; it isolates its guiding principles and heuristic hypotheses
("antecedent probabilities and presumptions"). In calling them
"hypotheses," we do not mean that they are sheerly assumed
propositions without a shred of evidence. But their application to
the case under investigation is not itself a matter of rule, a
demonstrable relation.

An example again will considerably clarify the relation. Take
two men setting out to answer the question, "Has God given a
revelation?" One man looks at the proffered evidence as a natural
event; he is concerned primarily with some physical trait of the
occurrence which he could isolate and repeat, not applying moral
criteria to the content of the revelation, and so on. The other man,
knowing that God exists, concludes that God could reveal Himself
and that if He did, His revelation would be ennobling, directed
to man's highest good, distinguished concretely by moral and other
qualities which would make His revelation identifiable as such. In
the light of their different views, the two examine various alleged
revelations. Naturally, they will come to rather divergent conclusions. But who can *prove* that an investigator must logically use
such or such principles? Certainly, we cannot give a formal,
logical reason for using particular principles and hypotheses. Of
course, their use in a given case is *reasonable*—but the reason
is not an abstract, formal, universal one; the "reason" is a "good
reason" only to the extent that it is concreted in this particular
matter and known as thus concreted. Yet the presence or absence
of appropriate, "reasonable" principles and hypotheses in an
investigation will lead to opposite interpretations of the evidence—
interpretations which will seem "logical" to both differing parties.

An informal inference must necessarily make use of real assents.
Hence, the conclusions of an informal inference must also be real
assents. An informal inference, then, enables us to ground real
assents to non-experiential and non-sensible realities.

Whereas notional and real assents are two alternative kinds of simple assents, so that every simple assent must be either real or notional, inference can be complex. Purely natural inference stands on the one side, purely formal inference on the other. In between are informal inference by itself, as a conscious and deliberate, reflective process, and a combination of scientifically formal inference with informal. In the latter case, the inference necessarily terminates in a complex assent. Not every kind of reasoning on every subject matter can be thus combined, of course. Some objects of thought and inference are only notions in themselves, as is the case with the objects of mathematics and formal logic. Other objects of thought are in themselves realities, but are known under such highly abstract conditions, without any relation to the subject, that they, too, are notions. One thinks of present-day physics, for example. That is not to say that many people do not give complex assents to many scientific—or, rather, physically interpreted scientific—statements. They do this precisely in view of the concrete images these statements call up in their minds; but this is not science itself, it is more of a mistake, a philosophical view masquerading as science. Scientific conclusions which are cast in the ontological mode[8] can be accompanied by real assents, whereas the constructural sciences should not be so accepted, at least as far as their own proper character is concerned. Strictly ontological sciences can therefore suitably be assented to with a complex assent, both real and notional, or they can be assented to with only a notional assent. The difference of assent in ontological sciences is not a difference in the object itself, but rather the way in which an individual knower exercises his knowledge. Nor is it a difference in the formal argument itself.

This last point is one which some contemporary discussions seem to be entirely ignorant of.[9] They notice that some students let their philosophical knowledge make a difference in their lives, and that others do not. Most people look for a formal difference in the argument. Thus, some writers conclude that metaphysics is not held by a real assent because the student has not grasped Aristotelian physics. Others say that metaphysics must be taught as a part of theology. Still others want to revamp Thomistic metaphysics so that it becomes one of the varieties of personalism or spiritualism or existentialism. Any brilliant teacher can probably find that what he does succeeds in bringing his students to real assents. But it is a mistake to think and assert that *formal scientific* differences have any real part to play here. A real assent is not generated by formal inferences, no matter how the formal inference is arranged, nor how many formal inferences are used to back each other up, for formal inference is *in principle* incapable of producing any real assent.

But we must return from this digression to see the different ways in which a proposition, or a group of propositions, can be held. The absolutely lowest way in which one can "hold" a proposition is that in which one asserts a proposition which one does not understand at all; this claim can well be called "formalism" or "verbalism." This affirmation is a merely external assertion without a corresponding internal assent, and we can compare this with Aristotle's statement that some people mouth the conclusions of a science though they have no idea of what they are saying. (1) The weakest of all true assents are those based on the most bare, abstract, impersonal notions, in which just enough is apprehended that something can be asserted at all. For the sake of a name, we shall call this kind of assent a "profession." (2) The next higher sort of assent is that of spontaneous assent to useful, and especially liberal, knowledge, when this knowledge is held in a generalized and stereotyped way. This is a notional assent to such opinions as we commonly take for granted, particularly those which make up common culture and the content of general education. Among them also are those which pertain to public morality and politics, as the ordinary, unreflective man holds them. This sort can be called "credence." (3) Credence can be reflected on, and then there is a "deliberate opinion." When we take a thing for granted, it is a credence; when we begin to reflect on it, we measure and estimate it, and possibly also modify it. (4) Next there are the assents to first principles. These assents are notional, because first principles are general and in that sense abstract. Real first principles are not subject to logic, but rather determine the whole process of reasoning. (5) Finally, the most perfect notional assents are found at the elaborated level of scientific knowledge. We are not referring so much to the stage of scientific inquiry as to the stage of scientific truth possessed. At this latter stage, the assents are clear, explicit, and most perfect of their kind; they are firm and conscious acceptances of propositions as true. Scientific knowledge is true and certain in the abstract order, and from the reflective point of view can well be called the perfect kind of knowledge.

The first three kinds of formal assent can be about particular things; and so, if they are enriched by living images, they can be turned into real assents. (A "formalism" needs to become an internal assent, and then it can become a real assent under the same condition.) If these assents are about universals, or about things which we cannot experience because they are beyond immediate experience, they cannot then be *turned into* real assents. Two things can, however, be done to them to improve them. (1) In their own order, they can be made more perfect, finally to become clear knowledge of principles and scientific knowledge of conclusions. (2) They can be accompanied by real assents deriving from informal inference, and then we should more properly speak of complex assents.

Where do these kinds of inferences and assents occur concretely? To answer this question, we need to consider the modes or levels of knowledge: common sense, humanistic elaboration, scientific knowledge.[10]

"Common sense knowledge" is the kind of knowledge that uneducated people have who have not reflected upon and organized their own knowledge. In general, common sense is an amorphous thing, and probably in no two persons has it exactly the same content. It includes direct experience and what is remembered from past experience, as well as what is gained by natural inference from that experience. It also includes what is learned from others —some of this is factual knowledge, some the "accumulated wisdom of the group," folk tales and sayings, and so on. And it includes much guesswork, personal and social; some metaphorical knowledge, some emotionally tinted or influenced ideas, and so on. This knowledge is not only composed of different kinds of elements; but these elements vary in truth value (since outside of the strictly perceptual elements, the chances of error are great), in certitude, in the kinds of assents which are given to them. Outside of that content which is derived from immediate direct experience that is necessarily common to all men, no generalizations can safely be made about the truth value, the clarity, or the kind of assent actually given by each person to what he knows unreflectively.

The second mode of knowledge is the one we can call humanistic. We must note in passing that no mode of understanding can be explained to a person who has not had a personal experience of it. But since this paper is addressed to readers all of whom have had an experience of liberal education, we can rest satisfied that they can all understand it with a minimum of explanation of the point of view taken on it. Throughout this expository delineation of humanistic knowledge, it will be viewed as it can be found most perfectly and ideally; later on, some qualifications will have to be made.

Humanistic knowledge absorbs the entire attention and concentrates it on the concrete object. Because of this absorption, an abstractive critique of the object is not possible, and similarly an abstractive critique of the humanistic mode of knowledge is not possible within humanism itself. The object, it has been said, is concrete. We deal, in the humanistic approach, not with abstract ideas, notions, but with persons and things. Or, if we deal with ideas, we deal with them as if they were persons or things, as in the technique of personification. Because we deal with the object as it is in its concreteness and particularity, we leave it an integral object. We do not divide or abstract.

The experience itself in humanistic knowledge is also integral, in that it involves all (or most) of the powers of knowing, both sensory and rational, and it involves them simultaneously, in combination. Granted that no normal use of the intellect is possible without a corresponding activity at least of the imagination, the imagination need not be involved other than as a kind of object, presenting, that is, the object to the intellect. But in humanistic knowing, the imagination is cooperating with the intellect precisely in the *act* of knowing. It is an intellectivo-sensory knowledge. The intellect is held close to the senses. For this reason, also, humanistic knowledge is never purely speculative, entirely innocent of emotion. Rather, by reason of the active sensory participation in the act of knowing, the emotions also are involved.

Nevertheless, we should not forget that humanistic knowledge is already reflective and conscious. Simple unreflective perception is real enough and integral, and it leads to real assents. Likewise, folk tales and folk songs, folk art and folk "ritual" can arise on the level of common sense, but works of artistic value do not spring so simply from the "soul of the people." We really should not speak of art and humanism till we reach a level where such knowledge is deliberately produced and cultivated. Some mature reflection is required. But it is reflection on the concrete and the concrete way of knowing. What is involved is a knowing we can call personal and penetrating, a deep understanding of the object. Rather than discursive elaboration of the object through other things, there is an attention fixed on the object in its relations in a unity. We call such deep understanding a realization, a savoring of the object.

As humanistic knowledge is reflective in a particular way, so also does it give a kind of explanation. This is not an explanation through abstractly known causes or through reduction to generic laws, but through empathy. We come to understand something through our own past experiences, and through concrete analyses, that is, from things to things. This is where humanistic knowledge rests on natural inference, in this movement from one concrete thing to another concrete thing.

And again, humanistic knowledge generalizes. It rises above

the strict singularity of sensory perceptual knowledge, above the vague generalizations of common sense. But this generalization is not through abstraction. Rather, the universal of humanistic knowledge is a concrete universal: a concrete instance seen as the type or prototype of all similar cases. Or it generalizes in axioms instead of principles. Most evidently, its generalization is that of metaphor: the same truth, law, and so on, is seen as embodied in a special instance which most perfectly shows forth the concreted truth or idea. Along the same lines, humanistic knowledge has a special terminology, but not really a technical terminology. We can say that it uses an "artistic" terminology, one that is purified from perceptual and pragmatic associations but not abstractly sharpened and limited by definition.

Lastly, humanistic knowledge is *one* kind of knowledge. Here again it contrasts with scientific knowledge which is specialized, distinguished into many kinds. Humanistic knowledge is one knowledge because it results from one attitude, a perspective of human relevance.[11] This is not merely subjective or arbitrary. Indeed, our lived world *is* a human environment, it is not merely and arbitrarily considered to be such. This is the concrete reality. The "world as it is in itself" is an abstraction from experience. Surely we admit the legitimacy and the value of such an abstraction, but scientists should realize that it is an abstraction, though apparently they hate to do so. They will go so far as to assert that "really" the object is as science (or philosophy) conceives it. If we honestly face the question, such statements are nonsense. I mean this quite literally, and I mean it just as much about the statements of the philosophers, great or small. The real world is *not* an abstraction—yet any scientific statement is an abstraction. If we ask Plato's question, What is really real? at least this much is clear: it is not the world of Platonic forms, nor the world of atoms, nor even the world of abstract matter and form, but the world of subsisting, acting things and persons. The highest level at which we can deal integrally with concrete reality as concrete and therefore as simply real is that of humanistic knowledge.

Because humanistic knowledge is integral, it is in a special way the perfection of man as a sensitivo-rational knowing-and-loving being. Intellectual knowledge is sought for, but only as a part of knowledge. Moreover, the knowledge is not merely a knowledge; it is related to appetite.

Humanistic knowledge is connected with emotion. First, it ordinarily is centered on objects which are also possible objects of emotion. Secondly, it concentrates on aspects of those objects which are more or less directly connected with emotion; as some say, it tends to be an evaluative knowledge. However, we should not be understood to mean that it is narrowly practical, pragmatic; indeed, it is not. And the emotion involved is not immediately the same emotion as would be present in the simple sense experience of the object which is now known humanistically—if one desires to eat the painted apple, he is not having an humanistic experience. This distinction is a well-known one; the humanistic emotion is sometimes said to be differentiated by "aesthetic distance"; though it is very easy to apply in some few cases, at times it may be very difficult, and may refer more to the reaction of the beholder than to a quality of what is presented for experience. Thirdly, and perhaps most significantly, the emotion is relevant to the very acquisition of the knowledge in question. Sometimes, emotion and feeling open the eyes of the intelligence. Thus, "empathy" with a character may be a necessary condition for understanding him. Concern over morality may be needed before the student can grasp the significance of some attribute of a situation.

This is a very important consideration when we are concerned with imparting the *first idea* to a student. When an idea is acquired not entirely by one's own personal effort, it is very difficult to have the student get more than a bare notion of what is intended. Its very meaningfulness may depend on the student's own reaction to it. But the bare notion cannot give rise to any reaction; the presentation must be such that the student can react as he learns. And it is precisely the function of traditional humanistic method and content to embody new materials in this way.

Finally, with regard to the relation between knowledge and action, we have already seen that knowledge *can guide* action. Even abstract knowledge can have this function. But abstract knowledge will never *move to* action. Only that which is concretely appetible will move anyone to action, and thus only real assents will move a man to act. Now, we have seen that humanistic knowledge is integral, making use of both the understanding and the sense powers. When these are all properly employed, the understanding will be accompanied with a living image, and thus will be either a real assent or a complex assent, both real and notional.

We must pause here to face the historical situation realistically. Humanistic knowledge in its perfection will be integral, value-laden knowledge. But humanistic knowledge often is to be found at a lower level: a level of spontaneous assent to opinions which people take for granted, and this is a kind of notional assent which we labelled above "credence."[12] When liberal studies produce no more than credence, I think we can say that they have failed of their proper purpose. They produce what we can call a veneer of liberal culture. Of course, such culture does influence behavior, at least exteriorly. But such behavior will be stereotyped and in some sense hollow. Nevertheless, even the lower level of humanistic knowledge is valuable in itself; it is not a mere instrument of moral goodness. Beauty, even when divorced from the full human goodness and truth, is still a good for man. There are those who deny the physical in order to safeguard the moral, just as there are those who deny the natural to safeguard the supernatural. Then there are the naturalists and the humanists (in the contemporary sense of these terms) who think it is necessary to deny or reject the moral and the supernatural to safeguard the physical and natural. Obviously, neither of these two attitudes is the completely Catholic one. Less obviously, neither is the truly and traditionally humanistic one. The humanism which we have described earlier is the integrally human one, which has its roots in what is most fundamentally real for those who hold it and is equally open to that perfection which is offered gratuitously to man by God.

The third mode of knowledge is the scientific, divided itself into several main types: the sciences, mathematics, philosophy. In contrast to humanistic knowledge, scientific knowledge is primarily speculative: it is a *pure* knowledge. It is the work of reflective intelligence precisely as knowledge. Because it is directed immediately to the intelligibilities of the object as it is in itself, scientific knowledge is divided into distinct genera and species, according to the formal differences of those intelligibilities.

Scientific knowledge characteristically employs formal inference upon notional apprehensions, and leads of itself to formal assents. Its great advantage is that in concentrating upon intelligibility, it enables the knower to reflect upon his knowledge as knowledge. Hence, its conclusions are known to be true (that is, at the level at which they are reached) and are in themselves certain. To deal with pure intelligibility, it must be an abstractive and therefore notional knowledge. Hence, its application to the concrete real must always allow for the complexity of the real things. Scientific knowledge by itself—in its narrowest sense—is hypothetical, since the conclusion is certainly true if the premises are true. But the premises themselves always partly escape the control of the science when the science is practiced in the narrowly logical sense. Similarly, the assent to a scientific conclusion is by itself a notional assent, and the multiplication of formal reasoning to its ultimate perfection cannot bring about any different kind of assent.

In many cases, there is no advantage in changing or adding to the notional assent proper to scientific knowledge, and often this would be impossible if the proper character of certain sciences is respected. In one case at least, that of philosophy, a real assent is evidently desirable. This is for two distinct reasons. One is peculiar to realism. In a realistic philosophy, the propositions make a claim to deal with the real in its most proper sense. Surely there is something strange when a student talks about *the real,* and does not refer the real to what is *most real for him.* Indeed, it is hard to see how a realism can get started without building on the experience of the real. But this is to build on a real assent. The other reason pertains to any variety of philosophy. Philosophy purports to be in some way the ultimate rational explanation. To make such an explanation limited to the sphere of notions can only be done at the cost of reducing reason itself to an epiphenomenal function, not significant for vital reality.

From what we have seen, the notional assent at the level of scientific knowledge (pure speculative theory) cannot itself be changed into a real assent, nor will it become a real assent by having other notional assents added to it. But real assents can be combined with notional assents into complex assents. This is done when real apprehensions accompany notional ones, and when informal inference accompanies and undergirds the formal inference.

If we abstract from the concrete educational situation, we could imagine a way of teaching philosophy so that the real apprehensions would be presented along with the notional ones, and the informal inferences actually be gone through concomitantly with the formal reasoning. Practically, this would mean that the student spent several full years studying philosophy.

In our actual situation this is neither possible nor necessary. For all our students have already had a humanistic training in high school and the first year or two of college. And, in regard to the most important conclusions of metaphysics and the philosophy of man, the faith of the students provides a real assent which can be combined with the conclusions of those disciplines. If we assume that our students are Catholics, or at least committed to the Judaeo-Christian faith, and that the humanities have made them liberally educated, then there is need only for the explicit connection to be made between the real assents and informal inferences which they have already made and the formal inferences and notional assents of philosophy and theology. I believe it must be emphasized that such a connection must be made—it will not happen of itself except in a few rare instances. Students do not interrelate and apply their knowledges unless they are made to do so by the teacher.[13] They are capable of doing it, but only capable; and it is a failure on the teacher's part if such interrelation is not made. Here the teachers of philosophy and theology have an important part to play in integrating knowledge and action.

On the other hand, I have said that this will happen "if we assume that our students are liberally educated." A good liberal education prior to the study of philosophy and theology is therefore necessary, and under our current conditions this cannot be done in the philosophy and theology classes themselves. Humanistic knowledge as I have described it above must already have been acquired throughout high school and college. If it has not been acquired, if early training has been merely formalistic or exclusively technical and scientific, it is going to be very hard even for a brilliant teacher to bring about complex assents. And so, if a high percentage of our students have only notional assents at the end of their course work in philosophy and theology, this is not necessarily the fault of those courses themselves. Similarly, though most of our students profess a Christian or at least a theistic faith, it is not clear that all of them give real assents to their faith. We might have to say that many of them have only a credence, a general, opinionative, notional assent to their faith. But two or more notional assents produce only notional assents, never a real assent; the fact that one of the assents is to a religious truth does not change the intrinsic character of the assent. Theology courses have a slightly better chance to help the student make real assents or complex assents, as the case may be. For theology, as it is now conceived, has humanistic elements insofar as it is scriptural and Patristic. Moreover, a vital living of the faith outside the classroom may also help to change what was once a notional assent to a complex one including a real assent.

In all of this, we must single out the role of the teacher as a person. True, what the teacher *says* constitutes the formal part of his instruction. But the teacher is a person, and being a teacher is a personal activity in relation to other persons. This interpersonal (intersubjective) relation is in the order of what is *real for* the students, at the level of humanistic teaching as well as of philosophy and theology. A teacher who does not appreciate literature will not bring many of his students to like poetry, no matter what he *says* about it. A teacher who does not live his philosophy or theology is talking at cross purposes. On the other hand, a teacher who lives as a thoughtful Christian will have an impact on his students, no matter how mediocre his formal presentation of philosophy or theology. As an aside, we may point to the special role which the layman can play in convincing his students of the truth of his philosophy or theology, inasmuch as he stands before them as a concrete example of a Christian in the world—an example which the religious as such is incapable of giving.

From what has been said to this point, it would appear that all the factors which would influence living are working together to lead the student to a richer and fuller intellectual, moral, and religious life.

But some think that the case is quite the opposite. They feel that the humanities are dangerous, that they will lead the student to a love of sinful things. This problem is not one which we can deal with here. Some persons also feel that scientific knowledge, especially that of some social and natural sciences and of philosophy, has a corrosive effect on faith and on simple real assents. That in fact the faith of students, even in a Catholic college, is sometimes weakened, and that the practice of their faith sometimes becomes slipshod, apparently must be admitted. Why should this happen?

There can be several reasons why scientific study might weaken faith and relax practice. One of these reasons concerns the very activity of reflective intelligence itself.[14] Because intelligence reflects on its own activities and discovers the difference between valid and invalid procedures, it becomes also *critical* intelligence. It is critical first of all within the particular sphere of its work. But because in any particular sphere a general ideal of rational evidence and a general ideal of method is discovered, reflective intelligence becomes critical of the whole content of tradition.

Tradition, even when purified by humanistic reflection, still will not be entirely acceptable to critical intelligence. Under the critique of reason, certain elements of tradition will be simply dissolved, others will be re-created and become somewhat different. When this happens, there must necessarily arise a tension between the critical and reconstructive tendencies of scientific thinkers and the conservative upholders of the tradition. But if all goes well, the tension leads to a richer yet critically validated tradition.

However, all does not necessarily go well. We can see among our non-Catholic colleagues that critical intelligence has often become skeptical; that it dissolves tradition and reconstructs only what can be established by scientific methods narrowly construed. What cannot be thus scientifically established is taken to be an outmoded opinion or is referred to some non-rational function, such as emotion, decision, power, and the like.

When reflective intelligence thus becomes skeptical in principle, it does so through a restrictive epistemology. Presumably there would not be any cases of this in our departments of philosophy and theology, though there might well be some—perhaps unconscious and indeliberate—among some of the scientists teaching in our schools.

Sometimes, too, critical intelligence, though not skeptical in principle, has a corrosive effect on the student's mind through ineptness or impatience. Teachers certainly must stimulate students to think, and this may mean sharp criticism, forcing them on the defensive, confronting them with new ideas. But beginning courses are not the place to do this; criticism should not precede constructive training; students should not be asked to defend what they do not yet understand. When mistakes like this are made by an individual teacher, a dean or department head will often be able to correct poor technique and restrain impatience.

However, critical intelligence can sometimes cause tensions for reasons entirely outside its own function. Thus, we might consider a case where humanism, in its love for tradition, has become traditionalistic and reactionary rather than conservative. When the past is considered good because it is the past, any effort to criticize it will cause tension, even when such criticism is fully justified and even necessary. A student, trained in such a humanism, can well turn against his earlier training when he meets with an effective teacher of philosophy or theology. Or, in his first encounter with the critical attitude, he may return to his former teachers for reassurance, perhaps thus increasing the reactionary tendency. Such experiences are often hard on students, and can cause them harm insofar as they are led to reject the good along with what is restrictive or reactionary. One might then think that scientific studies are adversely affecting action. Yet the trouble is not that the philosophy or theology courses are harmful or badly taught; rather, the humanistic studies need reorientation, so that they tend to preserve the past when it is good, because it is good.

Another situation where critical intelligence can cause tension and corrosion of ideas arises when a student of one of the sciences or philosophy has had an inadequate religious education. An example of this can easily be seen in a Catholic student who has perhaps learned his catechism but has never had any further education to develop his understanding of his faith. He may perhaps have had his entire formal education in secular schools, and no compensating study of religion has been undertaken on his own initiative or that of his parents. When such a student runs into a reflective but skeptical mind, the result can easily be that his faith cannot withstand the criticism.

To a lesser extent, a similar situation can arise even in a Catholic school. At times, a student will perhaps have had some formal religious education, but either it has been inadequate, or the individual student has failed to profit from a good education. (The reasons for the latter condition are various; usually they will be psychological ones rooted in the experiences of early childhood; we are not here interested in investigating this question.) If we suppose that a student with childish ideas about his faith becomes keenly aware of the exigencies of critical intelligence, he may be unable, even in spite of the support of his surroundings, to prevent his questions from destroying his faith. It really makes no difference whether this student learns the nature of critical intelligence from a science or from philosophy or from some contact he has outside his formal classes. Blame for the loss of faith should not be laid to his courses which teach him the nature of critical intelligence. As far as the school is concerned, there is an obligation to see that a proportionately mature understanding of the faith is given to the students. The high quality of the theology courses will enable a student to find a home for his maturing mind within his faith. If the difficulty for a particular student comes not from any deficiency in any of the courses, but from some personal problem, counseling may sometimes help; but, on the whole, this possibility is one which must be risked if the much greater good is to be achieved, namely, the training of the majority of the students in reflective intelligence in the sciences, philosophy, and theology.

There are two final considerations. One concerns a role which philosophy, and to a lesser extent theology, can play in protecting the human assents of the student against the skeptical influence of our culture. An over-protective attitude would incline one to say: The student must never hear about ideas that conflict with his basic natural and Christian commitments. But the flowering of critical intelligence cannot allow such ignorance in principle; and of course in practice the attempt to shield the student from all anti-Christian and anti-rational ideas is foredoomed. But I mean more than what the positive requirements of the scientific discipline itself involve; I mean an explicit laying out of contemporary positions with their objections against the Catholic faith and a realistic philosophy. Since in our contemporary world most of these positions claim to be based on natural reason, they can best be presented in the philosophy classes. After a student has come to understand his own positions positively and constructively, the teacher can present the difficulties many modern thinkers have with them. This has many advantages. First, because such difficulties are presented in a teaching situation, their impact can be controlled and the student can be helped to see how they are solved.

Secondly, the student has more confidence in his school and his faith when he sees that his teachers are well acquainted with all the difficulties. Thirdly, he will not be surprised in later life by an argument he has never heard of. Fourthly, even if he does not remember what the answer was, he will recall that this argument was given in its strongest form by his own teacher openly to the class, and that the arguments were answered at that time and the answers were satisfactory to himself and his fellow students. This result is not precisely a scientific one, but it can be very important in a student's life and in the over-all orientation of knowledge to action.

The second consideration concerns *virtue*. It may seem strange that in the discussion of the relation between knowledge and action the notion of virtue should not have been mentioned. The reason is that properly speaking virtue cannot be *taught,* not even intellectual virtue. What can be taught in the strictest sense is (a) information and (b) an act of reasoning. First principles can sometimes be concretely presented, and rhetorical devices used to help the student attend to the evidence. But habits as such cannot so be taught; they can only be acquired by personal activity.

Knowledge always has something to do with virtue, even with moral virtue. The knowledge that precedes the virtuous act can be taught to the extent that it is *general* knowledge in some sense of the term. The particular knowledge that precedes an act of moral virtue is prudence, and prudence as such can only be guided; it cannot be taught. In our earlier discussions about humanistic knowledge, we stressed the concrete character of that knowledge. Virtuous acts and virtuous men can be shown to the student in concrete examples, and he can at the same time be moved to practice them on his own account.

More valuable still than the examples of virtue that students read about are the examples they see in their teachers (and other school officials). A good teacher is most essentially an example of intellectual virtue: he shows in his teaching what it means to be a scientist, a philosopher, a theologian, and so on. It is less essential—but still essential—that the teacher himself be an example of other virtues also. Even in the classroom situation other virtues are practiced, and in the varying relations of teacher and student outside the classroom still more concrete and moving examples of virtue are given. This is all that can be done by the teacher and the school. If the student is to acquire those permanent principles of consistently good action, he can do so only by his own good activity, his own personal interior acts.

Notes

1. This paper is not an historical or textual study, but a background paper. It will try to expound relevant ideas in an organized way. Footnotes will be few, to indicate sources of ideas, or materials that carry a particular point further. A bibliography of useful and significant materials will be appended in lieu of detailed documentation.
2. For an expansion of some of these views, see Etienne Gilson, *Reason and Revelation in the Middle Ages* (New York: Scribner's, 1938).
3. This well-known Thomistic axiom does not mean that cognition is related to appetition as means to end. There are many controversies concerning the precise relationship of intellect to will, but to go into them would distract from the present purpose and make the paper impossibly long. Several articles that I have found illuminating are: Gerard Smith, S.J., "Intelligence and Liberty," *New Scholasticism*, XV (1941), 1–17; *idem*, "The Nature and Uses of Liberty," *ibid.*, XXVI (1952), 305–26; L. B. Geiger, O.P., "On Freedom," *Philosophy Today*, IV (1960), 126–36.
4. Bernard J. Lonergan, S.J., "St. Thomas's Thought on *Gratia Operans*," *Theological Studies*, III (1942), 533–78.
5. For a detailed textual analysis of St. Thomas on these matters, see John E. Naus, S.J., *The Practical Intellect According to St. Thomas* (Rome: Gregorian University Press, 1960).
6. Every reader will recognize that these terms are taken from Cardinal Newman. This paper, however, is not an analysis of what Newman himself held; in this section, the primary concern is to find clarifying distinctions. There is therefore no claim that what is presented here is what Newman wrote. Whether he did or did not, the question here is simply, Are these analyses true to experience and helpful to understand our general problem? Obviously I believe they are, and the reader is asked to consider them only from these two points of view.

   Nevertheless, I must indicate my debt to an excellent study, an unpublished doctoral dissertation of Sister M. Joyce Rowland, O.S.F.,

"The Acts of the Mind According to John Henry Newman" (St. Louis University, 1962).

7. This is, of course, "scientific induction," or "rational induction," as several writers have recently called it, not the kind of induction which gives rise to first principles, "intellective induction." See Robert J. Henle, S.J., *Method in Metaphysics* (Milwaukee: Marquette University Press, 1951).

8. The "ontological mode of science," or "ontological science" in brief, is one which uses "ontological concepts." An ontological concept is one which arises by direct abstraction or by "separation" from an experienced reality, or is developed by a reasoning process from such direct concepts. It is contrasted with "constructural concepts"—concepts which contain an imposed intelligibility, derived originally from some other reality and used to understand a reality opaque to direct understanding, the application of such intelligibilities being governed by precise rules and mediate evidence. The distinction corresponds to that proposed by M. Jacques Maritain between dianoetic and empiriological knowledge, *Degrees of Knowledge* (New York: Scribner's, 1959), pp. 202–205. See also Robert J. Henle, S.J., "A Thomistic Explanation of the Relations Between Science and Philosophy: The Theoretical Presentation," *Bulletin of the Albertus Magnus Guild* (October, 1956), and Klubertanz, *Introduction to the Philosophy of Being* (New York: Appleton-Century-Crofts, 1963), pp. 286–293.

9. In a paper for a Workshop on "Teaching Thomism Today" (Catholic University of America, June, 1962, to be published) I have discussed these positions more fully.

10. Much of what is said here about the three levels of knowing has been worked out by the Reverend Robert J. Henle, S.J., and if there is anything good in it, it derives from his original insights and elaborations. Unfortunately, he has not published all of this material, but the following can be consulted with profit: "A Philosopher's Interpretation of Anthropology's Contribution to the Understanding of Man," *Anthropological Quarterly*, XXXII (1959), 22–40, and "Science and the Humanities," *Thought*, XXXV (1960), 513–36.

11. On the way in which "originating attitudes" function to order, unify, and distinguish knowledges, see the very valuable paper by Jean Ladrière, "Freedom in Science," *Truth and Freedom* (Pittsburgh: Duquesne University Press, 1954).

12. It seems to be a common opinion that Cardinal Newman considered liberal education to lead only to a "credence," and to a veneer of culture, not to real assents and true moral activity. Some recent studies indicate that this may be a misinterpretation; see Edmond Darvil Benard, "The *Idea of a University*: Background and Theory," in *A Newman Symposium*, ed. Victor R. Yanitelli, S.J. (New York: Ford-

ham University Press, 1952), pp. 12–13, and Martin J. Svaglic, "Newman: The Man of Letters in Our Times," *ibid.*, pp. 112–18.
    But whatever Newman may have thought about liberal education, it seems true that a vital humanistic formation does lead to real assents.
13. That interrelation, application, and generalization must be explicitly worked for by the teacher is clearly brought out by Jaime Castiello, S.J., *Geistesformung* (Berlin: Düumlers Verlag, 1934), pp. 28–32, 34, 48, 60–61, 136–40. Father Castiello shows conclusively that almost all transfer from one course to another and from the classroom to life depends largely on the teacher's method. If the teacher teaches for transfer, both in formal statement and in instances of application, the transfer occurs in a high percentage of the students. If he does not, the fact that transferable matters are covered, no matter how excellently, does not bring transfer except in a very small percentage of cases.
14. On the idea of critical intelligence, see Robert J. Henle, S.J., "The Modern Liberal University: Reflective Intelligence Versus Tradition," *Confluence,* VI (1957), 184–95.

Selected Bibliography

Artz, J. "Newman's Contribution to Theory of Knowledge," *Philosophy Today,* IV (1960), 12–25.
Boekraad, A. J. *The Personal Conquest of Truth According to J. H. Newman.* Louvain: Nauwaelerts, 1955.
Castiello, Jaime, S.J. *A Humane Psychology of Education.* New York: Sheed & Ward, 1936.
Collins, James. *Philosophical Readings in Cardinal Newman.* Chicago: Henry Regnery Co., 1961. Parts 1 and 2.
Ganss, George E., S.J. *St. Ignatius's Idea of a Jesuit University.* Milwaukee: Marquette University Press, 1954.
Gilson, Etienne. "The Eminence of Teaching," *Disputed Questions in Education* (Garden City: Doubleday, 1954), No. II.
————. "Science, Philosophy and Religious Wisdom," *Proceedings of the American Catholic Philosophical Association,* XXVI (1952), 5–13.
Guzie, Tad, S.J. *The Analogy of Learning.* New York: Sheed & Ward, 1960.
Klubertanz, George P., S.J. "The Teaching of Thomistic Metaphysics," *Gregorianum,* XXXV (1954), 3–17, 187–205.
Pegis, Anton C. *Christian Philosophy and Intellectual Freedom.* Milwaukee: Bruce, 1960.
Schmitz, Kenneth L. "Natural Wisdom and Some Recent Philosophy Manuals," *Proceedings of the American Catholic Philosophical Association,* XXX (1956), 181–90.
Wade, Francis C., S.J. "Causality in the Classroom," *The Modern Schoolman,* XXVIII (1951), 138–46.

4

THE ACT OF FAITH AND MORAL BEHAVIOR

Vincent T. O'Keefe, S.J.

The object of this paper is to present some background thoughts for an exploration of the treatments of the act of faith and their relationship to the active life and moral behavior of the student.

Since the act of faith is man's response to God's revelation, the notions of revelation and faith are correlative and should be developed in relation to one another. Revelation is frequently described as a communication on God's part testifying to the truth of a proposition. The act of faith is then described as an intellectual assent to the truth of a proposition. In this context, the tendency is to identify revelation with a series of propositions and the act of faith with an act of the intellect alone.

Historically, before the development of the branch of Theology known as Fundamental Theology, faith was considered under the heading of the divine supernatural activity in man, the theological virtues. This is still true today in the treatment of faith in some seminary courses and in some theology manuals. The far more common practice is to treat the question of faith in Fundamental Theology.

A typical seminary treatment would cover the following points:

1. The *nature* of faith: it is an act which is formally intellectual, an assent to the truth of a proposition.

2. The *qualities* of faith: the act of faith is supernatural, the

firmest of all assents, obscure, and free; as a virtue it is necessary for salvation.

3. The *motive* of faith: its motive is the authority of God, who reveals a truth to us.

4. The *material* object: all divinely revealed truth as proposed by the Church.

5. The *preambles:* a treatment of the rational side of faith, how this act is in accord with the dictates of reason.

This represents a very brief but fair summary of the treatment of the act of faith in the classical and modern manuals. The prevailing mood has stressed the intellectual, not to say rational, side of faith. The emphasis has been on the notion of faith as an assent to a truth, and this ties in with the notion of revelation as a communication on God's part attesting to the truth of a proposition.

Some attention, but all too little, is given to the part played by the will in the act of faith, to the affective side. The treatments have been predominantly ontological in nature with relatively little done on the psychological side and little attention paid to the working of conversion as brought out by the testimony of converts.

Faith has been treated in the context of Apologetics in that a considerable amount of time and space has been devoted to the questions of the preambles of faith, the reasonability required for the act of faith, how to prove the reasonable or rational character of the act of faith. The following division is a familiar one:

1. *Judicium credibilitatis:* this is a speculative judgment which says the act of faith is reasonable because of the natural arguments in favor of the fact of revelation.

2. *Judicium credentitatis:* this is the practical judgment which says, "I am bound to assent to this as revealed."

3. *Judicium fidei:* this is the assent of faith whereby I freely affirm the proposition on the authority of God, who reveals it.

An emphasis on the intellectual and reasonable or rational elements is understandable in the light of the historical context within which the treatment of faith took shape. The pseudo-mystical and illuminationist doctrines of many Protestants brought about a reaction on the part of theologians who thought they had to attenuate the role of supernatural illumination of the grace of faith and who wanted to bring out the so-called faith of authority and dogmatic faith. A veil was thrown over the fact that faith is an assimilation to the intimate knowledge God has of Himself. The result was an exaltation of the aspect of submission to an authority and of acceptance of an ecclesiastical formula.

The eighteenth century was the Age of Rationalism. The truth of revelation and the intellectual validity of its content were denied. Rationalistic and positivistic attacks against religion led certain theologians to attempt a reply while remaining on the terrain of the rationalists and the positivists as though it were possible to introduce these people fully to faith while using their methods only.

The voluntarism of the late medieval Nominalists stressed the will's role in faith and remotely prepared Luther's conception. When teaching the *Epistle to the Romans,* it occurred to Luther that the faith portrayed there was an act of trust in a good God who wrought our salvation in spite of our sinfulness. This interpretation gave him peace, and he changed the then current notion of faith. It was no longer an act of the intellect, but an act of the will in which man grasped a loving God and in this grasp found his peace. Calvin took this interpretation, and the Reformers had a new notion of faith.

By the nineteenth century, the Protestants in the person of Friedrich Schleiermacher placed all the intellectual content of an act of faith in the category of indifferent impedimenta. Faith was an experience of God, strange, vital, luminous, but not intellectual. Luther's true position was now recognized: faith is a soothing and inspiring religious experience. Except for the Fundamentalists who still believe in the propositional revelation of the Bible, all modern Protestants in one form or other accept Schleiermacher's position.

Rationalism could not be met by the Catholics in the way it was by the Protestants. They insisted that faith was not intellectual, but the Catholics always insisted that it was a valid intellectual commitment. The Catholics had to answer the accusations of the Rationalists who tried to explain much of the Scriptures as erroneous. In order to meet the Rationalists, the theologians had to prescind from the theology of the issue and deal with them philosophically. In fact, there was a not infrequent tendency to prove too much by mere natural reason.

In our day there is a clearer emphasis on something which can be found in many theologians but which was not developed and stressed enough. This is the clear orientation to bring back to its rightful place the virtuous, religious, and supernatural character of faith, to mark the essential difference which separates natural belief from the theological act of faith, and to attach the latter act to the profound dynamism of the spiritual nature of the believer and not just to the exercise of the faculties of reason. This is in accord with the Catholic tradition as found in the great scholastic period and especially in St. Thomas.

It is by faith that man opens himself to supernatural life and orients himself in a radical fashion with reference to divine grace which is offered to him. This fundamental option surpasses the power of man left to himself and is a gift given by God. The act of faith is also an act which is eminently human and a profound manifestation of our personality where our responsibility is involved. Faith thus appears as a vital link between nature and the supernatural.

St. Thomas and his contemporaries were less interested in critical problems concerning the act of faith than in the theological virtue of faith and its religious value. The action of the grace of faith is put in relation to the role of the will in the intellectual assent of the believer. The clearest expression of this Thomistic explanation is, "The light of faith does not move by way of the intellect but rather by way of the will."[1]

In the Council of Trent the act of faith is characterized as the movement of man towards God, whose revelation is before all else a message of salvation. The religious character of the act of faith, which is not a simple enrichment of our intellectual knowledge, appears clearly. The essential role of faith in the origin of justification and its religious value are brought out, since the faith of the convert does not appear only as an adhesion of the mind to certain truths, but as the first orientation of man to God, who is faithful to His promises. The virtue of faith infused in the soul at the moment of justification is considered as a means of real assimilation to Christ.

The Vatican Council states that the true cause of the adhesion of faith and its firmness is to be sought in the action of God in the depths of man's soul. Faith is fundamentally the result of a grace of light and attraction. It does not suppose merely the testimony of God which is heard but also a more intimate and ultimate testimony, which acts in the interior of the soul, enlightening man's intelligence and drawing the powers of desire.

The constitution *Dei Filius* rules out the error of fideism and affirms, against a Protestant doctrine of illuminism, the existence and role of eternal motives of credibility. It is, however, the rationalist danger which seems most disquieting to the Council. There is an insistence that faith is a free and virtuous adhesion, which is the work of grace above all else, and that nothing would be more opposed to the Church's tradition than to want to assimilate it to the rational examination of a human doctrine. It is more in conformity with the general spirit of the tradition, not to limit the role of grace to making an act of faith salutary which one should logically consider as intrinsically natural, but to attribute to it an important part in the very genesis of the act insofar as it is an act of knowledge. Then, too, a prime place for moral dispositions and for the whole dynamism of the will is recognized.

This latter point is stressed by theologians who held on to the clear affirmations of St. Thomas. The role of the will in faith is not merely to rule out imprudent doubts, as some moderns seem to think. Drawn by what is good, the will positively draws the intelligence towards the divine Intelligible, Who exerts on us a very powerful attraction.

Once faith is conceived as the conclusion of a series of propositions, it is assimilated to any historical knowledge; and the role of moral dispositions is reduced to almost nothing. Presenting faith as a dry, extrinsic adhesion in abstract formulas and conditioned by an extrinsic credibility means insoluble problems.

Closer to our own time, Blondel and others have stressed the idea that faith is more a life than a simple cognition. To be converted is not merely to be convinced intellectually of the excellence of a doctrine, but to bring a new life to ourselves, a life higher than ours, and to attract God to us. Without this it would not be a supernatural faith which consists in an attitude of the whole being, which assumes a position relative to the supernatural order, which accepts the introduction into one's life of another Being, of a personal God, calling us to a deifying union with Him. Along with the element of belief, there is a larger role in all faith, human or divine, for the element of affective and unitive confidence. Beside the abstract knowledge of dogmatic propositions, Blondel sees in faith a concrete knowledge, a new relation of the soul to God, an ineffable relation of person to person, anticipating the beatifying union of heaven.

This obviously introduces into the notion of faith a certain number of elements which are strange to it and seems to confuse faith in the strict sense, which is an element of justification, with the whole processus of justification. Blondel's notion is closer to life. His concrete point of view leads him, at the risk of some confusion, to consider the ensemble of what is currently called faith and not to isolate different elements, as some scholastics do. He uncovers the complex aspect of this fundamental religious attitude in which the whole personality of man is caught up.

The problem of faith as posed concretely today goes beyond the question of an intellectual adhesion to a dogmatic ensemble. What enters in is the question of a personal attitude towards God and the supernatural. This involves the essential and intrinsic role of man's moral orientation and dispositions of will in the perception of reasons which will lead him to take this attitude. We must consider the action of the will in faith not as an element juxtaposed to the action of the intellect but as intimately united to it and conditioning its activity.

The Blondelians too often thought they had discovered for the first time things which the authentic Christian tradition had taught long before them. Their horror of intellectualism pushed them to avoiding precise concepts, arguments in form, and to being satisfied with imaginative but vague expressions which were at times ambiguous. The idea, which is true enough, that in faith there is more than just a simple assent to an abstract system of truths, led them to stretch unduly the notion of faith to the whole Christian attitude, to the life of faith, and to reason, as though faith englobed the practice of life in conformity with what one believes.

But on the whole, their reaction is sane. More than anyone else, they brought the problem of faith onto a concrete and religious terrain. Classical theologians were preoccupied with the rights of God and truth and placed the accent on the exterior and objective aspect of revelation and on the obligation that stems from it for men. The Blondelians' point of view is that of the subject. They sought to show how faith is inserted concretely into the spiritual life of man in conformity with his immanent law of perfection. Thus, they called attention to very important aspects of the psychology of faith.

Some objected that they were taking up the Protestant error of faith which is nothing but trust. But for the Blondelians, it is a question of something much more objective. It is not a blind and subjective confidence in one's own salvation but a confident abandonment to the intervention of God in one's personal life, and a free decision to open oneself to this divine action and to accept all that is implied by the renunciation of a purely natural vision of the world and the recognition of a supernatural end, with the possibility of a union with God, who enters into communication with man.

Christian Pesch is noted for his solid, traditional views; and yet, while remaining very traditional and fiercely hostile to all infiltrations of subjectivity, he understood better than most scholastics that there is in faith a moral element and an important part played by personal attitudes. Familiarity with Newman helped here. Faith does not have as its primary purpose the satisfaction of our intellectual curiosity. In its essence, it is cognition, an act of intelligence; and it would be confusing to bring into the definition the flowering which it finds in a life informed by charity. Pesch maintains that it is a special type of cognition. Instead of coldly discussing the truth of a proposition, it is a question of the believer's attitude vis-à-vis his Creator, which unveils for us the laws of the moral and religious world. Faith, an act of intellectual obeisance, supposes a free orientation of the whole person, intellect and will, toward God, who reveals himself as our final supernatural end.

Father Chenu also insists that religious faith is cognition of a special genre. It is testimony, but of God about Himself. Testimony here is the vehicle of real knowledge which gives us, although in mystery, as the object of perception and love, a reality, the divine reality. Faith is an assent to a proposition. But the act of the believer does not terminate at a dogmatic proposition, but at the divine reality which it expresses humanly.[2] This is the conception of St. Thomas, for whom faith is not only the objective datum of revelation but also the interior light: "there is not only the accepting of things to which we assent, but something which inclines us to assent, and that is a certain light of divinity infused in the human mind."[3]

Divine faith communicates not some intelligible matter but the very reality of our beatitude: it is God, substantial truth, satisfying end of all our desires. This is not merely a concept, propositions, a system of thought, but He in whom we recognize the whole of our lives, the object of our happiness. Through dogmatic propositions and thanks to them, faith is an adhesion to that which fulfills all our desires and the unique desire of our souls: beatitude in the possession of God. This shows the difference between the testimony of God in the believer and that of a man who is worthy of belief relative to a fact. Human testimony can beget certitude, but it is not in itself a vital knowledge which is the beginning of a further penetration right up to a vision.

Father Malevez has noted that the Thomistic act of faith is inspired by: "No one can come to me unless the Father, who sent me, draws him."[4] It is the Holy Spirit who places in us the principle of the adhesion of faith by way of an inclination which He gives us to eternal life and to its necessary means, faith itself, by way of an attraction which He has us undergo, and to which He gives us our power of freely consenting. This means that the Holy Spirit sees to it that our souls echo the essentials of the doctrine preached to them by the Church. He puts us in harmony with the exteriorly attested doctrine of our heavenly destiny by a motion which He exercises supernaturally in our wills. This motion inclines the whole ensemble to this new end and to the ratification by our intellects of the attestation given to us of it. At the same time as He reveals from without by the voice of the Church His plan to have us participate in His life in Christ, God connaturalizes us from within with this new world. This is in two ways: in harmonizing our power of desire with the new end which is offered; and in soliciting us to affirm the testimony given to this new order by the external word of Christ and the Church. If we are solicited to affirm this testimony, it is not because of signs which would found it rationally, but because of a different motive which is not of the order of rational motives. It is by reason of a pure infused desire to conform our thought to the first Truth because of the inclination which He gives toward this effect and which we seize obscurely as coming from Him.

The consideration given to the affective and unitive characteristics of the act of faith is most important in the relation of the act of faith to moral behavior. We can now indicate a number of points which provide much material for earnest discussion on treatments of faith and the active life and moral behavior of the student.

In dealing with the notion of revelation, it can be misleading to say simply that it is a communication on God's part testifying to the truth of something. This can give the idea that the revelation which makes up the content of our act of faith is a purely academic thing, something impersonal, which God puts out without too much concern over whether it is accepted or not. The whole process here tends to remain on the propositional level.

If we describe revelation as a communication of God, asking for faith, this brings out the personal nature of God's revelation, His "concern" that we accept the revelation, and the personal nature of our act of faith.

The material object of faith is God, but it is God our salvation, who is manifested in Christ, the Son of God by nature. Faith is theocentric and has God for its object, but God who wishes to bring about man's salvation. Thus the content of our act of faith is not merely a cold or indifferent proposition to be affirmed, but something bound up with our salvation. The total and adequate object of faith is the mystery of Christ and His Mystical Body. This brings together God, Christ, the Church, and the believer as the object of salvation which comes from God. To have faith means to believe that I am concerned in salvation which comes from God.

The term of our act of faith is not just the words of this act. Faith does not consist in merely pronouncing the words of the creed. "The act of the believer does not terminate at a proposition, but at a reality."[5] The movement of faith does not attain only the words of the act of faith. As in every act of authentic cognition, it seizes the thing itself. Faith has Christ himself as its term. There is a true union with Christ by faith. This is obviously not in the sense of a corporal inhabitation, but of a spiritual union which exists in knowledge and love and which constitutes a certain mysterious presence.

Faith has God Himself as its term.[6] Only God appeases the movement of faith, and it is God Himself, His personal reality. St. Thomas uses expressions like "man is joined to God through faith,"[7] whereas the unbeliever "is alienated from God,"[8] "does not approach Him."[9]

Sacred Scripture orients us in this direction, e.g., in I John. The expression "to believe in God"[10] introduced by St. John, has been understood by tradition in the sense that God Himself, according to His divinity, is touched by faith.

Hence the assent of faith is not just a conceptual assent, but a unitive assent, one of communion with God. Communion here is understood in the sense of an inchoative friendship, an initial assimilation. It must be distinguished from the communion of inhabitation which is the communication of God to the soul according to His substantial presence which permits the soul to enjoy this presence.[11]

The union with God through faith is a mediate union in that it is through the intermediary of a created reality which is the believer's faith. Faith is thus the beginning of eternal life. "He who believes in the Son possesses eternal life."[12] Faith is the actuality of revelation for the believer of today.

In treating the act of faith, careful attention can be paid to the notion of revelation, to the material object of faith, and to its affective and unitive nature, as well as its intellectual aspect. This would have a direct bearing on the active life and moral behavior of the student. This would not intermingle indiscriminately the act of faith and the much broader notion of the life of faith. It would also arise from a theological treatment of the act of faith and not from any "exhortatory" element added over and above the theology. A theological treatment of the act of faith will show a "built-in" factor which relates to action and moral behavior.

Notes

1. "Lumen fidei . . . non movet per viam intellectus sed magis per viam voluntatis." (St. Thomas Aquinas, *In Boethium de Trinitate,* q. 3, a. 1, ad 4.)
2. "Actus credentis non terminatur ad enuntiabile sed ad rem." (St. Thomas Aquinas, *Summa Theologiae,* II-II, q. 1, a. 2, ad 2.)
3. "Non solum acceptio rerum quibus assentimus sed aliquid quod inclinat ad assensum, et hoc est lumen quoddam divinitus menti humanae

infusum." (St. Thomas Aquinas, *In Boethium de Trinitate*, q. 3, a. 1, ad 4.)
4. "Nemo potest venire ad me nisi Pater qui misit me traxerit eum." (John 6:44.)
5. See note 2 above.
6. "Moventur in Deum." Heinrich J. Denzinger (ed.), *Enchiridion Symbolorum* (31st ed. rev. by C. Rahner, S.J.; Borcinone, Friburgi, Brigoviae: Herder & Co., 1957), No. 798.
7. "Homo conjungitur Deo per fidem."
8. "... elongatur a Deo."
9. "... non appropinquat ei."
10. "credere in Deum."
11. Cf. John 5:38,40,43; 6:45; I John 4:12,15,16; 5:10; I Cor. 2:16; II Cor. 4:6; Phil. 2:5.
12. "Qui credit in Filium habet vitam aeternam." (Cf. John 3:3; 17:3; I John 2:23–27; Eph. 1:14.)

Bibliography

Roger Aubert, *Le Problème de l'Acte de Foi* (Louvain: Warny, 1958) is the best book on the subject.

Part II

THEOLOGY

5

CURRENT APPROACHES TO THEOLOGY

Gerald Van Ackeren, S.J.

The purpose of this paper is to expose the current approaches to the study of theology and in particular to point up the implications of these different views for the teaching of theology in the colleges. It is intended to give some background in the pluralistic views on the nature of theology with the implications for the development and teaching of theology.

Kerygmatic Approach

According to Yves Congar, O.P., the two great questions in theological method during the period immediately preceding World War II were the question of kerygmatic theology and that of *Konkluzionstheologie*.[1] *Konkluzionstheologie* is now a completely dead issue, largely owing to the magnificent work of Father Congar himself. The thrust of kerygmatic theology, however, is still very much felt and is exerting a continued influence.

This conception of theology presents itself as a return to the original spirit governing the Christian message. As a new movement in theology, it had its beginning among the theologians at Innsbruck (Jungmann, Lakner, Hugo Rahner, Donder) in an attentive evaluation of present-day Christianity.[2] The kerygmatics find that the alarming number of Christians who really do not practice their faith points to glaring deficiencies in our pastoral work of preaching and teaching the message of salvation to the faithful.

83

It is not so much a lack of knowledge among Catholics that is so distressing as their lack of persuasion that Christianity is of vital importance in their lives. To them Christianity is true in the same sense that Mount Everest is 29,028 feet high—it might just as well be fifty feet higher.

According to these "kerygmatic theologians," the fundamental reason for the sad state of Christianity today is found in our scholastic theology. Scholastic theology, they say, is too much set up within the circle of its own concepts and theses, too preoccupied with outdated controversies and with defense against adversaries long dead. It has hardened into a dry set of impeccable formulas in which nothing is missing except life. School-theology, moreover, fails to prepare anyone to teach and preach the Christian revelation as meaningful for Christian living.

The kerygmatic thesis is that revelation has been given for Christian living and the study of revelation must unfold its message—the tidings of great joy, the good news of Christ and salvation. What is required is a rethinking-through of revelation and a rebuilding of present-day theology into a theology which can convey the urgency of the Christian message.

The kerygmatics do not deny that scholastic theology has its place. It must continue to penetrate ever more deeply, to assimilate and systematize the whole content of revelation, and to defend it against attack. However, these objectives do not provide for the needs of Christian preaching and living, where the important thing is the glowing vision of Christianity as a way of life, a message of salvation, a wonderful gift of a loving Father.

Secondly, the logical, systematic order of scholastic theology is not suited to the vital communication of the Christian message. Taking God as its object, it begins with the consideration of His essence (unity and Trinity), then studies His operations (the procession of creatures from God through creation and their return to Him). The demands of Christian living, however, require a different order of presentation—a psychological-historical order, in which the central figure is Christ, studied in His historical background, His life, His work, His Church.

Thirdly, scholastic theology makes use of a technical and somewhat shopworn terminology in its pursuit of clarity and precision. It constructs the message of revelation in an abstract system of categories which are far removed from Christian living and have no kerygmatic value. It is rather in Scripture and in tradition and the early history of theology that we find not only the kerygmatic content of revealed truth but also a method of presenting it which aims at making Christianity appealing and acceptable.

It was chiefly Lakner of Innsbruck who proposed to solve the problem of revitalizing theology by dividing theology into "school-theology" (positive and speculative theology) and preaching-theology.[3] School-theology is nothing else than the projection of God's view of things into this world. Since the blessed in heaven have already reached their eternal goal, for them the question of means to this goal is superfluous. For them suffices the view of the *true*, under which viewpoint they behold all reality; while for mortal men, the way to beatitude shines forth from their examination of revelation from the viewpoint of the *good*. Hence, the different formal aspects of scientific and kerygmatic theology. School-theology emphasizes the question of truth; preaching-theology that of salvation, in order to lay bare the meaningful values for life and thus provide a real incentive for pursuing our eternal goal. Preaching-theology presupposes dogmatic theology; nevertheless, it examines revelation from a new standpoint—"through men's eyes."

Preaching-theology as developed by Lakner is an independent, self-contained, scientific system, with its own formal object (the good), its own subject matter (Christ), and its own material object (truths which lead to our goal), out of which finally stems a corresponding mode of presentation which emphasizes the vitality of revealed truths by showing how they find their meaning in Christ and lead to salvation.

Catholic theologians from other parts of Europe (and even Karl

Rahner of Innsbruck) showed general agreement with the kerygmatics on the none-too-flourishing condition of our Christianity
and even on the deficiencies of present-day preaching and teaching
of theology. But they reacted vigorously and quite unanimously
against the proposal of setting up a new theological science which
would be distinct from and independent of scientific theology.
Such a new theology, they say, is neither necessary nor possible,
because theology of its nature is at one and the same time both
scientific and kerygmatic in character.[4] Overemphasis on either
aspect is equally wrong. Since revelation is in very fact the message
of salvation, any true exploration of revelation (and theology is
actually nothing more than this) is already in itself the science
of salvation. The effort to explicate what is implicit in revelation
and to develop what is there in germ is in itself a help to preaching
and a service to living.

Significant in the reaction of Catholic theologians is the criticism made by Michael Schmaus. After protesting vigorously
against an independent kerygmatic theology, he set out in his
Katholische Dogmatik to provide a theological presentation of
revelation which would correspond to the needs of preaching the
Gospel. As Schmaus says: Theology "is a service first of all for
the knowledge of salvation (speculative science), and secondly, it
is thereby also a service for the winning of our salvation (practical
science)."[5] Any study of revelation whose exclusive preoccupation
would be the constructing of a system for organizing revealed
truths *merely* in their ordered hierarchy of intelligibility would
tend to betray the profound motives which inspired God to make
the revelation. At the same time, however, if theology would re-
nounce strict methods of procedure and careful documentation, if
it would neglect the intelligibility of revelation as the ground for a
salvific encounter with Christ the Savior, if it would slight the demands of reason and the objections of adversaries, it would betray its character as a science.

It is significant that of the internationally recognized theologians of our day who have commented on the question, practically all have rejected not only the necessity but also the possibility of setting up a kerygmatic theology essentially distinct from scientific theology. Here we can name Father Yves Congar, O.P., M. D. Chenu, O.P., Karl Rahner, S.J., and many others.[6]

In reply to the rather violent criticism of a distinct kerygmatic theology, Father Jungmann insisted that it was never his intention to foster a new theology independent of and opposed to scientific theology. If the fruit of the whole controversy, he says, is an orientation of a scientific theology to pastoral needs, there is no need for a separate kerygmatic theology, since the original objective would be obtained.

The kerygmatic controversy itself has been a dead issue now for about fifteen years. But the kerygmatic thrust continues to make itself felt. With added impetus from the new biblical studies, the liturgical movement, and the emphasis of the role of the layman in the social worship and action of the Church, it has provided a true enrichment of our conception of theology. In recent years kerygmatic concern has for the most part turned about problems in pedagogy rather than the epistemological problem of a distinct science. Nevertheless, the movement has helped to bring theologians out of any ivory tower they had built for themselves and has made them face the problem of understanding the message of salvation in function of mid-twentieth-century Christian thought and life. It has also served to emphasize the Christocentric character of revelation and the consequent necessity for theology itself to be centered in Christ Himself. Father Emile Mersch[7] had already for more than a decade been championing Christocentrism in the construction of theological science, and the encyclical *Mystici Corporis* (1943) gave added impetus to this conception of theology. But it was chiefly the kerygmatic concern manifested in the catechetical revival in Germany and Austria and the consequent attempts at a kerygmatic theology that pushed Christocentrism to the fore in the mid-century re-evaluation of theology.

Scriptural-historical Approach

The emphasis put by the kerygmatics on the psychological (as opposed to the logical) approach to the Christian Mystery has led even classical theology to re-examine its methodology. Because Christ is the Way (and there is no other way) and because He is the Way in His human involvement in the history of salvation, we must study Christ in His background, His life, His mission from the Father, and His Work. This study must be directed specially to the Gospels, where the visible historical impact of his personality on the apostles and disciples is manifest to us. It is primarily in the Scriptures that we shall discover the very heart of the good news which is Christ.

Very encouraging and inspiring support for this approach was found in the new Scripture studies called forth by the encyclical *Divino Afflante Spiritu*. More enlightened studies of the story of God's interventions in history for the salvation of his people, of the genesis of the great themes of the Old Testament (such as the covenant, the kingdom, the people of God), the new understanding of the apostolic kerygma, and in particular the first steps toward construction of a biblical theology—all these advances have vindicated the validity of the scriptural approach in creating interest in a better understanding of our faith.

At the same time, however, they have cast a shadow of distrust over many of the abstract formulations of scholastic theology, which frequently carry the impression that we can know what a thing is from an already manufactured definition or that we can understand the meaning of a dogma by analyzing terms of an abstract proposition.

Moreover, since the personal possession of truth requires experience and reflection, the kerygmatics are most insistent on re-living the genesis of an idea or truth, not only in the history of revelation itself but in the development of the deposit of faith in the Church down to the present.

Biblical theology does not claim to be the whole of theology.

But it has found an intimate sympathetic response in the current kerygmatic concern. Biblical theology is not the same as a religious history of revelation, its genesis and its evolution. It goes beyond the stages of semantics and history and textual analysis to the discovery of unifying themes and an internal principle of order which can organize all biblical realities into an intelligible whole.[8]

Here we may note two tendencies: (1) Some biblical theologians adopt an historical order of treatment, taking up successively the different sources of the divine message. Although they are intent on finding the intended meaning of the sacred writers in their use of the thought patterns of the time, they insist on keeping the conceptual and historical categories of the Bible in the construction of a biblical theology. Their work is chiefly exegetical and historical, but also theological. Their concern is the movement of *Heilsgeschichte* as determined in God's historical self-communication to man. But they hesitate to break out of the framework of historical development and transpose into any new mode of conceptualization the content of their sources. For them to venture beyond biblical categories of unity would be to stray from their specific work as biblical theologians.[9]

(2) Other biblical theologians, however, do not wish to be restricted by these limitations. They conceive their function as an endeavor to come to grips with the object of faith, with the truth itself revealed in the Scriptures. Although they adopt the categories of thought of the inspired authors, they endeavor to rethink them, purify their concepts, and translate them into a language which is "demythologized" as far as possible and more universally intelligible. Their effort is not only to determine the origin and exact meaning of biblical conceptions in function of their usage at the time. They do not only try to perceive the full conceptual content of biblical terms, together with the overtones and affective values with which they have been enriched by usage. But they endeavor to transpose these materials beyond the realm from which they were extracted and unify them into a harmonious architectonic

whole, wherein each element receives its proper emphasis and value.[10]

This conception of biblical theology has a close affinity with speculative theology. But it does not call on the service of philosophy in the elaboration of the intelligibility of the content of revelation. Biblical theology presupposes no philosophy, no rational schema. It is not preoccupied with giving a reasoned account of the divine mystery nor with defending it. It is concerned exclusively with expressing in an intelligible whole the full biblical notion, the reality which God has wished to make known to men through His Scriptures.[11]

The Ecclesiological Approach

The modern liturgical movement which took its start in the great French, Belgian, and German Benedictine abbeys of Solesmes, Maredsous, Beuron, and Maria-Laach has unleashed a whole cycle of wider movements beyond itself which are having their part in enriching our conception of theology. Under the guidance of the Holy Spirit, the liturgical ferment has not only contributed to the rediscovery of Scripture and the Fathers of the Church. It has issued in a rediscovery of the Church itself which is recorded in an abundant and still growing literature.

The movement has refocused our attention on a key truth of Christianity: namely, the Presence of Christ, not only in history, but especially in the Church today and in the sacraments which are his saving actions in the reconstruction of human society.[12] It is the Church that brings Christ to us and brings us to Christ. We are not first united to Christ and through Him to the Church. It is in and through the Church that we are joined to Christ, by being incorporated into His Body.

The development of this insight has led to what might be called an ecclesiological approach to theology insofar as it can be distinguished from the scriptural-historical approach mentioned earlier. The main elements in this approach seem to be as follows:[13]

(1) Since no one can theologize except in faith and from faith as a starting point, we must begin theology with faith as we have it, namely in the Church. It is the Church that immediately touches our lives; in the Body of Christ we grow to full maturity; in this mystery we are united; to life in this Body we are committed. This is the situation in which we are, where we find ourselves; and we can only start from where we are.

Our approach must then be made "from the inside" as believers, who seek not so much to justify the Church to non-believers as to discover more deeply its living reality and the challenges to which our commitment in the Church calls us.

(2) Theology is the methodical pursuit of an understanding of this commitment in the Church where we stand. Here we can trace two lines of development.

First of all, we can study in detail the revelation of God about his Church as evidenced in her teaching and sanctifying action today. This involves an approach through the authentic teaching[14] and the current living tradition of the Church, which immediately present us with the object of faith and clarify the meaning of the commitment of faith. It involves a study of Scripture and tradition, but takes its start from the Church today, especially from her teaching and sacramental life. It is the Church today that is *prius quoad nos* in our living faith. And the knowledge of the Church, her life, and what she proposes today for our faith provides the premises on which further pursuit of understanding depends.

Then follows the "fleshing-out" of this knowledge: that is, a retrogressive study of the historical development of revelation and doctrine by which the Church in time has arrived at the current conceptualization of her living tradition (biblical and positive theology).[15]

In this process insights are gained not only into the structure of the development itself but also into the hierarchical value of the truths of revelation. It should be noted that throughout there is always question of clarifying one's original and unshakable commitment to faith and to the life towards which it continually beckons.

Another line of development pursuing understanding within the faith is as follows: While acknowledging our present commitment in the Church by faith, we proceed to relive, as it were, the development of this faith from its origins in God's election of his people, through the progressive revelation of his salvific designs in the Old and New Testaments, finally arriving by a kind of genetic method at the fuller understanding of our faith as it is formulated for us by the magisterium today.[16]

The theory behind this approach might be explained as follows: All life as we know it grows by a sort of dialectic imposed by its historical dimension on the internal dynamism of God's creation. It can be understood adequately only in view of its genesis and development in realizing its purposes in historical fact. A certain groping is intrinsic to this process. The struggles, conflicts, reverses, and victories all leave their stamp indelibly on the organism. Just as man cannot be understood apart from his background, birth, childhood, adolescence, and development to maturity, so the living faith of the Church today cannot be understood except in and through its genesis and evolution of *Heilsgeschichte*.[17]

Both the retrogressive and genetic procedures have certain advantages as well as disadvantages, especially from a pedagogical point of view. But we shall not delay on this point now.

Within the ecclesiological approach there is a further development which theologians regard as necessary in theology. Within faith there is a moment or an aspect of reason which must be elaborated as the rational ground of faith. This moment involves the fact of revelation itself as a communication of God to man in history. The necessity of this consideration within the commitment of faith is thus explained by Father Weigel:

A man who believes is already convinced of the truth of his belief, for otherwise he would not believe. A man who does not believe doubts or rejects many propositions of faith, and he will hold none of them on faith. The approach to the problem of the credibility of the Church will be different in the two cases. The believer has already become certain of the fact of revelation, but he may not reflect on the motives of this certitude. Consequently in his case the work of fundamental theology is to render explicit and reflective the motives for such a certainty. Even to him fundamental theology does not wish to prove the reasonableness of his faith; if his faith is serene, then he has already done this. It wishes only to marshal in methodic fashion the motives which implicitly and without reflection have moved the believer already. There is here no essay of proving, but rather of expressing proofs already implicitly [accepted] and with little or no reflection. This is done not that the man can believe, because he believes already. It is done so that a stable and firm rational discipline can be established on the basis of his faith.[18]

Rahner conceives this aspect of an ecclesiological approach in a somewhat different light. He says:

. . . dogmatic theology must develop out of itself and within itself a theology of *theologia fundamentalis*. It must, that is to say, declare as part of its own discourse, the existence, mode and meaning of a rational demonstration of the faith from without and with a view to those without, as possible and necessary. Dogmatic theology does not execute this demonstration; but autonomously determines the possibility, the sense and the limits of such a demonstration. . . .[19]

It is well to note that the ecclesiological approach is also Christo-centric, but it emphasizes the point that Christ as center is found in and through His Church.

A Theology for the Laity

The movement for a theology of the laity has been energized by the urgency of providing the layman with an operative intelligence of his faith in fulfilling his role in the social worship and action of the Church. This urgency is felt particularly in Catholic universities and colleges, where the problem is immediate and critical. Efforts to provide such a theology have made use of all the above-mentioned approaches. The new programs in college theology are kerygmatic in spirit, Christocentric; they lean heavily upon Scripture and the Liturgy; and they emphasize development from within faith into a vision of the organic totality of the Christian mystery in its orientation to the sanctification of the whole man in his historical and social situation.

The most successful attempt to describe a theology for the layman is that of Father John Courtney Murray, S.J.[20] He has avoided the pitfall of the original kerygmatics by stressing the analogous character of theological knowledge as it is participated at different levels of intelligibility.

He carefully set down three guiding principles for the construction of a theology for the laity: (1) theology is a science of faith; (2) theology stands essentially in the service of the Church; (3) the particular form that theology assumes is determined by the special service it seeks to render to the Church.[21]

The form that theology assumes in the clerical course consists in "that intelligence of the faith, especially in its relation to reason and philosophy, which is required in order that the magisterium of the Church may be able effectively to preserve, explain and defend the whole of revealed truth."[22] Theology for the laity, on the other hand, is that form of theology, "that intelligence of the faith, especially in its relation to human life and the good of mankind, which is required in order that the laity of the Church may be able effectively to collaborate with the hierarchy in accomplishing the renewal and reconstruction of the whole of modern social life."[23]

The differentiation between clerical and lay theology is determined by the role which the student of theology has in the Church. The priest may be, as Father Murray says, a sort of diminished bishop, but a layman is not a sort of diminished priest. Likewise theology for the laity is not a diminished sort of scholastic theology.

What seems particularly worthy of being pointed out here is

that Father Murray is not proposing two theologies but different modes or forms of one and the same theology. Moreover, the finalities of which he speaks are not in the realm of the objective purposes of the discipline itself, but of purposes and needs of the personal subject in pursuing the discipline. To be technical, the finalities used to differentiate the forms of theology are not *fines qui* but *fines quibus*. They stress the subjective conditions of the student and the mode or manner in which he is to benefit from theology to fulfill his role in the Church. This subjective aspect determines the mode or "form" that theology takes in relation to the learner, and its influence in determining the mode of communicating theology is in the area rather of material than of final causality. Here there is a question of the principle: Whatever is received, is received according to the capacities and dispositions of the recipient (*Quidquid recipitur, recipitur per modum recipientis*); it is not a question of strict final causality.

This analysis of Father Murray's presentation is necessary, I believe, if we are to understand his own thought and profit from the insights he has brought to the problem. The pedagogical principles which he calls upon for constructing the course for the layman are formulated in view of the layman himself and his needs: (1) the primacy of the teacher and (2) the law of congruity in regard to both the student's psychology and his existential situation in the Church and in the world.

In view of the layman's situation, this law calls for a "total and pacific exposition of God's revelation as a harmonious, ordered, organic whole, whose parts are illumined by reference to a single interior principle of intelligibility, and all vitalized by reference to a common focus—the sanctification of the total life of man. . . ."[24] The single interior principle is Christ Himself, and the central theme is the whole Christ.

In view of the student's psychology, the law of congruity calls for a method which follows the order of discovery. That is to say: (1) It must start with what is relatively more knowable according to our human mode of knowledge (not what is more knowable in itself). Hence it must give primacy to the visible, the immediate and concrete, the historical. (2) Presentation will follow the subjective and genetic order by which we discover the truths of revelation as distinguished from the objective and logical order within the body of revealed truth as such. (3) Giving primacy to the visible, concrete, and historical in the subjective, genetic order demands reliance primarily on Scripture and the Liturgy as sources in the presentation of the Christian mystery.

The ultimate religious finality of the lay course, Father Murray ventures to say, lies more in the realm of charity than of intelligence.[25] While it is important for the layman to understand his faith, it is more important that what understanding he gains awaken the desire of acting *ex fide* (out of and in accordance with this faith). This desire springs from a "yes" to life (*consensus in vitam*) on the part of the whole person rather than merely a "yes" to truth (*consensus in verum*).

If the lay course assumes the function of effecting a fully religious formation, of cultivating charity as well as intelligence, a major difficulty arises owing to the disproportion between the instrument and its intended effect. "Inasmuch as it is taught and learned, it is directed to the intelligence, and its proximate aim is to leave the student in possession of a sum of knowledge. Inasmuch as it is theological, its aim is to leave him with a knowledge that is complete, verified by reflection on its sources, and organized into a coherent body. Obviously, an academic course, methodically taught, can communicate ideas and form an intelligence. But can it communicate charity and form an apostle, who is a man not only of ideas but of dynamic love? At all events, there is the problem—how to make an academic course the instrument of religious formation."[26]

The ideal genetic process proposed by Father Murray for this religious formation involves four stages or moments which interact on one another: (1) *scientia fidei;* (2) *actio sacra;* (3) *sensus Christi;* (4) *actio Catholica.* "The formation of the social order in the spirit of Christ [*actio Catholica*] demands that one be oneself formed in the spirit of Christ [sensus Christi] by means of an intelligence of Christ, indeed [scientia fidei], but chiefly by sharing in the sacred action of Christ, the mass [actio sacra]."[27]

In other words, intelligent insight into the Christian mystery cannot be given experiential keenness except through active participation in the central Christian act of worship.

It is quite clear that this process involves much that is not the work of theology itself. The academic course even for the layman is only part of his Christian formation. The specific function of theology is not here clearly distinguished from the function of other agencies in the work of Christian education. And there's the rub. Father Murray himself is not unaware of the difficulty.

It seems that Father Murray's permanent contribution to the development of the notion of theology is his delineation and justification of the analogous forms which theology assumes in the Church. He has also set down with clarity the fundamental pedagogical principles which must serve in constructing an academic course for the layman. The problem remains, however: Is theology in any form of such a nature that it can be an adequate instrument of religious formation?

Theology and Christian Living

Father Yves Congar points out that there is danger here of confusing two different problems: (1) that of giving vitality to theology; and (2) that of giving a vitally persuasive presentation of the Gospel message for Christian living. The first problem, if not a false problem, is at least badly formulated.[28]

For theology supposes the immanent active presence of faith. Theology is essentially religious knowledge carrying within itself a dynamic for living. But theology itself cannot assume the whole burden of religious formation. For this formation we must go beyond theology to what St. Thomas calls sacra doctrina—salutary teaching in all its amplitude.[29] This teaching, committed by God to the Church, has several functions: it has a scientific function, namely theology; but it also has other functions, in particular a pastoral function.[30]

In the Thomistic view this pastoral function does not necessarily have its source in theology itself, but in the apostolic transmission of the faith through preaching, the liturgy, and the example of the Church, as it is assimilated by the faithful in prayer, contemplation, common worship, and Catholic action. This is a different function, more necessary than the scientific function and more closely connected with the mission of the Church.[31]

However, this pastoral work of the Church involves other functions beyond her salutary teaching, especially her sanctifying actions of worship in the sacraments. It is not only through her teaching office but also through her sanctifying office that full religious formation is imparted.[32]

If Father Congar's observations are correct, theology is simply incapable of assuming the whole burden of the religious formation of the laity. There are, in fact, *many* agencies at work in this formation.[33] Theology itself can only do its part: namely, provide an *understanding* of the faith and of Christian life. In fact, solid motivation consists in this understanding of the commitment of faith. As Father Rahner says: ". . . dogmatic theology cannot be something morally neutral. . . ."[34] But the presentation of this motivating understanding is not the whole of religious formation.

If our universities have assumed or have at least been given in our day the work of complete Christian formation, we have *de facto* become for our students their family, Church, community, spiritual guides, confessors, sodality moderators, preachers, pastors, and example. If our theology departments assume or are assigned these functions, they perform them not by reason of their office as instructors in theology, but by reason of their pastoral office in the Church. As teachers of theology, they can only give their students by word and example the vision of the Christian mystery —the Word—and trust that the Word will make them live.

Theology, however, as conceived in the Franciscan tradition is primarily practical, primarily affective and aimed at making us good. It therefore emphasizes the pastoral function of sacred teaching (i.e. the anagogic of faith which is in the realm of personal spiritual experience).[35] In this conception theology itself has as its primary aim total religious formation.

Undoubtedly in the mind of St. Ignatius our schools are to be training grounds for intelligent Catholic life and action in the reconstruction of human society. But is this training to be the work of the religion and theology teachers, or is every teacher, especially every priest in the school, involved in imparting some aspect of this formation? Can this formation be accomplished solely by the academic curriculum, or have we become responsible in our Catholic institutions for roles other than the academic? We have academic vice-presidents and vice-presidents in charge of student affairs. Perhaps we should add a vice-president in charge of pastoral needs of our students.

The solution to this administrative problem depends to a great extent on our conception of theology. The Thomistic tradition in theology has perhaps so emphasized the scientific character of theology that it has given occasion for its separation from its sapiential function and its relation to Christian living. In fact, until recently all Catholic theology neglected the fact that faith itself is a personal commitment informed by love.[36] Theology starts from faith and strives for an understanding of faith. Just as the Word was sent into the world because of the Father's love, so the fundamental initiative and dynamic of faith is love, an act of personal decision exercised by the will commanding personal intellectual assent.

Moreover, as the Word who is sent breathes forth love, so the Word sent into the mind and heart of man breathes forth, as it were, the life of the spirit. But just as the Word of God is not constituted by love, so the Word as it takes root and develops in man is not constituted by charity, but it originates in the commitment of love in faith, continues its development only under this commitment, and is destined to issue in an ever more total commitment.

Hence, in the Thomistic conception as well as in the Franciscan conception, theology both in its roots and in its fruits engages the whole man.

Secondly, in any theology God's Word implies an "I" and a "Thou."[37] It calls for a response, a dialogue, and hence a certain community life. If there is no listening to the Word, there is no response, there is no dialogue, there is no community. The Word dies because community is not established. Hence, theology—the understanding of the Word—cannot be impersonal. Moreover, the Word of God not only reveals the intimate life of God and his salvific plan, but reveals the meaning of man—not just man in general, but my own meaning in my own existential situation, my own dignity and misery, my own need for God's redemptive love.[38] Hence, no theology can abstract or prescind from myself and my life.

Thirdly, it is the Word of God that establishes the authentic Christian CAN, OUGHT, and MAY, in answer to the question: what must I do that I may enter the eternal life?[39] Hence, theology, the understanding of the Word, must not fail to unfold the Christian imperative, the urgency of love (*Caritas Christi urget nos*) to be incarnated in every human activity.[40] Theology, therefore, presupposes and builds upon religious commitment, nourishes it, and lays out the pattern according to which its inner-dynamic must work to assume mankind (individual, society, culture) into the current of God's salvific love. Thomistic "Theology" stops here; Franciscan Theology would go into the immediately practical order.

Finally, in both Franciscan and Thomistic conceptions, it is better here on earth to love God than to know Him. But the inner dynamic of love sketched by Augustine and analyzed by Thomas is such that love cannot and will not rest until it possesses its object. This possession of the ultimate good is achieved in its perfection only by intelligence in the beatific vision. Hence, the ultimate good for which we strive from the depths of our spiritual being in all of our human activity is the good of intelligence. Here it is that Thomas and Bonaventure part company. For Thomas, unlike Bonaventure, the absolutely ultimate end is truth, the good of intellect. And this inner dynamic of the spirit is manifest in their differing conceptions of theology.

It is not difficult to see, however, that even in the Franciscan tradition theology itself is only one agency at work in the progressive Incarnation of the Word in the World. The grace of faith itself must be operative in theology but does not do the work of theology. The Word can be presented in various degrees of intelligibility, but unless the student of theology is disposed by living faith to receive it, the Word dies. Unless the understanding of the Word comes to be mediated by prudence into active participation in Christian worship and social action, the desire to grow in understanding is thwarted. Thomistic Theology, unlike Franciscan, does not of itself attempt to effect this mediation; it invites us to it as the path of salvation.

Hence, we see that certain subjective conditions are necessary on the part of the student of theology and the theologian, if theological endeavor and teaching are to achieve effectively their own proper and immediate goal—namely, understanding of the faith. Moreover, these conditions depend for their actualization on God's gratuitous grace and the student's free active cooperation in bringing understanding to experiential realization through participation in Christian worship and social action.

From these reflections, the conclusion suggests itself that theology is only one phase or aspect of sacred teaching and religious formation; that it cannot be identified with sacred teaching and religious formation in all its amplitude. The completion of religious formation through spiritual direction, active participation in the life and worship of the Church and Catholic action must be accomplished by agencies in the Church other than the academic curriculum.

The Future of Theology

Theology thrives and develops not because it is a system but because it is the living human expression of the spontaneous impulse of intelligence transformed by the light of faith to assimilate the truth of God's salvific economy in which we are engaged.

This assimilation takes place gradually as the human mind moves from truth to truth, achieving insights of dependence and interconnection, arriving at views of individual truths in higher unities, until an all-embracing vision is discovered. Here I would like to quote a lengthy passage from Father Bernard Lonergan in which he illustrates the gradual assimilation of divine revelation:

This increase of theological understanding, knowledge and wisdom consists not in the fact that by means of increasingly probable theories we draw closer to a hitherto unknown truth, but rather in the fact that the same truth, which has always been believed, becomes more and more comprehensively known, understood and appreciated. Natural sciences, since they begin from sensible objects and grow in understanding through the discovery of increasingly probable and useful theories, cannot arrive at truth until they understand everything perfectly. With such sciences theology can in no way be equated, because it begins from a believed truth and grows in such a way that it constantly adheres to the same truth; and this adhesion is so necessary for theology that if it attempted to understand a truth other than as revealed, that understanding would not be theological. "How, then," you ask, "is it possible that the same truth, understood in the same sense is understood now more, now less?" The answer is that there is variation not in the object which is understood but in the manner of understanding. Just as the higher angels understand more things through fewer species, so also those who progress in the understanding of revealed truths understand not one thing now, and then another, but the same thing ever more comprehensively. This can be seen from the following examples.

First, let us suppose a man who reads the whole of Scripture and correctly understands each of its statements. He understands many things correctly; but since he understands each thing separately, he is simply lacking in comprehensive understanding.

Let us suppose another man who not only reads all the Scriptures and correctly understands their individual statements, but also goes one step further. He compares the various texts of Scripture with one another, prescinds from mere accidentals, discovers that the same thing, substantially, has been said in many places; he then conceives accurately and expresses in technical terms this substantial identity; and when he has gone through all of Scripture—comparing, abstracting, discovering, expressing—he comes at the end to express the same truth, understood in the same sense, in new and technical terms.

In this case, although the same identical truth is expressed, although it is understood in the same sense, nevertheless it is understood in a different manner. Whereas formerly he understood many things separately, now he understands many things together and in a unified manner. Whereas formerly he understood not only the essentials but also all the accidentals (who is speaking, with whom, on what occasion, in what circumstances, with what intention; what actions are related, and under what images, figures or parables; what emotions, sentiments and affections are aroused, etc.), he now prescinds from nearly all the accidentals and attends only to the essentials. Whereas formerly he used only biblical words and concepts, he now uses only new and technical terms and remote and essential concepts.

Now let us consider a third man, one who inquires even further. This man has not only read all of Scripture, understood its individual statements, compared different texts, prescinded from accidentals, discovered, conceived, and technically expressed the essentials, but has also penetrated more deeply. For revealed truths, even reduced to their essentials, are not easily grasped in their inner coherence. For example, God is one in such a way that there are three Persons; Christ is God in such a way that He is also man; everything depends on the gratuitous will of God in such a way that the heavenly crown is not awarded except for our own merits. And there are many other such truths which demand a new kind of understanding. The systematic exegesis of what is said in Scripture is one thing; the understanding of the facts and actions affirmed in Scripture is quite another. The man who understands the essentials of what is said in Scripture is doing a systematic exegesis and discovering theological problems; the man who seeks an understanding of what Scripture teaches to be true has entered upon the way of theology. . . .

The fourth and last manner in which the same truth may be understood constitutes a new step in comprehension. According to Aristotle, science is two-fold: it is science in potency when it is merely of universals; it is science in act when it is applied to particular cases.

Besides systematic exegesis, therefore, there exists an historical exegesis which no longer omits the accidentals but includes them in a synthetic manner. Besides systematic theology, there exists a more concrete and comprehensive theology which considers the economy of salvation in its historical evolution and seeks to understand it. This new step in comprehension has been in preparation for a long time, thanks to so much biblical, conciliar, patristic, medieval, liturgical, ascetical, and other research; but its synthetic character has not yet clearly appeared because of the fact that today's scholars resemble 12th Century compilers rather than 13th Century theologians, so too those today who with solid scholarship investigate biblical, patristic, and other areas can certainly look forward to a future theology which will be more concrete and comprehensive. However, the legitimate expectation of a future event is one thing; the bold and premature assertion that it has arrived is quite another. If in the other sciences all true progress consists in adding new elements in such a way that all the old ones are included (physicists, for example, do not revise their old measurements whenever they accept a new theory), it should be quite clear to all how much more this conservative law of progress governs theology, which never intends anything else but the fuller understanding of the same truth.

We have explained four ways in which the same revealed truth can be ever more comprehensively understood. If we add to these the manner in which God understands revealed truths and the manner in which the Blessed participate in the divine understanding, it is sufficiently clear that the same truth can be understood in many different ways.[41]

The various ways and degrees in which the same truth can be understood, already suggested earlier by Father Murray, is further emphasized by the fact that God's revelation is assimilated by man in terms of his own language, thought patterns, culture, and philosophy.[42] The transposition of God's revelation from language to language, from culture to culture, and its interpretation with the help of diverse philosophies have led us in the past and will lead us further to an enrichment of understanding.

Is any one language, any one culture, any one philosophy better suited than another for this full assimilation of the truth of God's revelation? These are questions we cannot discuss now. They

serve, however, to point up the fact that the confrontations of
God's revelation by different cultures and philosophies have given
rise to a variety of theologies.

In the Western world we have seen the rise of Augustinian,
Franciscan, and Thomistic theologies; and all of them have
flourished in so far as they provided some understanding of the
revelation of God for the inquiring spirit of man. If theology today
is in crisis, it is not because of the content of the revelation, but
because it cannot be heard owing to the form of presentation that
hinders modern man from approaching it; because it has not been
living in vital confrontation with our own times and the spirit of
our age.[43]

Theology has found its rise and decline in almost direct proportion to its life in the great universities. It was a tragedy of history
that theology came gradually to be ousted from the university and
removed to the seminary. The hope of theology today is its return
to the university, where it is forced to speak to the spirit and mind
of our age.

Notes

1. "Bulletin de théologie dogmatique," *Rev. Sc. Ph. Th.*, XXXV (1951),
   591–603.
2. See chronological bibliography on kerygmatic theology in *La Scuola
   Cattolica*, LXXVII (1950), 350–356; see esp. the fundamental work by
   J. A. Jungmann, S.J., *Die Frohbotschaft und unsere Glaubensverkündigung* (Regensburg: Pustet, 1936), now available in English: *The
   Good News Yesterday and Today* (New York: Sadlier, 1962).
3. F. Lakner, S.J., "Das Zentralobjekt der Theologie," *ZKT*, LXIII (1938),
   1–36.
4. Cf. *La Scuola Cattolica*, LXXVII (July–October, 1950). The whole
   issue is devoted to a discussion of kerygmatic theology.
5. *Katholische Dogmatik*, I (Munich: M. Hüber-Verlag, 1953), 7.
6. See esp. Congar, *Rev. Sc. Ph. Th.*, XXXV (1951), 592–593, and K.
   Rahner, *Theological Investigations*, Vol. I, tr. C. Ernst, O.P. (Baltimore:
   Helicon Press, 1961), p. 7.
7. Cf. E. Mersch, S.J., "Le Christ mystique centre de la théologie comme
   science," *Nouv. Rev. Théol.*, LXI (1934), 449–475; "L'objet de la
   théologie et le *Christus totus*," *Rech. Sc. Rel.*, XXVI (1936), 129–157.

8. See C. Spicq, O.P., "Bulletin . . . ," *Rev. Sc. Ph. Th.*, XXXV (1951), 34–60; "Nouvelles réflexions sur la théologie biblique," *Rev. Sc. Ph. Th.*, XLII (1958), 209–219 [*Theology Digest*, VII (Winter, 1959), 29–34]; see also *Sacra Pagina; Miscellanea Biblica Congressus Internationalis Catholici de Re Biblica*, ed. J. Coppens, A. Descamps, and E. Massaux, 2 vols. (Gembloux: Editions J. Duculot, 1959), esp. Albert Descamps, "Réflexions sur la méthode en théologie biblique," I, 132–157, and Máximo Peinador, "La integración de la exégesis en la teología," I, 158–179.

9. See, in addition to Descamps and Peinador, R. A. F. MacKenzie, S.J., "The Concept of Biblical Theology," *Proc. Cath. Theol. Soc.*, 1955, pp. 48–66.

10. See C. Spicq, "Nouvelles réflexions . . . ," *Rev. Sc. Ph. Th.*, XLII (1958), 209–219.

11. *Ibid.*, pp. 210–219.

12. See, for example, the work of E. Schillebeeckx, O.P., *Die Christusontmoeting als Sacrament van de Godsontmoeting* (Antwerp: 't Groeit, 1957); in French, *Le Christ, sacrement de la recontre de Dieu* (Paris: Cerf., 1960); in English, *Christ the Sacrament of the Encounter with God* (New York: Sheed & Ward, 1963). Also Y. Congar, O.P., *The Mystery of the Church*, tr. A. V. Littledale (Baltimore: Helicon Press, 1960). Also T. Soiron, *La Condition du Théologien*, Introd. et adopt. française par Y. Becker et J. R. Heunion, O.F.M. (Paris: Librairie Plon [no date: The original, *Heilige Theologie*, appeared in 1935], esp. pp. 125–142.

13. See, for example, R. Hasseveldt, *The Church: A Divine Mystery*, tr. W. Storey (Chicago: Fides, 1954).

14. The approach through the Magisterium is indicated by Pius XII, "Humani Generis," par. 21 (quoted from A. C. Cotter, S.J., *The Encyclical "Humani Generis" with a Commentary* [Weston, Mass.: Weston College Press, 1951], pp. 23–24): ". . . the authentic interpretation of the deposit our Divine Redeemer did not entrust to the faithful, nor even to theologians, but exclusively to the Magisterium of the Church. If then the Church does exercise this function, as she has often done in the past, either in the ordinary or in an extraordinary way, it is plain how false is a method which would explain what is clear by what is obscure, and that all must follow the opposite procedure. We see now why our predecessor of immortal memory, Pius IX, when explaining that the noblest office of theology is to show how a doctrine defined by the Church is contained in the sources, added these words, and with good reason: 'in the sense in which it has been defined by the Church.' "

15. The dogma and its presentation comes first. Then comes the study of how the dogma in question arrived at its present formulation from its foundation in Scripture through its development to the present time. Schmaus, for example, in his *Dogmatik*, uses this procedure extensively.

GERALD VAN ACKEREN, S.J. 107

16. In this procedure faith is presupposed, but its content and understanding are unfolded in genetic, historical fashion. Various attempts at this method are being made now; for example, see the new French series *Le mystère chrétien* now being published by Desclée & Co., Tournai (Belgium).
17. See in this regard Oscar Cullmann's work, *Christology of the New Testament,* tr. S. L. Guthrie and C. A. M. Hall (Philadelphia: Westminster Press, 1959).
18. *Summa Ecclesiologica* (Class notes, Woodstock, Md.), p. 6.
19. *Theological Investigations,* I, 18.
20. J. C. Murray, S.J., "Towards a Theology for the Layman," *Theological Studies,* V (1944), 43–75, 340–376.
21. *Ibid.,* p. 63.
22. *Ibid.,* p. 75.
23. *Ibid.*
24. *Ibid.,* p. 348.
25. *Ibid.,* p. 344.
26. *Ibid.,* p. 345.
27. *Ibid.,* p. 373.
28. Congar, "Bulletin . . . ," *Rev. Sc. Ph. Th.,* XXXV (1951), 592.
29. Congar, " 'Traditio' und 'Sacra Doctrina' bei Thomas von Aquin," in *Kirche und Uberlieferung,* ed. J. Betz and H. Fries (Freiburg: Herder, 1960), pp. 170–210, esp. pp. 183–187.
30. Congar, "Bulletin . . . ," *Rev. Sc. Ph. Th.,* XXXV (1951), 593.
31. *Ibid.,* p. 594. Cf. Joseph Ratzinger, "Theologia perennis," *Wort und Wahrheit,* XV (1960), 179–188 [*Theology Digest,* X (Spring, 1962), 72–73].
32. Congar, " 'Traditio' . . . ," p. 179.
33. Cf. T. C. Donlan, O.P., *Theology and Education* (Dubuque: The Priory Press, 1952).
34. K. Rahner, *Theological Investigations,* I, 17.
35. Tavard, *Transiency and Permanence; The Nature of Theology according to St. Bonaventure* (St. Bonaventure: The Franciscan Institute, 1954), pp. 183, 257; cf. J. Beumer, S.J., "Die Aufgabe der Vernunft in der Theologie des hl. Bonaventura," *Franz. Stud.,* 1956, pp. 129–149.
36. The works of Congar, Chenu, Beumer, K. Rahner, Lonergan, Schillebeeckx, etc., have re-emphasized this aspect of faith in the teaching of St. Thomas.
37. Soiron, *op. cit.,* pp. 81–94.
38. *Ibid.,* pp. 94–99.
39. K. Rahner, *Theological Investigations,* I, 17.
40. Cf. Richard McCormick, S.J., "The Primacy of Charity," *Perspectives* (Aug.–Sept., 1959), pp. 18–27. A good survey.
41. B. Lonergan, S.J., *Divinarum Personarum Conceptionem Analogicam*

Evolvit (Rome: Pont. Univ. Greg., 1957), pp. 17–19. Translation made by F. P. Greaney, S.J.

In regard to a more precise conception of the nature of theology and its method, I can only point to specific contributions made by theologians within the last two decades, all of whom are in the tradition of St. Thomas. (1) Father Congar has laid out for us the unity of theology in such a way that his work will be perennially helpful. (See esp. his article "Théologie" in *DTC*, XV, cc. 341–502.) (2) Professor Gilson has formulated the formal object of theology according to St. Thomas more clearly than anyone else. (Cf. esp. *Le Thomisme*[5] [J. Vrin, Paris, 1947], 1st chap., esp. pp. 23–25; also my comment on this chapter in *Sacra Doctrina: The Subject of the First Question of the Summa Theologica of St. Thomas Aquinas* [Rome: Catholic Book Agency, 1952], p. 111.) (3) Father Karl Rahner has brought out the fact that theology is not merely a theology of essence but a theology of existence. He has sketched an outline of theological anthropology, a theology of the Word, which is having its repercussions throughout the theological world. (*Theological Investigations*, Vol. I, chap. I.) (4) Father Lonergan stands in the forefront of theoreticians on the nature and method of theology. One aspect of his contribution is of particular importance to us: namely, his elaboration of the distinction between *via inventionis* and the *via doctrinae*—the method of discovery and the method of synthesis, the analytic and the synthetic procedures. (See esp. *Divinarum Personarum*, pp. 7–48.) Theology must begin with the way of discovery, with the *priora quoad nos*, that is, with what is more knowable to us, what is more immediate in our experience. Gradually it arrives at insights of higher unities, until it glimpses the ultimate principle of intelligibility and unity in the divine mysteries. St. Thomas presupposes this procedure in his *Summa* which follows the *via synthetica.*

42. See Jean Daniélou, "Unité et pluralité de la pensée chrétienne," *Etudes*, CCCXII (1962), 3–16 [*Theology Digest*, X (Spring 1962), 67–70]. Also Josef Ratzinger, "Theologia Perennis," *Wort und Wahrheit*, XV (1960), 179–188 [*Theology Digest*, X (Spring 1960), 71–76].

43. Daniélou, *Theology Digest*, X (Spring, 1962), 70; Ratzinger, *ibid.*, p. 76; K. Rahner, *Theological Investigations*, I, 8.

Selected Bibliography

Beumer, Johannes, S.J. "Die Aufgabe der Vernunft in der Theologie des hl. Bonaventure," *Franziskanische Studien* (1956:2), 129–149.
———. *Theologie als Glaubensverständnis.* Würzburg, 1953.
———. "Was ist Theologie," *Theologie und Glaube,* XLVI, No. 3 (1956), 161–172.

Chenu, M.-D., O.P. "La théologie comme science au XIIIᵉ siècle," *Archives d'Histoire Doctrinale et Littéraire du Moyen-Age,* II (1927), 31–71. Enlarged, revised, and re-edited as *La théologie comme science au XIIIᵉ siècle.*[2] Pro manuscripto. Paris: J. Vrin, 1943. P. 123.

Congar, Yves M.-J., O.P. "Bulletin de théologie dogmatique," *Revue des sciences philosophiques et théologiques,* XXXV (1951), 591–603.

————. "Théologie," *Dictionnaire de théologie Catholique,* XV[1], cc. 341–502.

————. " 'Traditio' und 'Sacra Doctrina' bei Thomas von Aquin," in *Kirche und Uberlieferung,* edited by J. Betz and H. Fries (Herder, 1960), pp. 170–210.

Crowe, Frederick E., S.J. "Development of Doctrine and the Ecumenical Problem," *Theological Studies,* XXIII (March, 1962), 27–46.

Donlan, Thomas C., O.P. *Theology and Education.* Dubuque, Iowa: Priory Press, 1952.

Dumont, C., S.J. "La réflexion sur la méthode Théologique," *Nouvelle revue théologique,* XCIII (1961), 1034–50; XCIV (1962), 17–35.

Gagnebet, R., O.P. "La nature de la théologie speculative," *Revue Thomiste,* XLIV (1938), 1–39, 213–255, 645–674.

Gilson, Etienne. *Le Thomisme.* Vol. V. Paris, 1947.

Hasseveldt, Roger. *The Church; A Divine Mystery.* Translated by William Storey. Chicago: Fides, 1954.

Journet, Charles, Msgr. *The Wisdom of Faith: An Introduction to Theology.* Translated by R. F. Smith, S.J. Westminster: Newman, 1952.

Jungmann, J. A., S.J. *Die Frohbotschaft und unsere Glaubensverkündigung.* Regensburg, 1936.

Lakner, F., S.J. "Das Zentralobjekt der Theologie," *Zeitschrift für katholische Theologie,* LXII (1938), 1–36.

Lonergan, Bernard, S.J. *Divinarum Personarum conceptionem analogicam evolvit.* Rome, 1957. Caput primum, 7–48.

————. *Insight: A Study of Human Understanding.* New York: Philosophical Library, 1957.

————. "Theology and Understanding," *Gregorianum,* XXXV (1954), 630–648.

MacKenzie, R., S.J. "The Concept of Biblical Theology," *Proceedings of the Catholic Theological Society of America,* 1955, pp. 48–66.

Malevez, Leopold, S.J. "Nouveau Testament et théologie fonctionnelle," *Recherches de Science Réligieuse,* XLVIII (1960), 258–290; *Theology Digest,* X (Spring, 1962), 77–83.

Mersch, E., S.J. "Le Christ mystique centre de la théologie comme science," *Nouvelle revue théologique,* LXI (1934), 449–475.

————. "L'objet de la théologie et le *Christus totus,*" *Recherches de Science Réligieuse,* XXVI (1936), 129–157.

Muniz, Francisco P., O.P. *The Work of Theology.* Translated by John P. Reid, O.P. Washington, D.C.: Thomist Press, 1953.

Murray, John Courtney, S.J. "Towards a Theology for the Layman; The Problem of Its Finality," *Theological Studies,* V (1944), 43–75.

———. "Towards a Theology for the Layman: The Pedagogical Problem," *Theological Studies,* V (1944), 340–376.

Proceedings of the National Jesuit Institute on College Religion, August 2–14, 1951. Edited by Eugene B. Gallagher, S.J., with the assistance of Robert H. Buchan, S.J., and Andrew H. McFadden, S.J. (Offset, bound, *ad instar manuscripti.*) Fairfield University, July, 1952.

Rahner, Karl, S.J. *Theological Investigations.* Vol. I: *God, Christ, Mary and Grace.* Translated by C. Ernst, O.P. Baltimore: Helicon, 1961.

Ratzinger, Joseph. "Theologia perennis," *Wort und Wahrheit,* XV (1960), 179–188; *Theology Digest,* X (Spring, 1962), 71–76.

La Scuola Cattolica, Vol. LXXVII, fas. 4–5 (July–October, 1950). The whole issue is devoted to a discussion of kerygmatic theology.

Sacra Pagina; Miscellanea Biblica Congressus Internationalis Catholici de Re Biblica. Edited by J. Coppens, A. Descamps, and E. Massaux. 2 vols. Gembloux: Editions J. Duculot, 1959. Especially Albert Descamps, "Réflexions sur la méthode en théologie biblique," I, 132–157, and Máximo Peinador, "La integración de la exégesis en la teología," I, 158–179.

Soiron, Thaddee, O.F.M. *La Condition du théologien.* Introduction et adoption française par Yves Becker et Jean-Robert Hennion, O.F.M. Paris, n.d.

———. *Heilige Theologie.* Regensburg, 1935.

Spicq, Ceslaus, O.P. "Nouvelles réflexions sur la théologie biblique," *Revue des sciences philosophiques et théologiques,* XLII (1958), 209–219; *Theology Digest,* VII (Winter, 1959), 29–34.

Tavard, George H., A.A. *Transiency and Permanence: The Nature of Theology According to St. Bonaventure.* New York: St. Bonaventure, 1954.

Van Ackeren, Gerald, S.J. "Basic Functions of College Theology," *Jesuit Educational Quarterly,* January, 1955, 133–146.

———. "Reflections on the Relation between Philosophy and Theology," *Theological Studies,* XIV (December, 1953), 527–550.

———. *Sacra Doctrina: The Subject of the First Question of the Summa Theologica of St. Thomas Aquinas.* Rome, 1952.

6

THEOLOGY AS
AN ACADEMIC DISCIPLINE

H. James Yamauchi, S.J.

In recent years there has been a great deal of discussion concerning the place of theology in the Catholic colleges and universities of the United States. Theology has attained or is attaining equality with the other academic disciplines, and in view of this situation the attempt is being made to delineate its formative influence on the student. It is certainly true that theology will have its role to play in the student's mature and intelligent participation in the life of the Church, for theological formation should not lie inert and unproductive. But the subject matter of this essay has been deliberately limited to the question of intellectual formation, to contemplation rather than practice. An attempt has been made to survey some important thinking on this subject.[1]

There would seem to be little disagreement among those who teach theology in Catholic colleges and universities that theology has a role to play in the intellectual formation of the Catholic undergraduate.[2] However, it might not be out of place to note that there are members of the academic community in these institutions of higher education who question the value of theology, or at least of theology as it is presently being given, in the formation of the student. The apparent basis for this opinion is to be found in some very practical (or, at least, they are thought to be so by their exponents) considerations. Interestingly enough, the difficulty seems to have arisen in recent years, when theology in the colleges and universities has become something more serious, requiring more attention and study on the part of the student. The exponents of this view do not think that theology is absolutely useless. Rather the problem for them involves a question of the hierarchy of educational values. At present, they contend, too many precious hours are taken up by theology (be it in class or study), and that to the detriment of the student's major and even minor fields of concentration. Philosophy and theology, with their perhaps thirty-four required hours (more in some places, a little less in others), are, they tell us, placing the student in our Catholic colleges and universities at a real disadvantage in comparison with his fellow student in secular universities. Given the number of these required hours, the student in a Catholic college is forced to take what amounts to nearly a whole year of additional credit courses and hence is not able to take sufficient elective courses either in his major field or in other fields, as is done in the secular college to the great advantage of the student. As a solution to this problem some have recommended that required theology courses be reduced to a bare minimum of one or, at most, two semester courses of two hours a week. It is thought that with such a reduction students in Catholic colleges would not be "penalized" (the word is theirs) in their competition with students in non-Catholic colleges and universities.[3]

This objection must be taken seriously, not only because it is seriously advanced but because it requires that the *raison d'être* of theology in our colleges and universities be clearly determined. At the same time this objection brings us to the very heart of the problem—the objective itself of Catholic undergraduate education. If this objective is the trained technician in a particular field, be it in science or humanities, one immediately sees there is a grave problem with theology in the curriculum. What then are we attempting to do in our undergraduate education?

Frequently it is taken for granted that the aim is the liberal education of the student. What does this really mean? It is expressed in various ways. A liberal education is not aimed at the production of an historian, a natural scientist, a doctor, lawyer or political scientist, but rather a man who knows the methods of history and natural science, the principles of literature and drama, and, consequently, is capable of thinking critically and intelligently. Or again: the aim is to establish the student in his proper self-possession and independence, to develop his whole personality to a certain level of maturity and dedication to truth. The liberal arts, therefore, present the basic approaches to reality—humanistic, scientific, philosophical, mathematical and theological—to the student in the hope that he will be able to appreciate these diverse dimensions of awareness of man, and by his own experience understand the nature and interrelationship of the various disciplines. Or, to put it another way, we are told that a liberal education has as its aim the handing on of an integral Christian culture by creating an awareness of those various aspects of our Christian heritage contained in the various disciplines ordinarily given in a liberal arts college. Hence a liberal education distinguishes itself by being non-technical, non-professional. It does not train a man to perform a particular task; rather it strives to make a man realize, actualize his inherent potential as a man. Christopher Mooney, writing in the context of theology and the college, tells us that a liberal education consists in the process of transmitting a spiritual heritage from one generation to another through initiation into a culture, i.e., into a set of values and ideals—religious, philosophical, artistic, scientific—which are seen as worthy of esteem and hence are accepted and lived by a community.[4] Gustave Weigel considers the liberal arts college's function as making the student pass through a program of humanistic dedication—dedication to literature, science and philosophy—not in order to become an expert in these fields but rather to see the different ways in which the human being can function on a level other than the pragmatic.[5]

With such conceptions of the function of our undergraduate colleges one would have little difficulty in defining the place that theology should play in the intellectual formation of the student. But is there not an inherent difficulty in adopting such a position?

Is it not simply unrealistic? No matter what we may think Catholic undergraduate education should be, we must face it in its stark reality. Have we not seen in the vast majority of Catholic colleges and universities a persistent increase in enrollment in the pre-professional courses of medicine, law, engineering, commerce, and finance, and the swing towards a specialized curriculum in the natural sciences? The reasons for such a change from the "good old times" are numerous. In the natural sciences, the faculty is interested in the preparation of their students for future graduate work, and graduate studies are becoming more the rule than formerly. Schools of Business Administration have sprung up and are a far cry from liberal arts colleges; and, dare we say, the calibre of the student is frequently not of the liberal arts level. Every department of theology worries about its "pre-something" students who seldom take a full course in theology and whose education is clearly specialized towards that "something." This is the reality, and it must be faced squarely by the modern Catholic educator. It is of such students that we must ask what role theology plays in their intellectual formation.[6]

All would agree that an intellectually mature grasp of the Catholic Faith should be high on the list of aims regarding theology's contribution to the intellectual formation of the student. The student's theological maturity must at least match or equal the intellectual maturity he acquires in other academic disciplines. But in what does such a grasp of the faith consist? In answer one might say that our faith must be seen by the student as a consistent whole, together with its relationships to other areas of knowledge. The student should perceive the organic relation of truth to truth, of moral precept and devotional practice with dogma. He must learn to appreciate the logical harmony, the historical continuity and the internal unity found in faith. John Courtney Murray has insisted that, faced with the contemporary secularistic *mystiques,* which are not merely coherent and articulated systems of thought but ardent militant ways of life as well, it is the task of theology in the college to present a system of thought yet more unitary, an even more dynamic and triumphant *mystique* whose engagement of the whole man is still more imperious than those of contemporary cultures.

What is needed is a profound and personal intelligence of faith gained through a pacific and total exposition of divine truth, which will reveal the Christian faith to be no mere set of propositions satisfactorily proved, but the "good news" which the angels announced with a song as "joy to all the people," for in its splendid organic wholeness it is the "power of God unto salvation," personal and social, temporal and eternal.[7]

But it is not sufficient for the intellectual formation of the lay Catholic that there be only this internal synthesis of faith. One must attempt to show the student the relationships of this vision of faith with truths contained in the other disciplines. For it is the specific task of the layman to be the mediator between the spiritual and the temporal orders—to Christianize the temporal, whether in its intellectual, social, or institutional structures.

This is a big order. What does it imply? Some will say that it supposes that the habit of theology be produced in our students, at least to that degree of perfection which is possible according to the cultural, mental, and moral development of the student.[8] Others say, and it is probable that they mean the same thing, that our aim is to form a student who is capable of thinking theologically, one able to meet religious problems intelligently and critically. A Catholic mind and attitude is thus developed which will view all things from a Catholic point of view.[9]

Many ways have been suggested to bring our students to such theological maturity. It is thought by some that such can be accomplished through an exercise in both historical and speculative theology (with little emphasis on the polemic or the systematic). Others will insist more on the study of the progressive development of revelation and hence of its theology, thus attempting to bring the student to a personal discovery of the truth, an assimilation of it as a reality. Still others would introduce the student to an intellectual tradition of theology and to scientific theological method. One might note that these divergent methods reflect various and sometimes opposing views concerning the nature of theology, and especially of that theology which should be given the college student. But at the same time it is interesting to note that all seem to seek more or less the same goal.

However, there is a difficulty which should be mentioned here; it concerns the question of the "habit" of theology. As John L. McKenzie has so well pointed out, we can hardly expect that college students will emerge at graduation with the habit of theology, the more so because it is rare that a seminarian after four years devoted nearly exclusively to the study of theology possesses this theological habit. As is obvious, Father McKenzie is speaking of the habit of theology in a very strict sense, which he suggests be defined as "control of theological sources, familiarity with theological methods, facility in theological thinking, which issues in confidence in theological expression,"[10] all of which should develop into the habit of creative theological thinking. Put in such terms it is rather obvious that such a theological habit cannot be developed in our college student.[11] That which is aimed at is clearly on a much lower level, yet certainly higher than mere catechetical instruction. Where to place and how to name this middle ground requires much reflection, but Eugene Burke, C.S.P., has put the matter rather well when he writes:

[The result of our theology courses should be] the living presence of the body of theological principles for both thought and action. This body of principles should be articulated and grasped on the same level as the rest of the student's education. It must be orderly, organic, and ultimately result in an intellectual grasp of them. This does not imply that the student possesses the intellectual habit of theology as does the theologian—but rather a personal possession by the educated Catholic of a body of theological principles necessary to, sufficient for, and on a level with the rest of his general education.[12]

But, and this is the all-important question, why such theological maturity? Why this theological formation of the Catholic college student? The answer to this question should furnish us with the *raison d'être* of our theology courses, at least with respect to the intellectual life of the student.

From the negative standpoint, one notes that without theology the student is given an incomplete if not a distorted picture of the most important realities of life—God, man and the universe. Had there been no revelation, had man not been raised to the supernatural order, philosophy would have in this regard an importance beyond measure. But God has intervened to reveal what the human mind could never have achieved on its own. To leave out of education this revelation and its repercussions on other fields of knowledge would deprive the student of his right to know the total truth. Nor should we forget what Edwin Kaiser, C.PP.S., has brought to our attention:

In the present state of fallen man it is not possible practically to come to a clear and complete understanding of the basic natural religious and moral truths, without insecurity and error, unless God comes to man's rescue by some means of divine help. . . . [Recall the teaching of the First Vatican Council:] "It is to be ascribed to this divine revelation that such truths among things divine as of themselves are not beyond human reason can, even in the present condition of mankind, be known by everyone with facility, with firm assurance, and no admixture of error."[13]

Cyril Vollert has argued for the importance of theology in the curriculum in the following manner:

If then, a university is, as Newman argues, an institution that "by its very name professes to teach universal knowledge" (*The Idea of a University*, Discourse II, Loyola University Press, 1927, p. 38), if the purpose of a university is, in the words of a contemporary educator "to provide a haven where the search for truth may go on unhampered by utility or pressure for 'results,'" (R. M. Hutchins: *Higher Learning in America*, Yale University Press, 1936, p. 43), if the primary concern of higher learning is "thinking about fundamental problems" (*Ibid.*, p. 106), the theology of revelation can be banished from the lecture halls only at the expense of abolishing the university itself. . . . Without theology, university teaching is one-sided, defective, distorted; for it presents a false, or at best an inadequate, concept of the universe, of the beginning and end of all things, of man and destiny, of God. Real learning is learning cognizant of *fact;* but the greatest facts of all are the facts presented by theology. To ignore these truths, which alone explain the world and the world's function, is to ignore reality and live in a world of make-believe.[14]

But there are more positive reasons for the theological maturity of the Catholic college student. Theology alone can tell the student of the Triune God who has been revealed in a Redeemer God. It alone can inform the student of the true and actual condition of man, be it as sinner or redeemed, in a supernatural order; and it is here that the whole of salvation history plays its unparalleled role in the educational process, immersing man in history, but a history that can only be perceived with the eyes of faith. To appreciate man and humanity as they concretely exist supposes a realization of their divinization by grace and their relationship to the Incarnate Word. The glorious and tragic aspects of human activity can only be seen profoundly in their relationship to the glorious and tragic activity of the Word made Flesh. Only theology can inform man what his ultimate destiny is in actual fact —the loving contemplation of Father, Son and Holy Spirit (and one cannot but think here of the necessary incompleteness of philosophical ethics, be it considered in its theoretical or practical aspects). The concrete reality of the supernatural has affected not only man but the whole universe as well, and thus theology alone can give the students a science of world order and lead the students to a

judgment of the proper place and proportionate value of all things within the framework of salvation. In this judgment the student perceives with his intellect not only the hierarchy of truths to be known but the hierarchy of goods to be loved. It is through this judgment that not only the objects of the intellect are put in order but also the objects which are pursued by the will. Thus sacred doctrine communicates a knowledge which is by definition salvific—a salvific understanding of world order.[15]

Put more prosaically, as our students grow in knowledge in the various fields of learning presented to them, there must be a concomitant growth in the ability to see the meaning of these facts and their place in the total picture; and this can only be accomplished through philosophy and theology. Otherwise there emerges an intellectual monster, with an expert's knowledge of chemistry, for example, and a child's knowledge of religion, or that dangerous type of graduate who is articulate but ill-informed. As Edwin Kaiser has noted, "much learning in profane subjects and little in truths of faith almost inevitably creates an imbalance which leads to a disdain for the little as unimportant or insignificant."[16]

In the same vein Etienne Gilson has written:

One can be a scientist, a philosopher or an artist without having studied theology, but without theology one cannot be a Christian philosopher, scientist or artist. Without it, one could well be a Christian on the one hand, and on the other a scientist, philosopher or artist; but without it our Christianity will never descend into our science, our philosophy and our art, interiorly to reform and vivify them.[17]

In seeking for the basic reason for the intellectual theological maturity of the Catholic college student, Francis Keating has suggested that the very role of the Catholic layman in contemporary society requires this. The layman must understand his basic responsibilities, he must place actions which aim at religious and moral renewal, the Christianization of the total life of mankind and actions which aim directly at the Christianization of the institutional structures of society. But such a view is not possible without an intellectual formation that is profoundly mature.[18]

It is rather obvious that if the aim of our colleges and universities on the undergraduate level is a liberal education, the theological formation of the student is a necessity. Christopher Mooney approaches our problem from this viewpoint. A liberal education, as he conceives it, attempts to transmit a spiritual heritage from one generation to another, through initiation into a culture, that is, into a set of values and ideals—religious, philosophic, artistic and scientific—which are seen as worthy of esteem and hence are accepted and lived by the community. In such a view, the college's function as one of the agencies of initiation into a culture is to develop a human personality to a mature level in and through the acquisition of knowledge. Clearly there is question here of intellectual growth, a growth that enlarges the student's capacity for conscious living, extends the reach and range of his relationships, and enables him to take possession of the world about him. Thus he is prepared to play a more useful and significant role in the social world of his generation and consequently contribute a greater share of the achievements of his community. American Catholic education, then, must build personalities at once fully Christian and fully American. Theology in the Catholic college injects into this educational process a totally new approach to reality in the order of knowledge—faith. The student is presented with a supernatural vision of human life and work, so that he will have a rational basis for reacting in a Christian fashion to the society in which he finds himself. Thus, with reference to America, such a student should be capable of making a rational synthesis of those very aspects of American culture that seem of themselves to be irreconcilable—the dichotomy between individual and community, the apparent opposition between the Christian's spiritual destiny and America's almost fanatical dedication to temporal progress.[19]

We might add that if Catholic liberal education's aim is to hand on to its students a Christian culture, as Mooney has suggested, then it should be obvious that theology, since it forms an integral part of that culture, must be in the curriculum. Religion has always been a focal element in the culture of mankind, and Christianity is certainly no exception. Knowledge of the "Great Books" of Christianity, be they the greatest of them all, Sacred Scripture, or the writings of the Fathers and the declarations of the magisterium, can hardly in such a case be neglected in a Catholic college or university. Our scientific contemplation of God is essential, for as Maritain has written:

Theological problems and controversies have permeated the whole
development of Western culture and civilization, and are still at work
in its depths, in such a way that one who would ignore them would
be fundamentally unable to grasp his own time and the meaning of its
internal conflicts.[20]

If, on the other hand, one conceives liberal education as the
development of the whole personality of the student to a certain
level of maturity and dedication to truth, theology's place is clear.
In such a view the perfection of intellectual formation involves a
conscious, reflective control of truth, an intelligence of meaning
which liberates the student from the concrete and individual by
placing him in the world of universal ideas while retaining a relation to the limited culture within which he must grow to a distinctive realization of human living and assume its responsibilities.
The student's spontaneous search for understanding of reality is
refined and made conscious by development of certain capacities
and habits and by conscious possession of certain techniques and
methodologies which give rise to the manifold sciences and disciplines. The basic approaches to reality are humanistic, scientific,
philosophical, mathematical and theological. Hence the student
appreciates the dimensions of awareness of man and nature distinctive to these approaches, and by his own experience of them,
understands the nature and interrelationships of the various disciplines. In such a context theology contributes to the student a
conscious appreciation of its own distinctive dimension of awareness and of relation to other approaches. The student's education
would be deficient if this appreciation were lacking. This theological dimension of awareness can be achieved through sustained
effort at a more refined understanding of revelation by methods
which are philosophical, or, as in the early Fathers, more properly
humanistic.

Finally, John Courtney Murray has insisted upon another, and
indeed, frightening reason for the necessity of theological maturity
in our Catholic college student. He has pointed out that the world
in which we live is hostile to the Christian; for it is a world

alienated from the Church, a world which does not support our faith. With approval he quotes the judgment of E. I. Watkin:

A sufficient Catholic education, which imparts a living organic and interior knowledge of the Catholic religion is now literally a matter of life and death. The Catholic today as he grows out of his childish acceptance must either go into an interior view of Catholic truth or go out of the Church. However many individual exceptions there may still be, due to the interference of other factors, this alternative faces us inexorably. Come in or go out. You cannot stay on the surface. There is no foot-hold left there.[21]

In such circumstances it is clear that faith, which stands next to charity in any Christian hierarchy of values, must at all costs be preserved. It is the hope, and, indeed, the prayer, of every teacher of theology in our colleges and universities that he can contribute in some way to the formation of "Christian men strong enough to be plunged into the modern secularized milieu and confidently left to the inner resources of a mature faith that is able to stand by itself, supported by the strength of its own deeply experienced reality. More than that, he desires to develop Christian men who will be intelligent enough and strong enough to reform the milieu itself."[22]

APPENDIX:
INTEGRATION OF THE
CURRICULUM AND OF THE
STUDENT'S INTELLECTUAL,
SPIRITUAL, MORAL, AND
RELIGIOUS LIFE[23]

Teachers and administrators cannot achieve integration in the student. They can only give him materials and tools with which to integrate, and work toward disposing him to achieve integration.

What is the meaning of integration? Integration means unification, and unity can be understood in several ways. It can be taken strictly as unity without real distinction; this meaning of unity is too strong to be applicable to the things to be integrated here (the elements of a curriculum, the activities of the intellectual, spiritual, moral, and religious life). Unity, less strictly, is order and relationship. In this sense, integration means "unification, ordering, or relating" of some kind of diversified manifold. There are then as many forms of integration as there are ways or causes of order and relationship.

Kinds of Integration

The first kind of integration is by final cause—teleological integration. In the case of the curriculum and the student's life, the end is both the ultimate (e.g., A.M.D.G.) and the specific end of undergraduates in a four-year program of liberal arts. Other specific goals will be analogous to this.

The second kind of integration is by formal cause, ordering activities (especially kinds of knowledge) according to objects and methods. Complete integration by formal cause seems out of the question here; but it is possible within limits, that is, in general terms, or according to large classes; here also would pertain one aspect of the integration through the history of the disciplines and of their objects.

The third kind of integration is through material cause, the student himself. Not only is he one being, but all the things he is to do in the undergraduate college are chosen for their human relevance: in their significance for him as a mature Christian person. Here, too, history functions in ordering and relating the student to his own time and other times and cultures.

The Role of Theology

What is the role of theology in integrating curriculum and student activities as defined in the theme of this Workshop? The term "theology" needs distinction.

Theology, taken in its complete form as including philosophy, would be able to integrate the curriculum through both final and formal causality. In the line of final causality, theology would be able to state and relate both the ultimate goal of education and the specific goal of the college to all the other activities of the college and of the student.

In the line of formal causality, it would be able to state, relate and order the elements of the total curriculum and the other activities of the college, not only in its inception but as a continuing process. (It seems advisable to state that this "ordering" is not to be understood as a dictatorial, imperialistic interference in the internal structures and objects of any other discipline.) In addition, it concretely presents an instance of integration, in that it uses the methods of many other disciplines. Another way of considering the causality of theology is to view it as a norm. As a "negative norm" theology has the duty of noting and marking for rejection all opinions which are explicitly and formally opposed to any truths of the Catholic faith. From a positive point of view, theology should bring out the bearing of this or that theoretical discipline on revealed truth as a whole. The means of accomplishing this integration are several. Inside the various disciplines taught in the college, theology itself should explicitly relate its work to relevant areas of other disciplines, and other disciplines should in turn frequently refer to those points or areas of theology that are germane to the points they are handling. The influence on other disciplines by theology can be best brought about by informal communication between the members of the theology department and other departments of the college. The presence of graduate students of theology on the campus would greatly increase the effectiveness of this informal communication, and would bring it proportionately down to the student body. Standing research committees on the integration of the curriculum and the other student activities could profitably be formed in each school.

Theology, in the form which is taught to the student—the yet-to-be-fully-developed "college theology"—is not theology taken perfectly and inclusively, but theology in a less perfect, or analogous sense. College theology integrates teleologically—not by sermonizing or exhortation, but by its own inner dynamism. This orientation is obviously to the ultimate goal of all life; it is also to some of the proximate goals to some extent: it can emphasize social responsibility (integration of teaching and life), for example, through the doctrine of the Mystical Body. It disposes the student to a personal integration of knowledge and action because of its own dynamisms. College theology also integrates by formal causality, as "incarnational theology," in that it concretely gives a profound meaning for action, including the intellectual actions of studying and knowing. It can prevent a misguided rationalism in philosophy by showing itself as an area of valid knowledge. It also initiates and helps the integration and systematization of values. According to material cause, college theology integrates by helping the student to see his own uniqueness before God and his own distinctive value as a person.

The Role of Philosophy

What is the role of philosophy in this integration? Again some distinctions seem in order. Philosophy is first to be considered in its complete perfection. It seems well to note, secondly, that a non-metaphysical philosophy would integrate only in the way in which history or literature would integrate. Often an alleged non-metaphysical philosophy implies a false metaphysics, and so could indeed integrate, but this would be a "false" integration. It seems, thirdly, that a philosophy, to be fully adequate as an integrating factor in a Jesuit school, must be one which admits, at least, that there is a valid revealed theology.

A philosophy, thus defined and qualified, would be able to integrate according to formal cause (cf. *supra,* as explained for theology). Inasmuch as it is the only discipline which includes in its object the modes of being and of being known, it is the only subject which *ex professo* orders the elements of the curriculum in this way.

In its influence on the student, philosophy is an integrating factor as far as it is understood. In addition, to the extent that it leads to habits of reflection, analysis, and abstract thinking, it will be an integrating factor perfecting the student's ability to see relationships.

The Roles of Other Factors

Are there other integrating factors which should be considered? Among these, it seems important to mention the following: the presence of Jesuits in all departments; the concept of the college (or university) as an academic community; then, among subjects, literature, the arts, history, and social sciences (possibly also biology); honors programs; the Sodality, especially in regard to the integration of knowledge and action.

Areas of Unfinished
Business in Integration

It was mentioned that integration according to formal cause is possible only in rather general terms. Most of the detailed work remains to be done; the development of an adequate philosophy of science that proceeds beyond generalities to specific cases; a philosophy of art; a philosophy of history; a philosophy of action; a philosophy of society as this is now developing.

As far as the role of theology is concerned, it is only after college theology will have been developed to a greater extent that the general indications mentioned above can be seen in any detail. Areas of effective integration are similar to those mentioned for philosophy.

It would be desirable to know whether there are any effects in our present-day students which could be called "integration," and it would be well to check these studies as courses become radically different, to see whether the results are more or less integrated.

Notes

1. In the preparation of this paper, besides published material, we have had the opportunity to use a number of reports from the departments of theology of Jesuit colleges and universities in the United States in which the subject matter of this paper was considered.
2. In speaking of the Catholic college student, it is the undergraduate that is in view. This deliberately leaves out the question of the non-Catholic and of the professional or graduate student in our Catholic institutions of higher learning.
3. Is it not interesting that such opinions are being ventilated in Catholic colleges and universities, while the plea for the teaching of religion or theology, together with separate departments in the field, is arising in the world of the secular university? Thus Robert Michaelsen of the State University of Iowa writes: "Religion is significant to the liberal arts curriculum. . . . The liberal arts curriculum should include the study of religion—as central in human experience and culture, as the study of man's approaches to ultimate questions, the manner in which he sees himself in the universe, the object of his loyalties and his loves, the rationale of his existence." "Religion as an Academic Discipline," *Liberal Education*, XLVII (1961), 72–83.
4. "College Theology and Liberal Education," *Thought*, XXXIV (1959), 326.
5. "The Meaning of Sacred Doctrine in the College," *Shaping the Christian Message*, ed. Gerard D. Sloyan (New York: Macmillan Co., 1958), p. 175. On this matter of liberal education see "The Report of the Commission on Liberal Arts Colleges," *Jesuit Educational Quarterly*, XIX (1956), 83–86; "Objectives of Catholic and Jesuit Liberal Arts Education: A Symposium," *ibid.*, pp. 87–93.
6. I have found it disagreeable to have had to bring up this matter of objectives. There is nothing more distasteful than the discussion of the objectives of institutions that have existed for centuries. The feeling is, no doubt, that if we haven't discovered the objectives by now, we might as well abandon hope. But in spite of all this, this question had to be treated in order to put the matter in hand in its proper perspective.
7. "Towards a Theology for the Layman—The Pedagogical Problem," *Theological Studies*, V (1944), 354.
8. Gerald Van Ackeren, S.J., "The Finality of the College Course in Sacred Doctrine in the Light of the Finality of Theology," *Proceedings of the Annual Meeting of the Society of Catholic College Teachers of Sacred Doctrine*, II (1956), 23.
9. In all this our aim would seem to coincide with what Pope Pius XI in his encyclical *On the Christian Education of Youth* puts forward as the goal of Christian education: "the supernatural man who thinks, judges and acts constantly and consistently in accordance with right

reason illumined by the supernatural light of the example and teaching of Christ; in other words, to use the current term, the true and finished man of character" (NCWC translation, Washington, 1936, p. 36).

10. "Training Teachers of College Theology," *Jesuit Educational Quarterly,* XIX (1956–57), 97.

11. For a contrary view see Thomas Donlan, O.P., *Theology and Education* (Dubuque: W. C. Brown Co., 1952).

12. "The Role of Religion in the Development of the Catholic Intellectual," Keynote Address at the Annual Fall Meeting of the Southwestern Regional Unity of the NCEA, College and University Department, October 20, 1956, p. 4 (mimeographed).

13. "The Nature and Function of Courses in Sacred Doctrine and Their Curricular Implications in Liberal Education," *NCEA College Newsletter,* October, 1956, p. 15.

14. "Theology and University Education," *Modern Schoolman,* XXI (1943), 20–21.

15. Van Ackeren, *op. cit.,* p. 16.

16. Kaiser, *op. cit.,* p. 15.

17. "L'Intelligence au service du Christ-Roi," *Christianisme et Philosophie* (Paris: Librairie J. Vrin, 1936), quoted in Donlan, *op. cit.,* pp. 128–29.

18. "The Finality of the College Course in Sacred Doctrine in the Light of the Finality of the Layman," *Proceedings of the Annual Meeting of the Society of Catholic College Teachers of Sacred Doctrine,* II (1956), 25–46.

19. "College Theology and Liberal Education," *Thought,* XXXIV (1959), 325–46.

20. *Education at the Crossroads* (New Haven: Yale University Press, 1943), pp. 82–83, quoted in John Courtney Murray, S.J., "Towards a Theology for the Layman: The Problem of Its Finality," *Theological Studies,* V (1944), 46.

21. *The Catholic Centre* (New York: Sheed & Ward, 1939), p. 54.

22. John Courtney Murray, S.J., "Towards a Theology for the Layman— The Pedagogical Problem," *Theological Studies,* V (1944), 350.

23. Editor's Note: This statement, here presented in slightly revised form, was prepared during the Workshop in Los Angeles by a Task Force composed of the following members: George P. Klubertanz, S.J., Chairman, Joseph K. Drane, S.J., Frederick P. Manion, S.J., Richard A. McCormick, S.J., and H. James Yamauchi, S.J. All participants recognized the complexities of this topic. This statement was not discussed formally by Workshop participants. It is presented because of its relevance to the preceding chapter and to other chapters of this book.

7

SOME REFLECTIONS ON THE TEACHING OF COLLEGE THEOLOGY

Theodore Mackin, S.J.

Occasionally one still encounters among professors of theology the fear of professionalizing the Christian faith by submitting it to a rigorous theology, a wariness about shunting it into the academic arena as if the faith were a secular peer among peers. Some have urged that even in Catholic universities the study of this faith be removed to a situation of transcendence, apart from and above the world of academics.

The anxiety is often enough a legitimate one, and it is not hard to find the reason why. The Christian faith and religion can be treated as though they were subjects of secular knowledge. Courses in comparative religion seem rooted in the illusion that a detached, non-committal study of Christianity can yield an accurate knowledge of it. But such a study must falsify the very evidence under scrutiny, since the meaning of the Christian religion is the meaning of a personal experience. And the personal experience depends on an inner dynamism working in a realm of existence simply transcending that secular milieu which is taken for granted and preferred by the student of comparative religion. This kind of student is about as prone to think accurately on his subject as is the cold-eyed analyst who writes about married love.

One may, nevertheless, suspect in Catholic professors who indulge in this fear, a certain junior-sized Jansenism about professional academics, as though academics were incurably secular and the world of career scholarship were by definition profane. One suspects, too, that they have either never heard of the intellectual virtues or have never understood their role in the growth of Christian holiness.

On the contrary, if one insists that the career of learning and high scholarship is germane to the Church's continuing work of redemption, this insistence is not a kind of polemic-apologetic one, as if the Church would be thought *simpliste* if she had no scholars, or as if she could otherwise not address herself, with conversion in mind, to the world of scholars.

Plainly and simply, any man who sets out to understand even the rudiments of Christian revelation with any accuracy must set his intelligence to work. To understand is to define in some way, and defining cannot be done either by good will or responsive emotions. There have been epochs in Catholic Christianity when anti-intellectualism was held in honor in some places. That there is more than a suggestion of this in the *Imitation of Christ* is evident. But it is not evident that the piety of the Lowlands which produced the *Imitation* did much to halt the splintering of Christendom in the fifteenth and sixteenth centuries.

Let us set this down as a principle: the first gift of the grace of faith carries within itself an orientation, an urging, to the use of intelligence. Faith really does contain an élan towards understanding. Except in rare instances, understanding does not follow unless intelligence is guided and instructed. Indeed, understanding is itself one phase of the journey to wisdom. Since wisdom consists of the consideration of the first cause and last end of our creation and redemption, it is itself the end (in both senses of that term) of the journey. As the end, this consideration of first cause and last end is properly called contemplation, which also is an operation of the intelligence.

In chapter four of the Final Report of the Jesuit Educational Association Workshop of August, 1962, there is this particularly relevant remark: "But most pertinently (and somewhat paradoxically) to deny theology its properly academic methodology is to militate against theology's necessary and wholly substantial contribution to the moral, religious and spiritual development of the student." What has been said above was meant to suggest that theology's contribution to holiness is neither ornamental nor custodial-directive. This is not meant as a challenge to the commonplace of ascetical theology that Christian holiness is formally in the will as charity. Or, more rhetorically, it is not a denial that the notorious washerwoman of simple piety may far surpass the theologian in holiness. But it is true, nonetheless, that the somewhat holy theologian is more integral in his Christianity than the very holy washerwoman. She may be more intense in her love of God, but more of the theologian is able to participate in his less intense love. All of a man is graced if he is graced at all. All that he can do can be suffused ("in-formed" is the traditional term) with the love of Christ, including even the sense of touch in the holiness specific to marriage.

If this is true of the senses, it is *a fortiori* true of the intelligence, because the intelligence participates more immediately in the operation of the will. This is evident enough. But what has this to do with the institutionalized and profanely conventional teaching and learning that is theology in the colleges? What has college theology really to do with the holiness of the Church?

Theology's guiding and rectifying relationship to holiness in the Church is clear enough in the light of the centuries of good-hearted heresies in the Church.[1] But even beyond this, theology in the colleges is necessary for the holiness of the Church in an organic and intimate way. When we confess that the Church is the Body of Christ we mean more exactly that she is the instrument of the continuation of Christ's redeeming action in history. This continually redeeming Christ simultaneously lives the beatifying virtue, namely wisdom, but he lives it in the unity of vision. We who are still exiles in terrestrial history can live the same virtue of wisdom, but we live it only dimly and fragmentally. But experience it we must, or else we fail to incarnate Christ with constancy and accuracy. Christian wisdom—the consideration of the divine cause that is both source and goal, the consideration precisely of God drawing us and of our response to God—is an incomplete but not inaccurate definition of theology. Somewhere in the Church this wisdom must be carried on if the Church is to be the Church. Somewhere this wisdom must be conscious of its own inner anatomy and operation if the holiness of the Church is to be integral. It may as well be in the universities.

Theology is unique among the academic disciplines of a university in that it lives and moves and has its being simultaneously in two distinct worlds. It is a science within the possibility of men, if one will allow a traditional and non-restricted use of the term "science." But theology cannot in any concrete instance get under way as a scientific enterprise except with a religious-moral act, the act of faith, an act organically continuous with and enduring through all that comes after. Not that this religious-moral act guarantees the honesty as well as the Christianity of the theologian, who then proceeds with his theology. But by this act theology is made the science it is. And indeed the act of faith surpasses in its nature the potential of human understanding—a fact which confounds secular scholarship.

If this is conceded, it is not hard to get rid of the fiction that an unbeliever can make progress in theology. He cannot. If theology is truly theology only when it arrives at objectively certain judgments that are conclusions drawn from premises proper to this science, then the unbeliever can come to only hypothetically certain conclusions—hypothetical in that they hang from this premise which to him is unverifiable: "If God has really revealed. . . ."

For theologians and students of theology it is much more difficult to rid themselves of the bad habit of proceeding in theology as though all were hypothetical. Let me explain by recapitulating briefly what I said above. The first principle of any science, understood functionally, is the first act of that science. In this first act the student first apprehends the subject unique to this science; he has his first experience of the aspect of existence with which this science deals. This experience becomes the first cause, within the student, of any accurate judgment he will ever make concerning any instance of that aspect of existence.

In the sciences dealing with material things the first experience is of movement, or change. In metaphysics it is the experience of existence apprehended as such. But in theology the first experience is of God's act of communicating, of His revealing.

This experience is obviously beyond the conventional limits of science because it cannot be controlled, cannot be measured, cannot be repeated at the will of the student. Not so obvious to many is the fact that this experience is innately moral and places a moral demand on the student. It is not just that he must be honest with his evidence, a moral demand laid on every scientist. In theology, the very assent to the evidence is a moral act. This it must be when the evidence is God revealing not only the goal of all human searching, but the way to that goal as well. And there is in the revealing this added dimension, namely the demand that the goal be accepted and the way traversed. This is more than suggested in the words of the New Testament, "He who believes and is baptized will be saved; he who does not believe will be condemned" (Mark 16:16).

The first act of the science of theology is elicited by God, by a demanding God, by "a jealous God." The first act of the novice scientist is a reaction to this unmanageable and transcendent agent. The intruding God begins the science in this student by demanding that he accept and surrender in his will, and then with his will command his intellect and emotions. The student's intelligence is literally driven beyond its natural capacity and his emotions are assaulted beyond any reasonable demands of nature.

This experience must be immediate, intuitional, of person with person. One begs the question if he insists that the student can have this experience in hearing and accepting the words of teachers who are authorized by the Church. Such teachers—who, in moral-legal terms, hold ordinary authority—may indeed have such authority. But it is a shared authority, and like any shared perfection it can be a valid object of moral choice only insofar as it is sustained by unshared absolute authority. To put it more simply, the teacher holding authority is a source of certainty to the student only when the student brings prior faith to the teaching which he hears.

The student must have a personal experience of the entry of the demanding Lord into his life in order to theologize formally. This suggests, first of all, that the prudentially guiding discipline in all of his studies must ultimately be moral theology. (Moral theology is here understood as one pole of the continuum extending homogeneously through ascetical and mystical theology.) Secondly, the necessary centrality of the liturgy in the life of the student wishing to learn theology dictates that he must meet God where in fact God communicates now with men. This is in and through the eternally chosen mediator, Jesus Christ. Since Christ acts in history in the sacraments, and since the disciplined, patterned use of the sacraments is the liturgy, the student's theological learning is also born there and must be continually nurtured there. It is no coincidence that on Catholic campuses seriousness about and joy in theological learning grow in proportion as liturgical participation in the sacraments grows.

Any professor of theology is aware that a number of his students come to his lectures indisposed for the learning of theology. There is more here than a mere shirking of hard work or a lack of instruction in the rudiments of Christian doctrine. As a matter of fact, often those who have had little exposure to religious instruction are for that very reason the more ready to learn theology.

The reason rather lies in that experience, analyzed above, which is the beginning of true theology. This experience is the act of faith, initiated by God and taking its first form within the student as a love of the divine good, i.e., an acceptance of God who is communicating to him personally. We understand that this is a communicating not alone of the divine being as true; but, more perceptibly for the student, of the divine being as will which calls all men to redemption.

This personal communication of God to the student contains

a kind of descriptive definition of the student. It implies a rather remarkable humanism of the student and of every other member of the race. It suggests to him that in spite of surface appearance all is not well with him, that he is in a condition of misery and of potential tragedy of which he ought to be aware, that he has a need to be rescued, that he is in a serious way, helpless. It implies in a larger sense that all men are in this helplessness, this need, this faintly palliated misery—that they all need rescuing from themselves and from the world they have made.

It goes without saying that only a few of the freshmen who face the professor at the beginning of the fall semester share this awareness. There are two reasons for this, both important, but one only superficial, the other quite profound.

The first and superficial reason is that so many are the children of a peculiarly shrunken American *Anschauung* that is nine parts confidence in its own success at having banished misery from most of the world. The kindly riposte to these young ones that perhaps misery has been banished from only *their* world is a wasted one. For them their world is *the* world. For them the kinds of analgesics available for ills of both body and emotions are virtually limitless. That these are available mainly for purchase is significant. As tuition rises steadily higher in Catholic universities we shall have the continuing guarantee that most of our freshmen will have bought most of them. Besides, so often their parents have been educated to the questionably virtuous persuasion that their off-spring are by all means to be protected from pain, since, in their ethic, pain is by definition evil.

This may account for an increasingly frequent phenomenon noted by counselors of new university students: the parochial misery with which so many young men and women are acquainted is so often the frustration attending their insurrection against too prolonged parental authoritarianism. Or is it the diffidence, guilt, and self-contempt consequent on the long lack of tangible love from parents who are busy with earning for them the expensive good things of life? But this kind of misery, though subjectively harsh for the student, is objectively trivial. It is narcissistic and tends to lock him off not only from concern about the genuine misery of others in the world around him, but from his own far more authentic misery of original sin as well.

The second and more profound reason is somewhat the same, somewhat different. It is the as yet dwarf-humanity of so many students, their innocence of experience, their shallow awareness. It is hard to know on whom to fasten the indictment here. By reason of the warm and cushioned circumstances of their suburban lives they can have had few experiences calculated to shock them into awareness. They see a great deal of death, but it is the two-dimensional, odorless, "commercials"-punctuated, never-more-than-sixty-minutes'-worth death of the Apaches circling the wagon train. That experience has been drained of its personal dimension and its potential for awakening to the human condition. With the experience of death ruined for them, what experience is left that can do the job? They know so little of the human condition because the human being available to their reflection lies inside, undisturbed, unawakened by great happenings, asleep. What could the doctrine of original sin possibly mean to a late adolescent who thinks the problem of evil is how to break the habit of self-abuse?

This is where the great and humane literatures of the Western world, and some from the Eastern, ought to have entered and done their incalculably necessary work. What the student has not experienced actually because circumstances prohibited it, he ought to have experienced vicariously. This is the key determining whether he can learn theology. In reflecting on himself, has he developed some feeling for all of humanity? Some sense of history? Has he tasted the tears of being a lost and wandering creature? God bless those secondary school teachers who have caused their charges to undergo this experience by making them read and read and read! God forgive those who have made them memorize answers!

To the question dealt with thoroughly and competently elsewhere by John Courtney Murray, and in this series of essays by

Gerald Van Ackeren, concerning what theology for the lay student ought to be, we add a question comparable in urgency: "How many of our students can be taught theology in the first place?" We suggest on good evidence that those who have not been educated liberally cannot be taught theology, or can be only with great difficulty.

Notes

1. In this regard the theology manuals ought to get rid of the term *adversarii*. The heretics have always been far less enemies than they were men who thought the rest of the army out of step.

Part III

PHILOSOPHY

8

CURRENT VIEWS ON THE INTRINSIC
NATURE OF PHILOSOPHY

W. Norris Clarke, S.J.

I must begin by justifying the existence of this paper. It may seem a waste of time to delay getting down to practical matters by a general speculative paper such as this would seem by its title to be. Yet I think the planners of this workshop have chosen wisely in including it.

If we lived in a more or less homogeneous culture, or even if among Catholics in America there were a single fairly unified consensus as to the nature of the philosophical enterprise, there would be no need to do more than recall the basic scholastic descriptions of philosophy and go on from there. But the precise reason, as Father Henle told me, why this topic was included was because it is no longer clear that the once almost unanimous consensus among us as to the nature of philosophy has the same sway any more. As new young Catholic professors of philosophy are taken into our philosophy departments, after being trained in various institutions here and abroad, it has been observed that the trumpet no longer seems to send forth the same note from the different parapets.

I am not talking here merely of different particular philosophical positions or theses. Differences here are inevitable, natural, irreducible, and healthy, and we are more or less used to coping with this sort of pluralism among us. I am speaking rather of the very idea of what kind of enterprise philosophy is, what it means to philosophize. This is a more basic ground on which significant

141

shifts in attitudes have been taking place in recent years, reflecting, of course, movements of thought in the wider contemporary philosophical world. And the shifts in attitudes, we might add, are observable not only among Catholic lay professors but also, to a slowly increasing degree, among university-trained priests and religious. This, again, to anyone who is realistically-minded and is sensitive to cultural change and the history of philosophy, is to a considerable extent natural, inevitable and, at bottom, healthy, if properly animated by prudence, sincere philosophical reflection, and a sense of tradition.

But it is very important that this kind of difference of opinion be recognized very clearly and its significance understood. Otherwise it can generate great confusion, puzzlement, or resentment, either within a department or between a department and busy deans or higher administrators who are trying to keep the whole ship running straight on its course. Thus a chairman or a dean can wonder why under the sun Doctor or Father X is so perversely stubborn in always insisting on this or protesting against that, whereas it seems perfectly obvious in terms of the traditional scholastic concept of philosophy as he learned it or teaches it.

Before I start in, I do not wish it to be felt that we are on the brink of some grave crisis of philosophical cataclysm. By no means. But I do think we are entering upon a period of rather profound evolution in Catholic thinking about philosophy, somewhat akin, perhaps, to deep new tides in theology and Scripture studies. It will require considerable wisdom and especially patience and mutual confidence, even in the absence of clear understanding, to navigate safely during this time until we can see more clearly just where we are going. And just in order to moderate the zeal of those who might be inclined to feel that a change in our attitudes toward philosophy is an unheard-of novelty of our own day, let me recall the exhortation of one of our early Fathers to his philosophy class, words which I am sure all of us would repudiate with amazement today. Writing in 1614, in true Renaissance style, he described the role of the modern philosopher as the most pleasant of tasks, requiring of us nothing more than to cull the fruits that the ancient philosophers have already both gathered and expounded so luminously.

To the most obscure matters they brought so much light that in this alone does our labor consist, that we may absorb with the greatest pleasure the things they discovered and explained.[1]

It hardly needs pointing out that by the Ancients he meant Plato, Aristotle, and Cicero rather than Thomas Aquinas.

Traditional Scholastic Notion of Philosophy

A brief word first on the above as a point of reference. On this view, understood very traditionally, philosophy is the science of the ultimate causes of all things insofar as they are accessible to the light of natural reason. Now scientific knowledge through causes (not, of course, in the modern understanding of the term "scientific" as restricted to the empirical or experimental sciences) means explaining, giving solutions to problems, which solutions are considered for the most part to be certain, with variable outer fringes of probability and uncertainty. These solutions, the notable majority of which were reached some time ago, either by Aristotle or St. Thomas, or Suarez, etc., are considered, once acquired, to be definitively true. Individual teachers may vary, of course, in assessing the completeness or incompleteness of the answer given, as well as the adequacy of its conceptual and verbal formulation. But all would still adhere more or less unanimously to the general thesis that a truth, though discovered in time, is, once discovered, independent of time. The job of the scholastic philosopher is then to try to rediscover personally, under the guidance of the great masters, both the problems and the already discovered solutions, adding whatever refinements he is capable of. Thus a body of solidly proved truth is slowly built up, and added to, down the ages which is perennially valid and may legitimately be called the *philosophia perennis*.

It has been suggested to me that at this point I should mention two opposing views current among contemporary Thomistic philosophers as to the proper internal structure of the discipline. These views do not properly concern the nature of philosophy at the very basic level on which we are going to discuss it. Still, the holding of one or the other of them has such serious repercussions on the ordering of the curriculum that it was thought wise to call attention to them as a point of reference.

Both of these views look on philosophy as a strictly systematic organized discipline which can be taught in a series of tractates ordered internally and with respect to each other in terms of fundamental principles. They differ on the question of just what is the proper ordering of the branches one to another.

The primary dispute concerns the relation between the philosophy of nature and metaphysics. The first view is that which has been the most commonly held and practiced in American Jesuit colleges. It maintains that all the other branches of philosophy depend intrinsically on the principles of metaphysics, which in turn does not depend on them either for the discovery of its proper object or for its principles. As a result, metaphysics should be the first treatise of philosophy taught after logic, with the philosophy of nature, psychology, and ethics following upon it and appealing explicitly to its principles, such as act and potency, causality, analogy, essence and existence, etc.

This view has come under heavy attack from other Thomists in recent years as inspired by the *a priori* deductive rationalism of Christian Wolff and as contrary to the traditional Aristotelian-Thomistic order as laid down by St. Thomas himself and followed in the Dominican school to this day. According to them, the philosophy of nature, including both cosmology and psychology, must precede metaphysics. Two main reasons are given. The first is pedagogical. One must begin with the more easily grasped particular subject closer to experience and rise to the more abstract, difficult, and elevated one transcending our finite world, according to the order recommended by Aristotle and St. Thomas: first physics or philosophy of nature (the same for them), then mathematics, then ethics, then last of all metaphysics, which then gives ultimate grounding to the proper principles of all that precede it.

The second reason is doctrinal. It is impossible to begin metaphysics scientifically without first establishing the existence of at least one immaterial being. Only thus can the object of metaphysics be identified as that which of itself can abstract from all matter, according to the famous "judgment of separation" of which contemporary Thomists make so much (i.e., the judgment that being cannot be identified with material being, hence provides a subject matter distinct from that of the philosophy of nature), and the science of metaphysics can then be set up in its proper place in the hierarchy of sciences according to the ultimate degree of separation from matter (third degree of abstraction). Furthermore, unless the existence of some immaterial mode of being is first known, it is impossible to know being as explicitly analogous. If one remains merely within the material world, being would appear to us as identical with material being and able to be sufficiently explained by the principles of the philosophy of nature, matter and form, etc. The question of analogy or the act of existence as such would never even come up (though why at least existence could not be brought up has never been clear to me). Now the role of the philosophy of nature would be to provide scientific proof of an immaterial being, either of the human soul or of a Prime Mover in the order of physical motion according to Aristotle's procedure in the *Physics*.

Hence the philosophy of nature is essential both pedagogically and doctrinally as a prelude to metaphysics. It must therefore be taught first, and it can in fact discover its own proper principles of matter and form, act and potency in the order of change, and efficient causality without recourse to metaphysics, although of course the complete understanding of these principles would depend ultimately on metaphysics.

Those of our professors who have been trained at Laval (probably Fribourg also and other Dominican centers) would strongly advocate this position for both the reasons given above, as contrasted with those trained, for example, at St. Louis, the Gregorian, or Louvain, although some of the latter would recommend the same order for purely pedagogical reasons.

New Emphasis on the History
of Philosophy

Let me speak first of a rather mild shift of emphasis, or, perhaps better, enlargement of horizons that is now very common among younger professors, not to mention a considerable number of older ones, and is destined only, one can safely say, to become stronger. This is the great importance attached to the history of philosophy as providing the indispensable background and perspective for understanding properly the philosophical problems themselves. Thus more and more of our philosophers feel that without a considerable dose of the history of philosophy in general, or at least of the history of particular problems, both problems and answers will be dangerously distorted and misinterpreted by the minds of the students. Hence their insistence on the need of devoting more and more time to historical material in their organizing of the syllabus. This presents no special doctrinal problem, it seems to me, as long as some prudent balance is preserved between history and the study of philosophical problems in themselves.

Philosophy as Identical with Its History

There is another view, however, of the relation between philosophy and its history which would wish to go considerably further than merely increasing the amount of history as a complementary background to the study of problems. It looks on philosophy as, in some essential way, identical with its own unfolding history. Philosophy is in the last analysis nothing else but the actual progressive dialectic of the great philosophers and their systems as they unfold in a significant order of succession through history. Philosophy is thus the very dialogue itself of the philosophers considered as a continuous process; it is the very search itself of the human mind into the great problems, considered as significant in what this very process reveals about man and his relation to the universe. Thus the focus of the philosopher himself, or at least of the philosophy teacher, is not on attempting to *solve* philosophical problems for themselves, to build up a body of intrinsically satisfactory and thus permanent truths in the speculative order about man, the world, and God. Its focus is rather on the very quest itself as a continuous and by its nature unending process, whose significant message is the very history of the human spirit seeking to understand itself and the universe. The particular problems and especially the "answers" proposed at different moments along the journey are to a greater or less extent always provisory, incomplete, revisible, bound to the limited perspectives of their particular time and place in the historical process, and hence significant more for the light they throw on the development of the whole process than for their own definitive truth value.

It is clear that if one accepts this view of what philosophy is, then the very form and essence of the subject as studied and taught will be the advancing dialogue of the great philosophers as it unfolds through the history of human thought. One can still, within this framework, given a certain amount of ingenuity, teach problems or subjects, but any isolation of individual problems from the whole thought of a philosopher will be impossible.

You may have noticed that I have left the central thesis of the above position somewhat vague and ambiguous, so that you may feel a bit uneasy about it and yet not quite sure whether you should be outrightly against it or not. This was deliberate, since this is just the kind of impression that it often makes on more traditional-minded scholastics the first time they run across it.

Also—and more important—there is a wide spectrum of particular positions within this general approach. At one extreme, to the far left, would be the radical historicism, or historical relativism, of philosophers like Dilthey, for whom all philosophical views are so bound down to their historical context that they cannot transcend the latter and deliver any permanently valid objective truth at all. According to this view there is not even anything permanent which can be called human nature. Man's unique nature is that he has no fixed nature but forges his own changing essence by his free choice in history. The chances are high that none of our philosophy professors would go anywhere near as far as this.

To the far right would be those who consider that although no age can produce the full and definitive truth on a given question, still a growing core of permanent truth emerges progressively as each moment of the historical dialectic unfolds its own particular new insight or new perspective on the whole. This position may actually seem to be at times almost indistinguishable from the earliest view we mentioned above, according to which the history of philosophy plays the role of a necessary background for a proper understanding of the origin of all problems. But I think there is a slight difference. For once history has passed onto its next significant chapter, according to the view we are discussing, it is no longer possible to pose the problems or answer them in quite the same way or in quite the same language as in previous periods.

Between these extremes of far left and far right, there are all shades of intermediary positions, the majority leaning certainly well toward the right. But in general the resulting attitude towards Thomism (or any scholasticism) would be something like the following. One would draw deep inspiration from the Thomist moment in the history of philosophy as bringing with it a great and decisive enrichment to human thought. Nevertheless, one could not expect in mid-twentieth century to continue looking at the world according to the same inevitably limited and incomplete perspective of Thomas himself, nor pose only the same problems or in the same way as he did, or answer in exactly the same way or especially in the same language. One would have to reflect carefully and sympathetically on the intervening chapters and finally, most of all, on the existential matrix of one's own culture and confront the world anew with twentieth-century problems, perspectives, needs, and modes of speaking.

Thus it would be pointed out that one of the reasons why the great riches of the Thomistic vision of the world, which all Thomists recognize who have genuine and profound contact with St. Thomas, have had so little impact on American thought and culture is that they have been cultivated here like a direct transplant from the thirteenth century, preserved in their own imported cultural soil, rather than replanted in properly American soil, crossed with native American plants and made to bring forth new but recognizably indigenous American fruits.

The different needs of modern man as compared to medieval man would also be pointed out. Medieval European man was still fresh and young in spirit, only a few centuries out of the woods in most cases, hence still close to experience and with strong elemental passions not yet fully tamed. His religious experience was also still fresh and strong. Hence what he needed most of all was to order his world, classify it, situate everything within it in an integrated total pattern, using the two great heritages of past wisdom to help him: natural and rational from the Greeks, supernatural and supra-rational from Christianity. Hence the great need and aptness of the Thomistic ordering vision of the fundamental structures of the universe.

Modern man, on the contrary, has become in a way too externally civilized, too organized within the multiple external forms of our tightly knit technological society. Life now comes to him sifted through so many sophisticated and artificial screens that one of his most pressing needs today is to recover again the fresh wellsprings of his experience, of his primary contact with life. This would dictate the need at the present day for a heavy stress on phenomenology, especially existential phenomenology, as it has been called, or the careful description of the fundamental areas of our human experience, in preference to abstract metaphysical analysis. Other examples similar to the above might be drawn from other characteristics of modern thought and culture.

A—to me—highly instructive illustration of the clash between the above view, even in moderate form, and the conservative Aristotelian-Thomistic outlook occurred in a recent three-day meeting in New York of Jesuit philosophy teachers to discuss aims and methods of philosophy teaching. One man justified his ordering of the curriculum in this way: Since the nature of man and of the human intellect is such as Aristotle and St. Thomas have shown, it follows that such should be the basic order of learning, as outlined by these same thinkers. The other man, who had been defending the historical development of thought as the basic framework for philosophical study and teaching, then rose and objected in this vein: But don't you see that your basic premise of the nature of man and of human knowledge is itself a particular philosophical position located at a definite point in history and therefore to a considerable extent conditioned by it? To accept such a position from the start as a norm for judging other philosophical doctrines and determining the method of teaching, without first situating it in the stream of philosophical history and assaying its limitations, is a form of *a priori* dogmatism. If created being is itself historical, then its unfolding as truth to our minds must also be essentially according to the historical mode. And history did not stop either with Aristotle or St. Thomas.

Here we touch upon what is perhaps the most clear-cut point of friction between the traditional systematic and the historical point of view. The former tend to start off right away within at least the general point of view of the system, which already powerfully influences the kind of problems to be discussed, the angle of philosophical vision, the methods, and the type of language. The latter find it very difficult—intellectually painful, we might say— to first make what seems to them a blind commitment to the system and its strongly "conditioning" point of view and method, without first situating it in the total history of human thought that lies not only before it (as Aristotle and Thomas both did) but also after it (as Thomists are considerably more reticent about doing). They would also feel considerable professional qualms about imposing this *a priori* "method of faith" on students, even as an initial pedagogical device. And it need hardly be remarked that contemporary students, by some instinct of sympathy with the historical-minded age in which they live, also very frequently show a quasi-instinctive resistance to such an initial act of faith, at least in philosophy—though it is noteworthy that they seem quite innocent of such suspicions with regard to their science courses.

There is no point in tracing out in a technical way for this audience the historical sources for this widespread contemporary view of the nature of philosophy. Let us note only that one of the great sources is Hegel, with his assumption of history within philosophy as the unfolding of the life of Spirit itself. Another is Darwinian evolution in the biological world, and the immense new range given to our sense of time and change by the opening up of paleontology and human pre-history. Another is the general penetration of historical perspective into almost all sciences in the nineteenth and twentieth centuries. The result is that "historicity" has now become one of the characteristic modes of thought of contemporary man in all fields. This point and others pertinent to our whole theme, I might mention, have been developed with great penetration and frankness in the book of Canon Dondeyne of Louvain, *Contemporary European Thought and Christian Faith*.[2]

I do not feel it would be appropriate for me to enter here on a critique of the above historicist view of the nature of philosophy. My role is rather that of the neutral reporter or observer than the judge, especially since in order to judge I would already have had to commit myself to my own view of philosophy. Let me say only this. The extreme historicist view is clearly untenable by anyone (and especially a Catholic, of course) who holds for some degree of objective philosophical truth, some transcendence of truth over history. In addition, it is self-refuting. For if all positions are purely relative to their limited historical context, so too the very historicist position becomes in its turn an historically relative position to be transcended. It cannot both admit that all truth is historically relative and at the same time pretend that it alone can escape the universal law it has proclaimed governing all of history.[3]

As one moves further toward the center and right end of the spectrum within this general position, it is clear that considerable elements of truth are to be found. How large, and how much they really or only apparently clash with the supposed traditional scholastic position, is a difficult and delicate question which it will take much thought and discussion to work out, with perhaps not a few "agonizing reappraisals" here and there along the way.

Phenomenology

In the space that remains to me I have time only to sketch briefly some of the other views on the nature of philosophy current today and influential among Catholic philosophers. The first is that philosophy should lay heavy stress on phenomenology, either in place of, or at least as a necessary prolegomenon to, metaphysical analysis. I am taking phenomenology here in the wide sense it has now acquired of any careful description of the essential traits of some area or object of our human experience. Its aim is not to *explain* the experience but simply to *unveil its essence,* so to speak, to make it "appear" or show itself clearly for what it is ($\phi\alpha\iota\nu\acute{o}\mu\epsilon\nu o\nu$). It is essential description rather than explanation or reduction to causes.

Most scholastic philosophy presupposes experience as an already given and, presumably, easily accessible starting point. It then devotes almost all its effort to what it considers the specifically philosophical act: not how things *are* or how precisely our experience is textured, but rather how it is *possible* that they can be as they are, i.e. explanation of what is evident through what is not evident, its ultimate principles and causes. But as we remarked earlier, many philosophers today feel that one of the most urgent needs of contemporary man—and a need that no other discipline save philosophy has the disposition or the equipment to meet—is to rediscover with great explicitness and reflexive attentiveness the dimension of his basic human experiences or contacts with reality in all their immediacy and freshness before they become overlaid with sophisticated interpretations and explanations. "Back to things themselves," as Husserl, the father of contemporary phenomenology, has said, or, as many phenomenologists would prefer to say today, "Back to experience itself."

Those who are in favor of a heavy infusion of phenomenology into scholastic philosophy argue that not only does contemporary man in particular have a special need to recover his vital contacts with immediate experience on all significant levels, but that as a general principle it is dangerous to launch into the process of explanation unless one has first taken full and careful inventory of just what it is one is trying to explain. Explanations of incomplete data may risk becoming themselves incomplete and hence distorted, especially when they claim to be ultimate.

Hence there is a widespread feeling that more time should be given to phenomenological description of reality as we experience it and less to explanation. When I recently consulted the group of Honors Program students who are part of my larger class this year as to what they felt was defective or missing in my own moderately Thomistic explanatory approach to reality, this was precisely the point they made with remarkable clarity and unanimity. "You are constantly explaining what you call the data of experience," they said, "whereas we are not yet very clear at all on just what the experiences are that we are trying to explain. We need first to get clearly in focus just what is the content of our significant human experiences before the problem of explaining them can become fully vital to us." And it should be noted that by "problems" they did not mean problems in their abstract metaphysical form, such as the "one and the many," which they had been given, but problems on the level of their lived experience made meaningful to them in the context of their culture.

I think there is a great deal of truth in what they say. But to meet this need one would have to sacrifice a considerable amount of traditional explanation. This would involve not so much a conflict with traditional scholastic philosophy as a reappraisal of the emphasis and time to be accorded it.[4]

Personalism and Subjectivity

These two trends in contemporary thought, which are evoking an increasingly warm response everywhere among Catholic thinkers, have close affiliations with the spirit and method of phenomenology as loosely described above. Their aim is to bring into clearer and more central focus the unique characteristics of the personal dimension of being, both as regards the inner subjectivity of the individual self and its interpersonal or intersubjective relations. There is no doubt in my mind that although St. Thomas and the great Scholastics had a clear and explicit awareness of the supremacy of the person as "that which is most perfect in the universe," still their main preoccupation was to analyze the objective ontological structure of the person, to situate it precisely in natura, in the objective hierarchy of being, in terms of objective scientific analysis, or what some have called "spectator analysis." It was not to describe from within, as a participant bearing witness, what it feels like to be and act like a person and to relate oneself to other persons as compared to impersonal things.

The reason why this new type of analysis must be done more explicitly in our age than in the medieval is twofold: first, because of the constant deepening of the reflexive self-consciousness of humanity as it grows in maturity through history, just as each individual grows toward more lucid self-consciousness as he experiences himself meeting and reflecting on the challenges of life; secondly, because the highly organized and mechanized forms of modern life tend, if not deliberately counteracted, to cramp and smother the more naturally personalistic modes of living of simpler forms of culture.

Yet this new preoccupation with the subjective and the personal is not so much a new concept of the nature of philosophy (except, of course, insofar as it involves the attitudes and methods of phenomenology) as a shift in the focus of its attention to a new dimension of experience. It can certainly be integrated with traditional Thomistic philosophy, so far as I can see, though the effort will undoubtedly precipitate a certain number of unforeseeable, perhaps profound, changes in traditional scholastic methodology.[5]

Philosophy as Linguistic Analysis

Just a word need be said here about a movement which has not yet penetrated in notable depth among Catholic philosophers in this country, so far as I know. I am not thinking here so much of the general semantic movement as a special branch of philosophy. We will certainly have to make more place for the latter in our curricula as its importance grows in a world so conscious of and dependent on communication, as its significance and implications become clearer, and as more people competent in it become available.

What I am rather thinking of for the moment as affecting the nature of philosophy more deeply is the current of British-originated "ordinary language analysis," as it is called. Although members of this school resist with increasing vigor reduction to any single common "essence" or platform, still they do share certain recognizable common attitudes. One is the conviction that at least a large part of philosophical disputes and difficulties arise because terms and concepts are lifted out of their natural matrix of the living ordinary language, seen as by its very nature a successful "form of life" for dealing symbolically with reality, and are then employed in artificial new uses which generate philosophical paradoxes and problems. If one reinserts these terms into the texture of ordinary language which gave them birth and analyzes carefully how they function there, many philosophical problems will be *ipso facto* dissolved. Some extremists in the school hold that all so-called special philosophical problems would be thus dissolved; others, more moderate, that the ground would thus be cleared for the fewer genuine problems requiring specifically metaphysical analysis.

There is to my mind considerable truth in the claims of the moderate wing of this school, though no one yet knows clearly just how far the application of the method can be extended. It is now becoming more and more apparent that as a matter of fact a considerable amount of the philosophical analyses of Aristotle and St. Thomas were of this non-metaphysical order.[6]

Philosophy as Free Commitment and Fruitful Hypothesis

I would like to add a word here about one last attitude toward the nature of philosophy that is becoming slowly more widespread among modern philosophers who still wish to hold on to meta-physical analysis. It is also discernible among Catholic philoso-phers here and there, although how widespread it is, is difficult to say.

This view holds, first, that since philosophical problems touch the deepest springs of our personal existence, which necessarily involves our freedom to take certain basic attitudes towards ourselves and all reality, the ultimate positions of a man's philoso-phy can never be fully disengaged from these deep personal com-mitments and laid out on the operating table for completely objective analysis and formulation. And since these commitments are of their nature so deep and personal as to be pre-philosophical, every philosophical vision of the world is actually the rational explicitation of the philosopher's free decision to be this kind of person.

Hence different philosophical views of the world would be presented not so much as objectively and impersonally true or false, adequate or inadequate, but rather as alternative intellectual hypotheses having greater or less power to illuminate life and give clear reflexive expression to an experientially fruitful and fulfilling mode of actual living as a person. Their norm of evaluation would thus be a kind of pragmatic test, but understood in the fullest and richest human sense taking in all the dimensions of the authentically human, above all, of course, the deeper exigencies of the spirit as existentially lived needs.

Thus basic metaphysical theories or systems would be looked on, somewhat by analogy with scientific theories, as freely elaborated human constructions that are not to be taken as definitive truths but rather judged on their power to illuminate and give meaning to personal existence. Thus they can compete freely among themselves, and when a person finds a new one more illuminating than his previous vision, he is free to discard the old—in fact he should do so—not so much as false but as inadequate and impoverished in illuminating and meaning-giving power.[7]

On this view there is not a little similarity between philosophical systems and works of art, each being in its own special way free, creative, symbolical and illuminating of reality. To some extent Whitehead, one of the most influential of contemporary metaphysicians, might be said to look on his own philosophical system in this way. Others have suggested that every great philosopher has chosen one or a few basic metaphors or analogies which he uses like an artist's palette and paintbrush to produce a symbolic re-creation of reality.

Needless to say, any strong statement of such a position would be difficult to reconcile with traditional views of philosophy as objective if incomplete truth about the world.

However, a very nuanced and moderate interpretation might well contain some important kernels of truth which would serve to moderate the ever present tendency of scholasticism to excessive rationalism. This might hold especially as regards the role of freedom at the roots of every philosophy, a good deal of which

is already included in Augustine's and Anselm's view of reason
as dependent on initial faith.

Philosophy as Awakening to
Problems and Personal Reflection

One last word on a view of what is the primary aim of philosophical training, if not even of philosophy itself. It is that the
specific result to be sought for from philosophical formation is the
ability to become aware, with some degree of deep personal realization, of the basic philosophical problems, to be awakened to a
sense of authentic philosophical problems latent behind the taken-
for-granted matter-of-fact-ness of ordinary unreflective life, and to
learn how to reflect deeply and personally on these problems and
to become aware of the theoretical and vital implications with
which they are pregnant. It is believed by its adherents that
authentic philosophical deepening is acquired more by seeing
problems and the profound natural mysteries of being and the
self into which they open out than by attempting to solve problems
by clear logical formulations and reasonings, at least in the beginning of one's philosophical career. Premature solutions of superficial clarity can do more harm than good to the proper development of the reflective philosophical mind deeply attuned to reality.
Hence the methods of teaching would concentrate more on raising
problems and making them live in the student's mind with as
much depth and richness of implication as possible, than on teaching clear-cut positive solutions to be learned by the students. The
procedure is widely followed in secular institutions, partly because
it is considered improper in a pluralistic society for the professor
in any way to indoctrinate his students, even by the indirect way
of self-commitment.

It is clear that moderate doses of this spirit of problem and
mystery must be used by all good teachers of philosophy. An
objection arises only when the attitude is turned into the dominant
and adequate method of teaching.

Conclusion

In sum, these seem to me to be the principal new concepts of the nature of philosophy current today *and* influential among Catholic thinkers. (Movements like logical positivism and empiricism have naturally been omitted as not tenable by those who wish to be consistently Christian in their philosophy.)

During the discussion from the floor the question arose why I made no mention of existentialism and of the problem of Christian philosophy. As regards the first, it has turned out to be more a spirit or attitude than a total unified theory either of reality or of what philosophy is. I intended to include the essential lines of it, insofar as they are assimilable by a Christian, under the headings of personalism and phenomenology, since most of the Christian personalists (at least the European-inspired versions of the twentieth century, if not always the older American personalism) are existentialist in approach and spirit; and all existentialists use the technique of phenomenological analysis as their principal tool. Gabriel Marcel is probably the existentialist who has most influenced Christian philosophers (rather than the atheistic Sartre or the agnostic Camus), and he is par excellence a personalist thinker. Heidegger is indeed influencing some of our American Catholic philosophers, but he objects to being called an existentialist and, at least in his later work, is more properly a metaphysician than a phenomenologist.

As regards the question of whether there is a properly Christian philosophy, or only a philosophy done by Christians, this is not a new problem but one that has divided Christian thinkers since before the turn of the century. I do not have sufficient information to be able to pinpoint with any precision just where the majority of the younger Catholic thinkers in this country now stand. But there is certainly a strong sympathy among many of them toward the view that Christian philosophy can and should by rights have a uniquely recognizable character of its own both in spirit and in content, since, following the clearly identifiable influence of professors like von Hildebrand and Pollock at Fordham, for example, they believe that the Christian experience itself should be part of the data of basic human experience that forms the starting point of the realistic philosopher.

Let me now sum up for convenience the various trends outlined above.

The first is philosophy as identical with the actual historical dialogue of the great philosophers, as it advances through history by the dialectical process of position, counter-position, attempted synthesis, new position, new counter-position, etc. It is the whole process that is significant and therefore must be the direct object of philosophical study and teaching. The more moderate holders of this view would certainly maintain that a growing body of objective truth emerges steadily from this process. But such truths are always subject to the limitations of their incomplete historical perspectives on reality. And since succeeding moments in the dialogue are constantly throwing new light on the preceding achievements, it is impossible to stop the process and select one chapter, no matter how rich and significant, especially if it is in the distant past, and use its problems, methods, perspectives, and language as an adequate norm for judging all other philosophical positions or as an adequate medium for philosophical instructions. The method of teaching dictated by this view will naturally be that of the great texts of philosophers in some historical order, rather than any one system, even so great a one as that of St. Thomas.

The second is the conviction that heavier stress must be laid on phenomenological description of the essential facets of human experience as contrasted with metaphysical explanation or reduction to causes.

The third is a shift of focus, either partial or total, away from the purely objective or spectator analysis of reality, especially personal reality, toward a more personalist and subjective angle of vision. This is usually closely allied with the phenomenological approach and methods of analysis.

The fourth is the interpretation of philosophy as consisting, at least to some notable extent, of linguistic analysis, i.e., analysis of philosophical terms and problems by studying the meaning and use of these in their original natural context of ordinary language, the successful symbolic "form of life" that gave them birth. Recently a quasi-metaphysical orientation of such analysis has been opening up, showing marked affinity with the practice of Aristotle and St. Thomas and promising considerable fruitfulness: namely, the thesis that any explanatory philosophical theory will be rejected on principle if it renders the basic structures of ordinary language discourse either false, unintelligible or meaningless, or inconsistent.

The fifth is the conception of philosophy as a free, personal, quasi-artistic creation of world-hypotheses, motivated to some notable extent by pre-philosophical existential attitudes towards life, and tested not so much by the norm of abstract truth or falsehood as by the breadth and richness of their illuminating power with respect to reality and especially their efficacy in helping the person to achieve the greatest possible intellectually luminous personal fulfillment in actual life.

Lastly, there is the conception of philosophy, and especially of its teaching, as primarily the awakening to a deep awareness of the problems involved in any human attempt to understand reality deeply and ultimately and the theoretical and practical implications of these problems and the various attempted solutions put forward for them. Thus philosophical teaching would focus primarily on the awakening of the student to problems and the habit of deep personal reflection rather than on the learning of any particular systematic solutions.

Among all of the above, the first three and the last seem to me to be at present the most widespread and influential among the rising generation of Catholic professors of philosophy.

Let me conclude with a respectful word of warning as regards trying to settle quickly and "efficiently," especially by decree from above, the fundamental debatable issues arising from the pluralism of concepts now spreading among us as to the nature of philosophy. It seems to me psychologically unrealistic and in the long run deleterious to ask young university-trained scholars simply to repudiate the kind and content of the graduate training they have received because it does not fit in with the tradition of the place in which they are assigned to teach. This can lead to intellectual frustration, psychological resentment, and other concomitant troubles. On the other hand, even necessary changes in a tradition must ordinarily be made organically and slowly from within and not abruptly or by violent rupture.

I foresee that we are entering a period, at least a transition period, where considerable pluralism of views about the nature and methods of philosophy should prudently be tolerated, and in fact will have to be tolerated, in order to allow full scope for authentic progress as well as to avoid greater evils. The problems resulting can be worked out only by constant responsible fraternal discussion by competently trained, truly Christian-minded professional philosophers. Such a period will be difficult indeed to navigate peacefully for all concerned, and at times will be painfully confusing and irritating to efficiency-minded administrators. But I see no help for it in our radically pluralistic contemporary world, which our own colleges and universities cannot but mirror to a considerable extent, and should in fact mirror, I think, within prudent limits. And I believe we should have enough confidence in our own younger generation of Catholic thinkers, lay as well as religious, to trust that more good than evil, more growth than destruction, will come out of this fluid period ahead.

Notes

1. "Tantum rebus obscurissimis lucem attulerunt, ut in eo solum noster sit positus labor, ut quae ab eis inventa sunt et exposita, ea nos summa cum voluptate intueamur." Francisci Remondi Divionensis, S.J., *Poemata et Orationes* (Antwerp, 1614), p. 158, quoted in J. Herman, S.J., *La pédagogie des Jésuites au XVIe siècle* (Louvain, 1914), p. 79, n. 3.
2. Pittsburgh: Duquesne University Press, 1958.
3. For a deep and penetrating analysis of this whole problem see Emil Fackenheim, *Metaphysics and Historicity* ("Aquinas Lecture"; Milwaukee: Marquette University Press, 1961).
4. For one of the best examples of a Catholic synthesis of the achievements of personalist phenomenology see W. Luijpen, *Existentialist Phenomenology* (Pittsburgh: Duquesne University Press, 1961).

5. For treatment by Christian philosophers see E. Mounier, *Personalism* (New York: Grove Press, 1952); R. Troisfontaines, S.J., *Existentialism and Christian Thought* (London: Dacre Press, 1950); J. de Finance, S.J., "Being and Subjectivity," *Cross Currents,* VI (1956), 163–78; R. Johann, S. J., "Subjectivity," *Revue of Metaphysics,* XII (1958), 200–234.

6. See R. Rorty's challenging confrontation of realist metaphysics and analysis, "Realism, Categories, and the Linguistic Turn," *International Philosophical Quarterly,* II (1962), 307–22; and M. Charlesworth, *Philosophy and Linguistic Analysis* (Pittsburgh: Duquesne University Press, 1958).

7. For a moderate statement of this view see W. Walsh, "True and False in Metaphysics," *Cross Currents,* XI (1961), 269–82.

Selected Bibliography

Ayer, A. J., *et al. The Revolution in Philosophy.* New York: St. Martin's Press, 1956.

Blackham, H. J. *Six Existentialist Thinkers.* New York: Harper Torchbook, 1959.

Charlesworth, Maxwell. *Philosophy and Linguistic Analysis.* Pittsburgh: Duquesne University Press, 1958.

Collins, James. *The Existentialists.* Chicago: Regnery, 1962.

Dondeyne, A. *Contemporary European Thought and Christian Faith.* Pittsburgh: Duquesne University Press, 1958.

Fackenheim, Emil. *Metaphysics and Historicity.* "Aquinas Lecture." Milwaukee: Marquette University Press, 1961.

Ferré, F. *Language, Logic and God.* New York: Harper, 1961.

de Finance, Joseph, S.J. "Being and Subjectivity," *Cross Currents,* VI (1956), 163–78.

Johann, Robert, S.J. "Subjectivity," *Review of Metaphysics,* XII (1958), 200–234.

Luijpen, Wilhelmus. *Existentialist Phenomenology.* Pittsburgh: Duquesne University Press, 1961.

Mounier, Emmanuel. *Personalism.* New York: Grove Press, 1952.

Nédoncelle, Maurice. *What Is Christian Philosophy?* New York: Hawthorn Books, 1960.

Troisfontaines, Roger, S.J. *Existentialism and Christian Thought.* London: Dacre Press, 1950.

9

PHILOSOPHY AS
AN ACADEMIC DISCIPLINE

James V. McGlynn, S.J.

The contribution which philosophy makes to the intellectual formation of the Catholic college student may be discussed in several ways. In this paper I propose to consider the problem first in terms of some general considerations common to all the ways philosophy is taught in Catholic schools and then in terms of the various approaches to philosophy discussed by Father Clarke in Chapter 8. Roughly, these will be the divisions of our paper.

Before we begin, however, it may be in place to remind ourselves that we are not talking (primarily, at least) about the students who are majoring in philosophy. Presumably, these students are taking philosophy because they are interested in it, because they consider philosophy as valuable liberal background for law, education, or business, or because they plan to do graduate work in philosophy itself and eventually teach it. These students are but a small minority and are not the main concern of this volume. Hence in what follows we will not be discussing the value of philosophy for these students, but rather for the non-majors, who form the great bulk of the enrollment in college philosophy classes.[1]

I. GENERAL CONSIDERATIONS

Our first question is the general question: What does philosophy (more or less prescinding from the particular approach adopted in any given school) do for the intellectual formation of our students?

A. *Training in Exact and Abstract Thinking*

I suppose that the first, though certainly not the most important, result of the teaching of philosophy in college is the training of our students in careful and exact thinking and their habituation to the use of an abstract terminology. Philosophy has traditionally been praised for this and, I think, justly so. It is one of the satisfactions of teaching beginners in philosophy which every conscientious teacher enjoys. He can hardly miss seeing these skills developing in his students. As the student is liberated from slavery to the imagination, the successful teacher cooperates in this gradual emancipation of his charges from thinking through pictures.

These results are facts. Philosophers may tend to exaggerate them and administrators may want to minimize them; but, in varying degrees and in different proportions of students, significant progress is made along these lines. The exact variation in quantity and quality of these effects may never be determined. It will probably continue to be the subject of debate between those who favor as much philosophy as possible in college and those who would like to eliminate the traditional Catholic college emphasis on philosophy and relegate it to the status of music and fine arts, giving it only token representation in the curriculum.

It might be well, before leaving this point, to mention two aspects of training in exact and abstract thinking which are pertinent to this discussion. The first is the question of transfer of training. I really do not know the answer to this. We are not talking about any specific, easily tested skills, but rather about an attitude similar to that induced by the study of mathematics—a certain openness to the abstract and a certain caution in using language. Although this is nothing spectacular, it is the type of thing generally considered an integral part of a liberal education. And most graduates acquire it in at least a rough sort of way.

The second aspect of training in exact and abstract thinking which should be mentioned is that this is not something peculiar to philosophy. Other subjects, especially mathematics and the sciences, are at least as important as philosophy in developing this type of thinking. In fact, if this were the sole value or the main value of a philosophy program, it might be argued with much justification that it could be achieved much more economically and practically in mathematics and science. Consequently, few backers of philosophy would want to say that this is the primary function of our teaching of philosophy. Nonetheless, even if it is not peculiar to philosophy, this training in exactitude and in the use of abstract concepts is an important product of the philosophy program. And the contribution of philosophy to it should not be minimized or denied.

B. *Contact with Great Minds of the Past*

A second function of the teaching of philosophy, and one which most of us would consider more important, is that of putting our students in contact with the ideas of some of the great thinkers of history. In one way or another, every philosophy teacher who takes history seriously accepts this function of the undergraduate curriculum. This is not to say, of course, that he is interested in history as history; rather, his interest is in the history of philosophy as philosophy. Consequently, it would be a mistake to think that to urge contact with the great minds of the past is to opt for a philosophical relativism. It is true nevertheless that some Catholic teachers of philosophy do consider St. Thomas as only one great mind among many and agree to teach systematic Thomism only from this viewpoint, presenting it as a masterful synthesis and one of the landmarks in the history of Western thought.

Perhaps a word of explanation (even at the risk of repeating part of Father Clarke's discussion) would be in order at this point. There is a whole spectrum of ways of teaching Thomism systematically and historically. Only the extremely rigorous Thomists want to teach the doctrine of St. Thomas in complete independence of its historical context. Thomism is taught by these people as a timeless synthesis which can be studied in itself without any serious investigation of its Greek or medieval historical roots.

As we move from this type of Thomism across the spectrum, there is a greater concern for history. Thus some quite strict Thomists will have their students read Plato and Aristotle and work out the relationship between their ideas and St. Thomas' theses. It must be admitted, however, that the greater emphasis is on the conceptual relationships between the positions of Thomas and Plato and Aristotle. Not much is done to put all of this into historical perspective.

A third position among those who would teach a systematic Thomism is favored by many who take their inspiration from Gilson and the Medieval Institute at Toronto. They are neo-Thomists who have worked out a Thomistic philosophy for the twentieth century. They are very careful to situate St. Thomas and his ideas in their historical context and understand his ideas in this concrete situation. Using the truth which St. Thomas said for his day, they work to discover the truth which must be said for ours.

A fourth position would be on the borderline between the systematic and the historical approaches. Teachers in this category would use St. Thomas mainly for extrinsic, non-philosophical reasons; for example, because his Christian outlook fits in with that of our students. They would emphasize, however, the historical significance rather than any doctrinal content.

Thus, practically all Catholic courses in philosophy do something to bring students in contact with the great minds of the past, although each thinker will do this in his own way. The historical school puts greatest emphasis on this function of philosophy. In fact, for them, this is almost the whole point of doing philosophy. The Catholic phenomenologists and analysts belong to schools which do not have a strong historical orientation, but generally they put more stress on the history of philosophy and on St. Thomas than their confreres do. By and large, the same holds for teachers in our schools who fit the remaining categories listed by Father Clarke.

Consequently, as a general rule, we can say that in one way or another, teachers of philosophy in our schools consider that one of the important functions of philosophy in Jesuit colleges and universities is to put our students in touch with some of the great minds of the past.

We might ask again whether this value might not be achieved more easily and efficiently in some other department. The history department, I suppose, would be the obvious choice for this task. But I personally do not think that any but the very exceptional historian is at all capable of handling the philosophical writings and ideas which we are talking about. The average historian simply does not have the philosophical competence to deal with the technical writings of St. Thomas, Plato or Aristotle. Hence, if our students are to achieve any significant dialogue with the great philosophers, the philosophy class is the natural place for this to happen. For the guide to meaningful contact with the great philosophers must himself be well trained in philosophy and its history.[2] The task he has to perform is no job for an amateur.

C. *Consideration of*
   Important Questions

A third function of our philosophy program is to make our students aware of the great philosophical questions of the ages, the perennial metaphysical and ethical questions that each of us has to answer for himself if he is to live the examined life. And, as Plato said, no other life is worth living. To inculcate the reflective spirit which asks about the meaning of life, we have to ask about the nature of reality, of man, and of our moral commitments. We have to know what ends are open to us as men, what our capacities are, how we can fulfill ourselves as human persons. These are the questions par excellence of philosophy. And today more than ever before, when distractions flood in on us, when our mechanical culture so surrounds us with man-made objects that we cannot see beyond them to being, and when the temptation to pour ourselves out on external, material things is stronger than ever in human history, today we must strive more mightily than our forebears to bring our students into contact with reality and face to face with the problem of the meaning of life. The great traditional problems of philosophy must be faced, and Christian philosophy has not turned away from them.

Practically everyone teaching in our schools would agree with what we have said about the role of philosophy in confronting our students with the great questions which every man must face. There would be much less agreement about the type of answer philosophy can give to these questions. The traditional Thomist will maintain that St. Thomas has worked out definitive answers which should be transmitted to our students in their philosophy courses. The historical school and the other schools will emphasize the questions more than the answers. Philosophy for them is a search which each generation must undertake anew and which does not lead to clear-cut, decisive answers.

It will be worthwhile to insist at this point that the type of important question we are referring to here is different from the important questions of the natural sciences. For within the structure of our philosophy there are very important personal convictions and insights for the student. Perhaps the most important of these is an appreciation of the evidence for a rational and intelligent conviction with regard to the existence of God. Our philosophy courses should produce this appreciation in a large number of our students. Similarly, our philosophy should teach our students that the modes of knowing in philosophy and science are quite distinct and that they should not demand that theological and philosophical evidence follow the rules for empirical knowledge.

An important factor in the philosophy teacher's attitude towards these basic questions is his conception of the relationship between philosophy and theology. The Catholic philosopher of whatever school who looks on theology as a sort of answer-key to the problems of philosophy will hardly take the questions of philosophy very seriously. Philosophy is not a vital occupation for these people, but only a sort of low-power substitute for the higher power of theology. Those who are interested in Christian philosophy have something in common with this view in so far as they refuse to separate philosophy and theology. However, instead of looking on theology as furnishing the answers to philosophical problems, they look to theology to give the context in which the Christian philosopher must do his philosophy. For, as they say, everyone must philosophize in some context, and each philosopher, consciously or unconsciously, chooses his context. The Christian chooses the theological context of Christianity, and this conditions his whole thinking. Naturally, the answer-giving role of philosophy will be de-emphasized by these thinkers. Other Catholic thinkers want to keep philosophy and theology completely distinct. For them an autonomous philosophy can give rationally satisfying answers to the basic philosophical questions. Theology goes beyond philosophy but does not enter into philosophy in the way the "Christian Philosophy" school maintains that it must.

But whatever relationship between philosophy and theology the various schools prefer, they all will hold that the great questions of traditional Western philosophy must be asked. Nor would they want to admit that any education which excluded consideration of them could honestly be called "liberal." There may be various reasons for studying these basic problems, but they should find their place in our philosophy curriculum.

D. *Integration of Other Knowledge*

A final important function of our college philosophy course is that of integrating the different types of knowledge and training which the student acquires. Perhaps the extreme left wings of the historical, analytical, and phenomenological schools would hesitate to endorse this sort of integration, since for them philosophy has a much more humble role. Practically everyone else, however, looks on philosophy as asking the most general questions and so, of necessity, integrating our knowledge by putting it into a total perspective. This general framework expresses our world view or philosophy of life, which no serious teacher of philosophy can afford to overlook. In fact, almost any philosophy instructor in our schools with any feeling for the traditional outlook would be most unhappy with a philosophy which abdicated its role of integration. For these thinkers the pure historian, the pure analyst, and the pure phenomenologist are not really philosophers at all. Hence, although there may be room for them in a professional graduate program, they have no place on our undergraduate faculties, especially in the required courses.

The integrating function of philosophy must not be considered apart from the role of theology. Philosophy does not give us the whole picture, and so cannot be the ultimately integrating discipline. Only theology can do this. But it must be a speculative theology, which uses philosophy as an essential instrument. Consequently, philosophy will have an important role to play in the total integration of learning.[3]

These are four general ways in which philosophy aids in the intellectual formation of our students. There are others, of course, but I think that these are the most important and the least controversial. Not all of the members of the workshop will agree with me. There can be various reasons for this disagreement. Some teachers have had traumatic experiences in their undergraduate philosophy courses. Others have a more pragmatic idea of education than we would accept. Still others will be somewhat cynical in their estimate of the educability of our students. But whatever the reason, a fair number of teachers are convinced that eighteen to twenty-four hours of philosophy in today's crowded curriculum is too much to give to something, the visible effects of which are negligible. Unfortunately, or fortunately, as the case may be, there are no tests to measure the real effectiveness of the teaching of philosophy to undergraduates. This is probably equally true of every required course in the humanities. Notoriously unreliable personal reflections can be gathered. But in these, I suppose, the nostalgic remembrances of old Professor X, who made metaphysics "live," can be balanced out by the bitter memories of logic chopping and complete evasion of all problems in the epistemology classes of Professor Y. It is extremely difficult to get an objective judgment of the actual impact of philosophy on our students. It is easy to be flattered by alumni who come back to say how much their philosophy has meant to them. One might question their judgment in the matter or one might suggest that they are too small and selective a sample to furnish any adequate evidence.

For my own part, I have talked to enough students before and after graduation to be quite pleased with the effect our philosophy courses have produced. I have seen young men and women become more reflective, develop into more mature and rational agents, and acquire a deeper sense of the meaning of life from their courses in philosophy. This success, even on the limited scale on which I have observed it, is enough to convince me of the value of our philosophy program. Perhaps the discussion which will take place in this workshop will give the best educated opinion which can be formed on this point.

II. SPECIFIC CONSIDERATIONS

It will be in order now to turn to the more specific problems of the different approaches to philosophy in use in our schools. We have already included a fair amount of this, so we can afford to be brief.

A. *Traditional Scholastic View*

Following Father Clarke, we will first consider the traditional scholastic view, which holds that philosophy is the *science* of ultimate causes and that, as such, it can give us at least a hard core of certain knowledge. The more traditional and conservative members of this group have the advantage of giving their students clear and definite answers. They are able to tell their students just how things are and how all the other disciplines fit into the picture under philosophy. They situate the natural sciences within the philosophy of nature and the social sciences within the philosophy of man and moral philosophy. When presented sensitively, this method awakens in the student a live awareness of the problems of philosophy as they affect the meaning of his own life. As a result, the student who learns to appreciate the solutions offered by traditional Thomism as answers to the important questions which he must learn to face can acquire a philosophical orientation which will transform him from a heedless adolescent, who takes life around him for granted, into a mature young adult, who is beginning to understand what his values are and why he holds them. This approach has the further advantage of giving the student a sense of security, for he is presented with a clear-cut world picture which reinforces his Christian outlook. The traditionalist may or may not think that philosophy is independent of theology, but in either case the philosophical and theological syntheses fit together very nicely. On a lower level, this approach emphasizes clear and exact definition and tries to avoid fuzzy thinking.

On the negative side, the traditionalist can become very unrealistic, presenting philosophy in an intellectual and historical vacuum. The cold formulae of St. Thomas may be transmitted with little penetration into their real meaning. Instead, the various branches of philosophy may be presented like abstract mathematical systems, having no obvious connection with the world we live in. Another way of putting this is to say that the students taught in this traditional way are given answers before they know what the questions are. This, of course, robs the answers of any real significance. Two other dangers of the traditional position come from the reaction of some students to its apparent rigidity. Science students especially, when they find it difficult to reconcile their scientific work with the Thomistic theses they have learned, are inclined to reject the whole system and end up with no philosophy at all. For other students the emphasis on Thomistic orthodoxy leads to a confusion between it and Catholic orthodoxy, so that if they find it impossible to agree with the Thomistic position, they feel that they are bound to reject the Faith as well.[4] This may sound surprising, but I have been told of students who have been greatly relieved to find that they could disagree with St. Thomas without endangering their status as members of the Catholic Church.

B. *Historical School*

The approach which emphasizes the history of philosophy has different advantages. In general it tends to situate philosophical knowledge within the total range of human culture and experience. In general the student will get a better idea of the questions to be answered and will be shown how these questions arose. Consequently, having seen how thinkers in the past have been led to ask philosophical questions, these students will find it somewhat easier to relate philosophy to their own experience. A further advantage of the historical approach should be a deepening of the sense of history in our students.[5]

The main drawback of the historical approach is that it tends to substitute history for philosophy. As a result the students can come out of the philosophy courses with little or no grasp of any outlook on life, Thomistic or other. This is certainly not what philosophy was meant to be when it was prescribed for Catholic schools. Another weakness of the historical approach on the undergraduate level is that it may merely confuse the students. Exposed to half a dozen theories of metaphysics, they may conclude that philosophy has nothing to offer them and that they have no need of it. Thus, instead of becoming aware of the need for an explicit philosophy, these students may be thrown back on an unexamined, implicit philosophy, which is subject to all the pressures of society.[6]

C. *Other Approaches*

The other approaches are less common and so can be treated even more briefly. The strength of phenomenology is that it helps keep us in touch with experience and forces us to make sure that we are not building foundationless logical constructions. Negatively, as long as it remains purely phenomenological, it can never reach a metaphysics. Perhaps its real value is as an antidote to the rationalistic abstraction of latter-day scholasticism. Personalism and subjectivity are valuable in so far as they force us to root our philosophy in our personal experience instead of in an over-objective world. This personal dimension had been lacking in most of the neo-Thomistic literature, but has begun to appear in the last decade. On the debit side, personalism and subjectivity by themselves lead to a philosophical relativism without objective roots since they lack a general metaphysics. Linguistic analysis can be valuable in alerting us to the study of language and its importance in all philosophical discussion. But it can also be stultifying by burying real philosophical problems in a trite discussion of words. It is especially dangerous because of its unconscious commitment to an exaggerated empiricism. It has never completely emancipated itself from the verification principle of the logical positivists. Philosophy as free commitment and fruitful hypothesis has something to offer inasmuch as it emphasizes an aspect of philosophy which scholastics tend to overlook, namely the free choice which every philosopher makes when he decides on the rules which he will follow. The scholastic tends to be more rationalistic. Free commitment and fruitful hypothesis, however, have no safeguard against relativism, and this is their great weakness. Likewise, philosophy as awakening to problems and personal reflection will emphasize the personal activity of the student more than the ordinary scholastic approaches and so has some value. But again it can easily lead to confusion and disillusion, as well as to a radical relativism.

The burden of this paper has been that philosophy for our undergraduates should give them a training in exactness and abstract thinking and that it should give them a Christian world outlook. The several ways in which philosophy is taught in the Catholic schools of the United States seek this double goal in different ways and with different emphases. It would seem that no one way of approaching philosophy has a corner on the best ways of training our students. It might well be that each department (if not each instructor) should be allowed to use its own approach, tempered by some use of other approaches. Possibly our best teachers combine elements of all the approaches without formally identifying them as such, or even without being able to identify them. In any event, the intellectual formation of the Catholic college student which philosophy can give is not some easily identifiable skill. It is, rather, a combination of several things which the different approaches to philosophy produce in varying combinations and in different degrees. There is probably no best way to inculcate these values, but some sort of combined approach is better than any of the seven ways by itself.

Notes

1. I am not sure that all philosophy teachers will agree with this limitation. Some may think that it is like fighting with one arm tied behind one's back. I feel, however, that this is the only realistic way to discuss required courses, especially since the very fact that they are required is one of the elements which condition the students' response to them.

2. It is interesting to note how many of the reports submitted by our philosophy departments for this workshop indicated that solid preparation in the history of philosophy (especially at the doctoral level) should be a normal part of the training of members of our philosophy departments.

3. Since a successful speculative theological synthesis is impossible without a valid philosophy built into it, the theologian needs to be expert in philosophy. Many Catholic philosophers are unhappy about the frequently skimpy philosophical background of our theologians. As a result of this lack of philosophy on the part of theologians, philosophy tends to usurp the integrating role of theology. This situation is aggravated by the practice in our schools of teaching "theology" to students who have had little or no philosophy and so lack the proper instruments to handle

speculative theology. It is also aggravated by the pastoral orientation of so many "theology" courses.

4. Let us say here once and for all—both the actual advantages and disadvantages will vary from teacher to teacher. We are speaking of tendencies in the various approaches. To what extent these are actualized will depend on the instructor and the spirit of the department. A full discussion of this personal equation would require a separate paper.

5. One of the most glaring weaknesses I find in our undergraduates is an almost complete lack of a sense of history. They seem to feel no need to understand events or ages of history in terms of their antecedents. One might almost think that they were *Animae Naturaliter Cartesianae*, interested only in timeless, clear and distinct ideas.

6. A combination of the traditional and the historical may perhaps be the best approach for undergraduates. It gives a systematic philosophy backed up by history, and so it avoids the exaggerations of both approaches in their pure forms.

Selected Bibliography

Collins, James. "For Self-Examination of Neoscholasticism," *The Modern Schoolman*, XXI (1944), 225–34.

―――. "Toward a Philosophically Ordered Thomism," *New Scholasticism*, XXXII (1958), 301–26.

Conway, James, S.J. "Reflections on the Function of the History of Philosophy," *New Scholasticism*, XXI (1947), 419–37.

Gilson, Etienne. *Christianity and Philosophy*. New York and London: Sheed & Ward, 1939.

Henle, Robert J., S.J. "An Essay in Educational Theory," *The Modern Schoolman*, XXV (1948), 107–25.

―――. "Philosophy of Education," *The Modern Schoolman*, XXVI (1949), 148–58.

Maritain, Jacques. *An Essay on Christian Philosophy*. New York: Sheed & Ward, 1955.

Maziarz, Edward A., C.PP.S. "A Plan for Integrating the Catholic College Curriculum," *New Scholasticism*, XVIII (1944), 376–84.

McCormick, John, S.J. "The Student and Philosophy," *The Modern Schoolman*, XVII (1940), 51–53.

O'Brien, John J., S.J. "On the Pursuit of Catholic Wisdom," *The Modern Schoolman*, XVIII (1941), 24–27.

Pegis, Anton (ed.). *A Gilson Reader*. New York: Doubleday, 1957.

Phelan, Gerald B., "St. Thomas and the Modern Mind," *The Modern Schoolman*, XX (1942), 37–47.

10

THE TEACHING OF PHILOSOPHY
Carl J. Burlage, S.J.

Before inviting the reader's consideration of the following presentation, I wish to note two things that characterize it. First, it is very long. Secondly, it states and discusses many propositions that may seem obvious and elementary to professional philosophers.

It seems to me that many treatments of the present problem have failed to achieve agreement or even mutual understanding simply because certain basic positions and commitments were not made sufficiently clear—sometimes not even to those who held and had made them. The situation thus arising is analogous to one which most contemporary teachers of philosophy have frequently encountered and criticized: the "confrontation" of terminal propositions derived from different intellectual "systems" with the assumption that, since there appears a verbal and logical contradiction between them, one of them must (on the principle of the excluded middle) be true; the other false. It is evident that this "adversary" mode of treatment is seldom either fair or fruitful, for the obvious reason that it assumes a fundamental univocity in the terms employed in the contradictory propositions which is hardly ever realized in fact.

It is my hope, therefore, to avoid the trap of merely adding one more to an already superabundant accumulation of sterile and contentious discussions of the problem of reason and faith. To do so, I have gone back as far as I could and made as clear as possible what seem to me the fundamental terms in which the discussion should be conducted, advancing from these fundamental terms to the statement of a developed position.

Before proceeding to any discussion of the "essential" relationship between philosophy and theology, let us first try to make clear certain matters of fact. All Catholic undergraduate colleges in the United States offer extensive and detailed programs in philosophy and theology. Furthermore, these programs have a special and notable characteristic not found with respect to the offerings of any other department. This elaborate and long series of courses is required for *all* students.[1] Evidently, the decision to require such a series of courses is not taken lightly, nor can it be explained as a mere traditional survival: *"quod semper, quod ubique, quod ab omnibus."*[2] Why has it been taken?

Only one answer is possible. Catholic colleges are convinced that these elaborate programs are necessary to the fulfillment of their proper and essential goals.[3] To these goals we must, therefore, devote some brief attention.

Here it may be useful to make certain distinctions and specifications. First of all, it may be noted that the ultimate finality of the Catholic college, like that of any social institution, is a social and not an individual one. As such, the total specification of the activity of the college is to be found in the attainment of the *common good,* not of any mere sum of individual goods. This is the reason why the personal charm, admirable motives or even outstanding sanctity of any individual person are quite irrelevant as motives for admitting, retaining, or graduating any student, or for employing or retaining in employment any teacher, when any of these decisions would inhibit the social good which the college exists to obtain. But there are some activities within the college which its social purpose determines only *mediately.* This is eminently true of undergraduate instruction.

Let us explain. The purpose of the teacher in an undergraduate class is certainly determined by the over-all finality of the institution as a whole. He is not there merely because he likes to be, nor is he there simply to do what he likes to do. Nor is it the precisely individual and personal needs of the student (even the undergraduate) which justify and account for the existence of undergraduate education.[4] Both of these are subordinate to the ultimate goals for which society, secular and religious, establishes and supports the college as a social institution. But: the structure and relationships established for undergraduate instruction operate precisely on the assumption that the best way to attain the common good is by seeking to achieve the most perfect development of each individual student in the college. The function of the teacher is to do his practical best to transmit to each developing human person in his class (within the limits proper to his department) the intellectual heritage of the past—to develop in each student according to his capacity the academic knowledge and skills appropriate to his future adult life—to produce in him that degree of personal development, that enlightened maturity, which will equip him to assume his proper share of the social responsibilities appropriate to the position he will assume in religious and secular society.[5]

Granted, then, that the activity of the teacher is specified by the personal capacities and needs of the individual students he meets in his classes, it becomes necessary to see what those capacities and needs are.

Here we may at once dismiss as not germane to the present discussion certain specific orders or classes of student need. Thus we need not concern ourselves here with those aspects of undergraduate education which are met, not by the special activity of the teacher of philosophy or theology, but by the college program as a whole. Here we have in mind such things as providing the social climate for academic growth and personality development, or offering to the student a sufficiently broad acquaintance with the variety of human activities to found or confirm a proper vocational choice. Nor need we be bothered in this present context with what may be called the narrower needs of particular groups of students. Thus, one of the things that any undergraduate department does is to equip the student with the basic knowledge and skills necessary for further study and achievement in its particular field. Student needs of this special order are not the issue here.

This last statement deserves some further elucidation, precisely because it seems to have been overlooked in many previous discussions of our problem. In general, it might be said of most departments in a college that they exist primarily for the benefit of those students who take the particular field of that department as their academic major and who may therefore be supposed to be planning further study or research in that field. A department of engineering, for example, is concerned with and directs its teaching activities toward those who are going to become engineers. A department of medical biology is concerned with providing the basic scientific knowledge and skills appropriate to those students who will ultimately pursue their studies for a medical degree. But for the undergraduate departments of philosophy and theology in a Catholic college, the situation is different. The department of theology does not exist primarily to prepare students for graduate work in that discipline; the undergraduate department of philosophy does not find its reason of being in discovering potential scholars in the field of philosophy and providing them with the background of knowledge and academic skills appropriate to the future Ph.D. in philosophy.[6] The primary purpose of these departments is to meet certain personal needs *common to all the students for whom the undergraduate program of the college is designed.*[7]

Here, then, we may come to a more precise statement of the question which must be answered if we are profitably to discuss the teaching of philosophy and theology in the Catholic undergraduate college. *What are the needs, common to all students, which the required program of philosophy and theology courses prescribed by the college is expected to meet?*

Our search here is for the essential and central, not the accidental and peripheral. We may, therefore, dismiss from present consideration certain alleged benefits which may or may not actually result from the teaching of philosophy and theology to undergraduates, but which certainly do not represent the fundamental reason why these disciplines constitute so extensive and prominent a part of the curriculum of the Catholic college. For instance, that "training of the mind" which is the last refuge of the defenders of obsolete curricula is not the basic reason why students are required to study philosophy, though it may be one of the results of that study. Nor is it to enable the student to make converts to Catholicism, or to equip him with a ready-made *"apologia pro fide sua,"* or to promote his growth in personal sanctity and the life of grace—although, again, some of these effects may in fact be achieved. It is our position that the basic, essential and universal need which accounts for the existence of departments of instruction in philosophy and theology is the need every educated and intellectually self-aware human person has: *to be able to make certain basic, absolute and genuinely intellectual commitments about the ultimate truth of things: specifically about his own nature as a human person, about the goals and values which must ultimately determine his life and his attitudes toward it, about the nature of the world and the social order, and especially about the God who is (or is not) the one source who gives meaning and intelligibility and purpose to all of reality.*

We are here at a central thesis which must be accepted or rejected if any further discussion is to be profitable. It is because the Catholic college does accept it that the teaching of philosophy and theology to the undergraduate in such a college is and must be different from the teaching of these disciplines in institutions which either deny the possibility of such commitments by the educated man, or who at least deny to the college any responsibility for encouraging *and specifying* such commitments. Because, on the contrary, philosophy and theology represent for the Catholic college indispensable means to the making of such commitments, they can never be regarded there (as they often are elsewhere) as just two among the many interesting sorts of human activity worth a "gentleman's interest" on the part of anyone with a pretense to culture, offering further rewards of personal satisfaction and scholarly opportunity for the student who chooses to "specialize" in them, and manifesting some kind of marginal (and perhaps diminishing) "social utility."

At this point we beg leave to make two flat statements whose justification will, we hope, emerge later. First, *the interest of students in the Catholic college in the courses in philosophy and theology is this personal interest* resulting from their very real (if not always articulate) conviction that the making of the kind of commitments we have been talking about is the most important thing in their lives—is the most important thing in the world! Second, *the interest of these students is primarily (and properly) a theological interest.*

For evidence as to the first point, we can only call upon the experience and the testimony of the teachers of philosophy in Catholic colleges. Setting aside the (really very limited) number of "barbarians" present in any college—those whose only interest, or whose only admitted interest, anyway, is the financial and social benefits dependent on the attainment of a college degree, what teacher of philosophy or theology has not experienced an evident correlation between student interest and the personal relevance for time and eternity of a philosophical discussion? Students may yawn or nod their way through a class devoted to Aristotelian hylemorphism—but show the relevance of a decision about the substantial unity of the human person to moral commitments and watch them wake up! Even more simply—in the treatment of any philosophical question, raise the question of the relation between that question and what we can know or say about God—and observe the quickening of response. It is perhaps a matter for sobering reflection that we should have to remind ourselves that students in our Catholic colleges are *interested* in God!

If the reality of student involvement with the problems of philosophy and theology as primary and personal be admitted, we may proceed to two further observations. First of all, this reality must prevent us once and for all from trying to substitute for a genuine (if sometimes elementary) intellectual consideration of the problems of these two disciplines some mere sterile and artificial conceptual scheme conceived of as containing within itself in some absolute and in-every-way unchanging and unchangeable form all truth about God and the world. Concretely, we cannot satisfy the student's genuine intellectual hunger for the truth by offering him a kind of papier-mâché substitute in the form of a set of propositions to be committed to memory. Perhaps the propositions *are* true—but this is of no use, and we do not fulfill our function as teachers of philosophy until we have at least begun to introduce our students to an appreciation of the evidence which grounds the truth.

Here again, a comparison with the almost specifically different purpose of the introduction to scholarship which defines the work of the graduate department may prove helpful. The formal and proper purpose of the graduate school is not, as we understand it, to produce philosophers; on the contrary, its whole intention is *to produce scholars in the field of philosophy*—a quite different kind of thing. In other words, graduate work in philosophy is designed to provide the student with techniques and practice in research, and with a familiarity with the de facto accomplishments of those whom the verdict of history denominates "philosophers." Quite different is the purpose of the undergraduate department of philosophy in the Catholic college, which is not primarily concerned with the technique of research, nor with seeing that the student *remembers* what the significant positions of John Locke are as compared, say, with those of Descartes. If it urges the one or requires the other, it properly does so only in terms of the contributions thus made to the understanding of ultimate problems— the comprehension, limited but real, of basic truth. The undergraduate program does seek, within the admitted limits of the practicable, *to make students philosophers*.

On the other hand, the reality of student interest in the problems of philosophy and theology raises another question. Why is it there? We are all familiar with the familiar dictum of the Philosopher (re-affirmed, incidentally, by St. Thomas) that the study of philosophy, and specifically of metaphysics, is reserved for the fully mature (not to say aged) human person. Yet we propose this study to men and women in their late teens and early twenties and find them responding to our proposal. Why can we do this?

To this there can, we submit, be only one answer. It is this: It is the religious faith of our students which (a) predisposes them to an interest in the problems of philosophy, and even specifies the problems in which they will primarily be interested, and (b) provides that "rectification of appetite" only otherwise to be expected from long and disillusioning experience and the waning of bodily powers, thus liberating the mind from preoccupation with the "here and now" and making possible that consideration *sub specie aeternitatis* which belongs to the philosopher. If this be true, it is manifestly idle to speak of an undergraduate course in philosophy completely self-constituted in a splendid isolation from and irrelevance to faith and theology. The connection is there, in the minds and attitudes of our students, and no attempt to define it out of existence will really destroy it. Our problem is not to be solved by denying the real relationship every Catholic student finds between (for instance) natural theology and revealed theology. It can be solved only by achieving some understanding of that real relationship and its consequences for the teaching of philosophy in the undergraduate college.

Here we are confronted by a specific and precise instance of a more general and universal problem encountered over and over again in the history of Christian thought: the problem of relating faith and reason.

The history of this problem is a long one, manifesting many subtleties of doctrine between more or less frank rationalisms maintaining some kind of simply absolute independence of reason from the influence of revelation and faith to perhaps more frank anti-rationalisms which simply deny the genuine utility of natural reason altogether, or at least so diminish that utility as to reduce philosophy to a state of at least practical insignificance. It is not our purpose here to review that history in any specific detail. At the same time, it seems to us that many discussions of the problem have failed to be profitable because they have considered it in abstraction from the lessons and insights which the history of Christian (or, perhaps even better, Catholic) thought can make available. To approach the problem solely in terms of definitions constructed *a priori* of what philosophy (in the abstract) and theology (in the abstract) ought to be, is at least to run the risk of prejudicing the solution of the problem. At worst, it may result in failure to appreciate the real nature of the problem altogether.

The reason why this is so is that neither of these intellectual disciplines, expressing the reflective, self-conscious achievement of rational understanding, exists in the abstract. They exist only as the actual or habitual[8] achievement of human intellects engaged with the problems posed for such intellects by the data of supernatural faith or natural experience.

This consideration is so important, in our view, that we will risk trying the patience of the reader by amplifying it. It is misleadingly easy to separate the "sciences" of philosophy and theology if we restrict ourselves to essential and abstract considerations only. After all, they begin with different bodies of data, one supernaturally revealed and guaranteed, the other attainable by the exercise of purely natural powers; their criteria of certitude are different, relying in the one instance heavily on authority, in the other renouncing all appeals except to the universally available natural evidences of things. And are not other reflectively developed rational disciplines evidently attained and maintained in a state of complete independence and isolation from the statements of faith and the developments of theology? Why not philosophy?

Briefly, because philosophy deals with problems different in their nature from those of other rational disciplines. Mathematics, biology, physics (with reservations with respect to all of them, insofar as they tend, especially today, to approach considerations about the nature of truth, the ultimate meaning of "life" as a physical phenomenon, and questions cosmological and metaphysical in their implications) do not deal with central issues about God, man, the world—the meaning and value of existence. Philosophy does.

Whenever, then, an existing human person comes to grips with the problems of philosophy, he cannot, if he accepts as certain the statements of supernatural revelation in these areas, *really* abstract or isolate his considerations, investigations and conclusions from these certitudes. In this sense, we find ourselves forced to agree with M. Gilson that if we admit that only a rational discipline developed in total independence from the certitudes of faith and theology can be termed "philosophy," then "the famous statement of O. Hamelin that Descartes comes immediately after the Greeks as though there had been nothing else between [is fully justified]."[9]

How could it be otherwise? It is evident that whatever variant attitudes Christians have taken in the past both toward the activity of "philosophizing" and toward the historical achievements of past philosophers, they must (so long as they *are* Christian) remain undisturbed in a genuine agreement about a thesis universally held: *the revelation of truth by God through Jesus Christ is absolute, unique, transcendent and primary; commitment to this truth by an act and habit of supernatural and meritorious faith is the single most important demand on every human person: the "one thing necessary" to the achievement of integral (and in this sense* authentic) *and genuine human goodness.*[10]

In the concrete human person, turning his attention to the "central problems" we mentioned above, it is not really possible to make a complete and total precision from the truths thus known by supernatural faith. From the beginning, he must be aware of the implications of one for the other. And if he is, the philosophizing he does will necessarily reflect his awareness of these implications.[11] The problem is to understand, not deny, this fact of existence: to see how it is that this state of things can exist, and there can yet be the attainment of true and genuine philosophy.

Stating the question this way, we should expect to find *a priori* the conditions actually revealed by history. Inevitably—not in the first ages of Christianity only, but in every time—there will be Christians so impressed by the transcendent character and importance of revealed truth as to make them minimize, neglect or even deny the validity and importance of natural modes of rational access to truth. Furthermore, within the body of revealed truths, they find one—the doctrine of the Fall—which readily lends itself to an interpretation extending its effects from the loss of means necessary to the attainment of man's integral supernatural good to the loss (when nature comes to be thought of as an "in itself") of even natural powers.

Interestingly enough, this attitude tends to characterize those Christians who find themselves in either of two sets of historical circumstance: those who have become familiar with Christian truth, or, at least, who have made a full commitment to it, only *after* they have become familiar with the achievements and limitations of a pagan and purely rational philosophy on the one hand; those impressed with the destructive potentialities (or actualities) of some philosophy or philosophical method applied to matters relevant to faith (even though developed by Christians) on the other.[12]

In striking contrast—and as a continuing challenge—to the attitude of Christians who minimize or deny the importance of the exercise of the natural powers of reason with respect to the ultimate and "central" problems of human experience is the long history of what we may call Christian Intellectualism. At least in the Western Catholic Church, the pursuit of the natural evidences of things by rational methods has always been a characteristic, even dominant, feature, of Christian activity. Nor has this been (as is sometimes suggested) something reluctantly tolerated by ecclesiastical authority, merely; from at least the foundation of the medieval universities, it has been something consistently encouraged as good, indeed necessary, in itself.[13] There is, surely, no more illustrious and evident example of this than that of St. Thomas Aquinas. Granting that there is evidence of an evolution in Thomas's attitude toward the *ease* and simplicity with which the achievements of historically attained, purely natural evidences can be assimilated to the truth known from divine revelation,[14] nothing is plainer, nothing more fundamental throughout his work, than the calm certainty and confidence that the proper application of rational methods to the data of experience produces genuine truth, and that this truth can, should and must contribute both to the *speculative* appreciation of the truths of faith, and, *per consequentiam,* to the *practical* attainment of the life of faith in the Christian toward which man is, in this life, ultimately ordered.

Far from seeing the normal condition of the intellectual Christian as one of tension between the certitudes of faith and the rational evidences of nature, he views the attainment of truth by philosophy as naturally and normally contributing to, even something demanded by, the existence of faith.[15]

This situation has sometimes been explained by pointing to Thomas Aquinas as the man who uniquely appreciated the self-constituting and independent nature of philosophy—the man who (if not first) at least most clearly appreciated the necessity of submitting philosophical positions and statements to the test of natural and rational evidence alone, and thus emancipated it from its "Augustinian" dependence on a precedent commitment to truth through a supernatural act of faith. In other words, St. Thomas is the type not only of the Christian Intellectual, but also of the Christian Rationalist. Now there is, in our opinion, a sense in which all these conventional, even platitudinous declarations about St. Thomas are true. Yet we do not think that this truth is properly understood by those who would attribute to him the position that philosophical investigation is and should be in every way and absolutely dissociated from the truths of faith and the demands of theology, nor even by those who assert merely that accidental and fortuitous relationship commonly maintained by those who describe faith as *only* a "negative norm" for the work of the philosopher.[16]

Since we have located this discussion in the context of history, it may be appropriate at least to suggest some attention to the historical results attending the efforts of those who have (in practice and not just in abstract theory) actually tried to be (separately) "Christians" *and* "Rationalists." Here the name of Siger immediately presents itself, along with such more recent examples as that of Descartes. It is impossible here to pursue in detail the many condemnations issuing from the *magisterium* of the Church with regard to such "Rationalisms" and the truths of faith. But we would ask (and here we are genuinely seeking information): Where *is* there, in all the history of thought, the example of a philosophy developed in total independence of revealed truth, whose world-view *is* in fact consistent with the truths of faith, let alone revealing in regard to their meaning?

What *is* the basic position of St. Thomas on this problem? The position which enables him (obviously in his own estimation, as well as in that of not a few subsequent scholars) to achieve a rational insight into the natural evidences of the real at once in harmony with faith and productive of further understanding of the truths of faith?[17] In our opinion it is this: he simultaneously rejects the *essential* dependence of the valid operation of natural reason on faith implicit (in many Augustinians, if not in St. Augustine himself) in the familiar "*Credo ut intelligam*," and the assertion of the *existential* total independence of philosophy from faith, which is the charter of every Rationalism, Christian or otherwise. Not in abstract theory then—in its Platonic essence, so to speak—is the insight into natural evidence dependent upon revelation. To say that it is, is simply to destroy philosophy. But, in the concrete order of existence—in the brute temporal reality of the actual engagement of real human intellects with the problems of nature—it is only contact with divine revelation, only the enlightening and liberating effects of the Christian redemption, which permit the thoroughly valid exercise of human reason with the "central problems" of even natural experience.

This is not a textual investigation. But we should like to offer at least some brief evidence for our position here. Note the words of Thomas immediately following the previously quoted assertion of the in-every-way necessary precedence of supernatural revelation to man's attainment of the supernatural good: "Even as regards those truths about God which human reason can investigate, it was necessary that man be taught by a divine revelation. For the truth about God, such as reason can know it, would only be known by a few, and that after a long time, and with the admixture of many errors."[18] In other words, to get man into the "situation" where he can expeditiously, as a general thing, *and* without "admixture of error" pursue *concretely* the rational evidences of things, the influence of revelation is needed.

Still further enlightenment may result if we see St. Thomas (in our view) actually manifesting the effects of "the situation of faith." More than one student has been perplexed by the doctrine of St. Thomas in *Pars Prima, q.* 2, *a.* 2, *ad* 2*m*. Here, after having established in the preceding article that man cannot get himself (by whatever dialectical exercise) into a situation where the proposition "God exists" becomes self-evident *to him,* he affirms that the truth of this proposition can be made *mediately* evident. How? By means of God's effects, St. Thomas says, and then hastens to add that in a demonstration of this sort ("especially in regard to God") it is necessary to accept as a middle term the meaning of the name, and not its essence, "for the question of its essence follows on the question of its existence." We do not feel that we are misrepresenting the position here, if we say that, for St. Thomas, the *effectiveness* of our insight into the implications of the existence of things is dependent upon the *meaning* we can in fact give beforehand to the term "God," *antecedently* to the philosophical insight into the natural evidences for His existence, and antecedently to the verification of the "notes" attachable to that meaning by the natural investigation of what a cause of existence *must be.* What, in concrete reality, provides this "meaning"—for St. Thomas's students as for our own—except Christian revelation?

We repeat: our position here, whether or not it is St. Thomas's own, is that the adequate penetration of the natural evidence of things—the real achievement of this evidence in an existing human intellect—*practically:* in the order of men *as they are*—requires at least the favorable social, and preferably even the personal, situation *concretely* provided by revelation. We would go still further: the reality of Christian faith in a human person is the most powerful and effective stimulus to the attainment of a true and genuine philosophy.

We do not mean here merely the attainment of an "indifferent" or "neutral" philosophy: one of which it may be said "It does not contradict faith." Still less do we mean that the Christian will want (or at least be satisfied with) an "apologetic" philosophy which refutes anti-Christian assumptions and makes mak-

ing an "act of faith" reasonable, nor those "theologized" rational
schemes which search the statements of historical philosophers
for those that can be "interpreted" in a Christian sense, or certain of whose "positions" offer facile rationalizations of the mysteries or paradoxes of faith.[19] We mean the most thoroughly ex-
ploited rational investigation into the evidences of things, and
nothing less. . . .

Suppose someone came to you, having in his hand a little book,
and said, "In this volume are contained all the most important
things in the world. Master its contents, and there is nothing in all
the world worth having that you will not have; follow its precepts, and there is no good you cannot achieve, no height of perfection open to man which you cannot scale," *and you believed
him*. Gratefully accepting his gift, you rush home to your study,
dispose yourself to receive the message of salvation, and open the
book to its first page. Lo! the book is written in Urdu—and of
Urdu-knowledge you have not a trace.

Remember—you believed the man. Obviously, if this is so, you
are going to devote yourself to the study of the Urdu language; in
no other way are you going to be able to decipher the message of
the book. But the point of the parable is this: who is going to be
more concerned with really *mastering* the language? You, for
whom good and evil, and the fate of the whole universe, are dependent on knowing *what the book really says,* or the man for
whom the study of Urdu represents only the least undesirable way
of passing the time, or a respectable profession, or even *that human activity most desirable in and for itself?* We submit that there
can be only one answer: for you there cannot be a subtlety of
phrase, not a point of punctuation, whose significance you will not
feel compelled to search out. Does not the true good of all things
depend on your understanding? No other man can feel such interest. Even the man who loves Urdu for itself: to him these
things make a difference—but not that much difference!

Our parable, we suggest, validly represents the situation of the
Christian intellectual. Revelation communicates to us the *certitude* of its propositions, but not (if it is, as it is in the Christian

instance, clothed in words and propositions derived from our experience of the world of nature) the fullness of its meaning. The greater our certitude; the greater our conviction of the primary importance of making our own the truth revealed: the more necessary, the more imperative our understanding *what these truths mean.* To know with the certitude of faith that the proposition, "There are three distinct persons in one divine nature," is true is one thing; to understand what "person" and "nature" *mean* is another.

It will be obvious that what we are here describing is precisely the genesis of theology. From the first moment that the Apostles "did not take His meaning" to the moment when Anselm provided his magnificent formulation—*Fides quaerens intellectum*—to the last moment when an act and habit of faith shall exist in a rational creature, this demand must make itself felt in the degree appropriate to the history, experience, and genius of every Christian. *But the demand for the understanding of faith is a demand for the understanding of nature:* only so does the "unknown language" of the statements whose certitude and whose importance the Christian accepts by faith, yield up to him its transcendent message. It is the need for theology which (in the believing Christian) postulates and imposes the need for philosophy—and precisely for a philosophy adequate, genuine, and thorough in terms of its own demands and its own evidences.[20]

It is perhaps unnecessary to note, with the late Senator Sumner, that "an immense space has been traversed." But we have, to quote another source, "come out through that same door wherein we went." Our conclusion is that for the *teacher* of philosophy in an *undergraduate* class which is a *part of the sequence prescribed for all students* in a *Catholic* college, the ultimate finality is to awaken in his students that *genuine insight into the naturally available evidences* of the truth of things *accessible by properly rational methods* which meets the personal needs of the student for *an increased and increasing appreciation of the meaning and significance* of the truths of divine revelation which are his by reason of his Catholic and Christian faith. We do not concede that this finality destroys the independence of the philosopher; on the contrary, we have labored to show how, in our view, it authentically establishes and maintains it, and that—in contrast to certain positions on the problem which we have ourselves criticized as inadequate—recognition of this finality communicates to the search for the rational evidences of things not only a special dignity and value, but an existential excellence, *even in its own order,* which it cannot otherwise attain.

A brief final word may be permitted here on two problems not themselves central to our discussion, but necessarily intimately connected with it. The first is the question of the general method to be employed in exploiting the theologically derived need for philosophy which we have attributed to our students. It seems to us obvious that the principal means will be the use of historically recorded instances of response to that need: for us personally, it goes without saying, pre-eminently the response of St. Thomas Aquinas. Must we say that we do not mean the dead text of Thomas, treated as closed repository of answers to all questions? We hope not. What we do mean is encouraging the student to share in that intellectual adventure which is the always-living, always-being-re-created engagement of the Christian intellect with the problems of experience; not, however, leaving the student without any guide, but bringing to his assistance the help and enlightenment of the man who, if he was not the pioneer, is still the uniquely great achiever of the objectives of Christian philosophy.

It may be—it has been—objected that to do this is to cut off the student from "communication" with his (and our) contemporaries. To this a variety of answers might well be given—among them the fact that "communication with his contemporaries" is not the primary objective of the teaching of undergraduate philosophy. We would, however, be the first to urge reservations to this answer. First of all, the search for the "meaningfulness of faith" which we have described as the ultimate finality of the activity here in question is not a timeless absolute, but one which is necessarily always, for each man and each generation, "contemporary." Secondly, the Christian student is not an isolated individual seeking a merely personal perfection, but a "man with a message" who needs to communicate with his contemporaries— not least because such communication is the most fruitful source for appreciating the needs for further insights into the meaning of faith which in turn demand further rational insights into the natural evidences of things.

Our own position we might sum up under two heads with respect to the assertion that "emphasis on traditional theological-philosophical statements frustrates communication with our contemporaries." The first we might put simply thus: to "communicate" you must first have something to communicate. This "something" is precisely a genuine and fruitful insight into the truth of things, however limited in perfection, which it *is* the primary business of undergraduate philosophy to produce. To throw the student head-over-heels into a nebulous mass of pseudo-scientific-pseudo-philosophical-pseudo-religious "dialogue" is to do no service either to the student, to "communication," or to our contemporaries. If that is all we want, we might better recommend that the student invest his money in subscriptions to a variety of periodical publications which need not be named, rather than in paying tuition for our courses in philosophy. It seems to us that the student expects some guidance in the undergraduate phase of education, and that this guidance most properly and rightfully comes through asking of him a reasonable mastery of the achievements of the best in Christian philosophical and theological tradition.

Secondly, we would say in reply to the objection: "We don't believe it." First of all, it is not true that the traditional vocabularies of traditional Christian statement are *that* obsolete, that no one except the antiquarian in medieval philosophy understands them. Most people do know a cause from a cabbage, even though they cannot express the difference in precise technical terms. Secondly, while it is true that some students of other institutions have a far wider *acquaintance* with the terminology at least of more modern and contemporary philosophies, we have encountered no substantial evidence that they have a correspondingly more profound appreciation of the problems and meaning of these philosophies than our own students have. In any case, fruitful communication by our students with their contemporaries requires far more of them than a similar superficial acquaintance with terminology; our students need to understand the problems. But they can do this only if they can relate modern and contemporary philosophies to the real evidences of things in such a way as to understand why these philosophies have the problems they have, and what evidences of reality frustrate or prescribe their solutions. Let us face it; you cannot beat Hume by joining him. It is proper to try to understand him, but futile to hope to erect an anti-Humean metaphysic on Humean foundations. Finally, we find it simply inconceivable that the genuine contemporary *teacher* of philosophy in a Catholic college either can or will leave his students in the state of abysmal and utter innocence about contemporary thought that the objection assumes. He cannot help "relating," and passing on to his students some appreciation of the relations involved. And, doing so in a context of history, tradition, and living involvement with the real issues of Christian philosophy, he orders them to effective "communication" about as well as can be asked of anyone working not in an order of hypothetical "ideals" but with the real needs of real students.

One last (personal) note. It seems to us that frequently objections to the "traditional" approach of "Christian Philosophy" are grounded in a legitimate criticism of what (in some instances) the teaching of this philosophy has sometimes been: a "rationalized catechism." Now nobody is advocating that sort of thing. To reject an authentic and living Christian philosophy because some people have been too preoccupied with its dead relics is indeed to throw out the baby with the bath.

Notes

1. An exception to this statement is apparently to be found in the exemption of non-Catholic undergraduates from the regular theology program. Aside from the fact that there is usually some sort of "theology" program provided for them, too—a phenomenon which emphasizes the

point we are about to make—special provisions for them are not really relevant here. The educational program of the Catholic college is designed only *per accidens* for the non-Catholic student.

2. The contemporary trend, in fact, seems to be toward increasing rather than decreasing undergraduate requirements in these fields. Some institutions have, for a variety of reasons, chosen to disguise theology requirements under some such appellation as "Christian Culture," but in the field of philosophy the only such expedient seems to be the transfer of "Philosophy of Man" courses to the department of psychology. We might say that the norm today may be to require the student to devote as much as a full one-quarter of his class attendance to philosophy and theology—much more than was demanded in many institutions twenty or so years ago.

3. Anyone who thinks the word "necessary" too strong here has never tried to persuade a dean or an undergraduate board to consent to the inclusion of courses everybody admits to be highly *desirable* (but only that) among undergraduate requirements.

4. Obviously the *effective* teacher must achieve a substantial identity between the institutional goals of the college and his own personal ones, just as the student cannot be a good student unless he feels that the program of education to which he is being subjected is meeting his own personal needs. Sometimes, however, both sides of the desk may have to settle for the kind of "liking" we have for bitter medicine the doctor says is good for us. *En condition humana!* (Which may be freely translated: "That's the way the cookie crumbles!")

5. A brief digression may serve to clarify our point here. Note the difference between the finality specifying the activity of the *teacher* and that specifying the activity of the *scholar*. In judging the value of scholarship we quite properly apply a specifically social norm. "Does this work represent a genuine contribution to the publicly available knowledge in its field?" we ask, and are not at all concerned as to whether achieving it has made a better man of the scholar. It is true that there is (or at least could be) some kind of correlation between some scholarly work and teaching excellence. But as soon as we enter this field we return once more to a judgment based on the teacher's success in contributing to the personal development and perfection of the students in his classes. It might be suggested that this is at least one reason why universities have found it so much easier to establish standards of promotion and compensation based on scholarship than to establish standards based on effective teaching. In one instance publication and (the hypothetically purely objective) response to publication of other authorities in the field provide a publicly available measurement of the accomplishment of what is properly a public and social activity. In the other case, where the "end of the work" is the production of some perfection in the human person, no such method of

measurement is available. Of course, it does ultimately become evident in a concrete and human sort of way that some men are truly great and inspiring teachers—but this sometimes happens too late to permit the university to acknowledge it in tangible form.

6. Of course, the department has the discovery and preparation of future specialists in the field of philosophy as one of its goals. Every teacher will naturally (on the principle that good is diffusive of itself) be delighted to find among his students some who manifest a particular aptitude and liking for the discipline to which he is devoting his own personal energies, and will be anxious to provide for these students the necessary undergraduate preparation. Usually it is the hope of the college that the special requirements of the major program will accomplish this. Whether they do so or not is an entirely different question from the one at issue in this discussion.

7. We may note that some other departments in the college have to attend to this common or universal aspect of student needs, too, but none of them to the extent that the departments of philosophy and theology do. The departments of English, history, mathematics, physical science, all find that one of the duties they have is to provide courses suitable for students other than majors, and therefore in one way or another "required" for those who are not going to be specialists as well as for those who are. But in no other case is the specific, primary and principal purpose of the department dealing with problems and needs common to all students as it is for the two here under consideration.

8. We will consistently use the word "habit" in its conventional scholastic sense.

9. Granting (what should probably not be granted) that the philosophizing of Descartes actually conforms to this definition.

10. If this last phrase sounds too "Augustinian" to the reader, we would direct his attention once more to the term "integral." Cf. the statement of St. Thomas: "Man *is* directed to God as an end that surpasses the scope of his reason. . . . But the end *must* first be known by men who are to direct their thoughts and actions to that end. Hence it was *necessary* for the salvation of man that certain truths which exceed human reason should be made known to him by divine revelation." (S.T. I, q.1, a.1) The necessity spoken of here may, if one prefers to discuss the matter in the order of abstract essence, be spoken of as "hypothetical"; in the order of existence, however—the order in which every man actually is—(which is the order both St. Thomas and our students are interested in) the necessity is simply absolute.

11. The "awareness of these implications" is not restricted to convinced Christians. Not too long ago a contemporary agnostic of our acquaintance reacted to a (purely philosophical) paper on the nature of evi-

dence thus: "Brilliant, Father! But if I accept it, do I have to ask for Baptism?"

12. In the first class we would rank most (or at least many) intellectual Christians of the patristic period. The most striking example, evidently, is that of St. Augustine. To the second may be assigned many of the "Anti-rationalists" of Christian history—Bernard, à Kempis, *et id genus omne.*

13. As, for instance, in the prescription of philosophical studies as a major part of the training of clerics. One sees no justification for the gratuitous assumption that such prescriptions are insincere and jesuitical.

14. Between the "harmonizing" tendencies of the *Commentary on the Sentences* and the sharp rejections of (for instance) certain characteristically Averroist positions in late works, there is evidently a considerable gulf. And that St. Thomas should devote himself to the long labor of the *Commentaries* on Aristotle (incidentally going "out of his field" to do so) seems to us to indicate more than a mere defensive response to the "historical accident" of "misinterpretations" of Aristotle by members of the Arts faculty at Paris.

15. Again, it is suggestive that this harmonious conjunction of rational evidences with the certitudes of faith develops historically not in those "converted" from philosophy to the faith, but in those who, *having the faith,* apply themselves to the study of philosophy.

16. We should like here to re-emphasize the consideration advanced in the preceding note. The picture of the work of St. Thomas sometimes communicated to the student is that of a man who *first* achieved a developed system of rational evidences based on the writings of Aristotle and *then* applied himself to utilizing these evidences for the development of a theology. This attitude is at least in practice maintained by some of our contemporary "Thomists" (who shall be, here, otherwise discreetly nameless) who insist that students must first master the Prior and Posterior Analytics and the entire "Science of Nature" of Aristotle before they can be permitted to murmur a metaphysical question, let alone seek an answer to it in the writings of St. Thomas. At the risk of seeming frivolous, may we express our doubts that the mother of the infant Thomas replied to his first lisping questions about himself and the world with some such statement as this: "Every substance which changes into another substance must be recognized as composed of a potential principle called 'matter' and an activating principle called 'form,' " and going on from there? Indeed, Thomas seems to represent one of the most fortunate convergences of "the man and the hour" to be found in history: a self-aware, intellectual, deeply committed Christian coming to the fullness of his rational powers at the precise historical moment when the philosophical monuments of antiquity could present themselves to him in a form quite "unhistorical" in any schol-

arly sense, and relatively free from all those controversies about the
true and genuine meaning of the Aristotelian text which have complicated all subsequent efforts to repeat the achievement of Thomas.

17. We realize that we are raising here one of the most difficult problems
    of Thomistic scholarship. It is not our intention to offer anything like
    a thorough textual justification of our position. Strictly speaking, we
    are not so much concerned with establishing that it is the position of
    St. Thomas. We, too, are interested "in the truth of things."

18. S.T. I, q.l, a.l. Note that the connectives in the Latin text are *et*'s, not
    aut's or *vel*'s.

19. We do not mean to deny that *some Christians* have in the past settled
    for one or the other of these things and called it "philosophy." Many
    sincere Christians have tried to reduce philosophy precisely to a state of
    existential neutrality with respect to faith. ("It doesn't really matter
    whether you can demonstrate the existence of God philosophically, since
    our students accept it on faith anyway.") Others *have* seen Heraclitus as
    a prophet of hell-fire or the "end of the world"; Plato as describing the
    "beatific visions." And others, finally, have produced eclectic rational-
    isms with one eye on the "solution" of theological problems. For
    example, it might be suggested that one reason for the popularity in
    some historical scholastic quarters for the "pincushion" theory of acci-
    dents which Locke later made famous was its apparent utility in solving
    the problem of Transubstantiation. Our point is that the genuinely
    intellectual Christian cannot find satisfaction here.

20. Evidently, the influence of the motivation described above will not be
    restricted to philosophical investigations. A similar motive must and
    often does extend its influence in stimulating historical, cultural, anthro-
    pological, textual, linguistic investigations which throw light upon the
    authentic meaning of revelation. While there may be reasons both *a
    priori* and historical for suspecting that some of the statements of some
    of the investigators in these fields, as in the field of philosophy, occa-
    sionally reflect an apologetic, rather than a theological, motivation, it
    is evident that there is, in the present state of scholarship, no genuine
    reason whatever for equivalating religious commitment with scholarly
    incompetence or bias, let alone dishonesty. Furthermore, the precise
    point to be made here is that a genuine theological motivation imposes
    the highest possible dedication to the pursuit of natural evidences in
    every related order. A piously distorted description of Palestinian cul-
    ture in the first century A.D. produces a distorted understanding of the
    person and work of Jesus of Nazareth; a piously distorted philosophy
    produces a pious distortion of the meaning of revealed truth and must
    prevent, rather than promote, that genuine progress in understanding
    which is the only real objective of the theologically motivated intelli-
    gence.

Selected Bibliography

Books:

Dawson, C. *The Crisis of Western Education.* New York: Sheed & Ward, 1961.

Farrell, A. *The Jesuit Code of Liberal Education; Development and Scope of the* Ratio Studiorum. Milwaukee: Bruce, 1938.

Gilson, E. *Christianity and Philosophy.* New York: Sheed & Ward, 1939.

————. *God and Philosophy.* New Haven: Yale University Press, 1941.

————. *History of Philosophy and Philosophical Education.* (Aquinas Lecture, Fall, 1947.) Milwaukee: Marquette University Press, 1948.

————. *The Philosopher and Theology.* New York: Random House, 1962.

Horrigan, A. *Metaphysics as a Principle of Order in the University Curriculum.* Washington: The Catholic University of America Press, 1944.

Lawler, J. G. *The Catholic Dimension in Higher Education.* Westminster: Newman Press, 1959.

Marc, A., S.J. *Raison philosophique et religion révélée.* Paris: Desclée de Brouwer, 1955.

Maritain, J. *Education at the Crossroads.* New Haven: Yale University Press, 1943.

Nedoncelle, M. *Is There a Christian Philosophy?* New York: Hawthorn Books, 1960.

Ryan, J. J. *The Idea of a Catholic College.* New York: Sheed & Ward, 1945.

————. *Beyond Humanism: Toward a Philosophy of Catholic Education.* New York: Sheed & Ward, 1950.

Salman, D., O.P. *La Place de la philosophie dans l'université idéale.* (Conference Albert-le-Grand.) Paris: Librairie J. Vrin, 1954.

Trethowan, I. *An Essay in Christian Philosophy.* London: Longmans, 1954.

Articles:

Bonnefoy, J., O.F.M. "La théologie comme science et l'explication de la foi selon saint Thomas d'Aquin," *Ephemerides Theologicae Lovanienses,* 1938, XV, 491–516.

de Finance, J., S.J. "Être et Subjectivité," *Doctor Communis,* II (May–August, 1948), 240–258.

Garrigou-Lagrange, R. "De relationibus inter philosophiam et religionem," *Acta Pontif. Academiae Romanae,* 1938 N.S. 3, pp. 379–405.

Gilson, E. "Concerning Christian Philosophy: The Distinctiveness of the Philosophical Order," in *Philosophy and History: Essays Presented to E. Cassirer,* edited by Klibansky and Paton (Oxford: Clarendon Press, 1936), pp. 61–76.

Labourdette. "La théologie, intelligence de la foi," *Revue Thomiste,* 1946, pp. 26–34.

Phelan, G. "Theology in the Curriculum of Catholic Colleges and Universities," *Man and Secularism* (National Catholic Alumni Association; New York, 1940), pp. 128–140.

11

THE NATURE AND
FUNCTION OF PHILOSOPHY
IN UNDERGRADUATE EDUCATION

Harry R. Klocker, S.J.

In considering the role of philosophy in the American Jesuit College and University, the delegates to the convention held at Loyola University in Los Angeles in the summer of 1962 arrived at certain basic conclusions. These conclusions concerned: (1) the nature and function of philosophy; (2) basic commitments in philosophy; (3) the pluralism which is current in the teaching of philosophy; (4) the contribution which philosophy should make to the moral, religious, and spiritual formation of the student; and (5) the relation of philosophy to theology and to other departments of the college or university.

I. THE NATURE AND
FUNCTION OF PHILOSOPHY

Philosophy is a distinct discipline with its own proper methodology and its own proper goal. It is distinguished from so-called common sense and from humanistic knowledge by reason of its more rigorous method, its attempt to explain reality in terms of causes, and its abstract expression of those explanations. It is distinguished from the natural sciences and mathematics in so far as it seeks an ultimate explanation of finite being, of man, and of

God. Philosophy is, therefore, a speculative science which develops in the human intellect the tendency to think in terms of ultimates, to refer the contingent to the necessary, to see the relative as explicable finally only in terms of an absolute. Theology, of course, also treats of an absolute and of all things in relation to this absolute. But theology begins with a revelation and proceeds to investigate that revelation under the light of reason illumined by faith. Philosophy, on the other hand, begins with the given of sense experience and interprets and explains that given in so far as it is explicable in terms of human reason alone.

It is precisely in relation to the nature of philosophy that its function in the college or university must be understood. There are, of course, side benefits connected with the teaching of philosophy, but we are not concerned with these here. If philosophy is to be meaningful to the student, it must orient the student to what is of ultimate concern to him as a human being living in a world which is intelligible.[1] If, then, the teaching of philosophy is to be successful, it must at least provide the student with certain basic intellectual insights about the ultimate meaning of reality, of man, of God. And it should prepare the student to develop, at least inchoatively, the habit of thinking in terms of ultimates in these areas.

II. BASIC PHILOSOPHICAL
COMMITMENTS IN A JESUIT
COLLEGE OR UNIVERSITY

Those who are teaching philosophy are aware of the pluralism that is characteristic of the contemporary philosophical enterprise. As W. Norris Clarke has pointed out,[2] there are varied approaches to the teaching of philosophy, all of them in use at the present time. There is the historical approach, the phenomenological, the existential, the personal and the subjective, the rationalistic, and the systematic. The situation is complicated to some extent by the fact that some of those teaching philosophy in Jesuit colleges and universities have been trained in this or that method, and departments of philosophy engage professors whose backgrounds include one or more of the approaches mentioned above.

I do not think this is undesirable. Any philosophical system, to remain vital, must also remain open to current trends and insights. To possess truth is one thing. To deny that this truth can be purified and deepened would be ridiculous. It is from this viewpoint that an approach like the historical or phenomenological can be of real value, not only to the philosopher himself but also to the teaching of philosophy. In this sense, a philosophical pluralism can be a healthy influence on the *philosophia perennis* as well as on the philosophical life of the college or university. It can keep the student abreast of modern developments in philosophy, and it can make good use of the varied backgrounds of the members of the department of philosophy.

At the same time I think we must recognize that a certain amount of philosophical truth has been discovered and that this truth is contained in that *philosophia perennis* which can be communicated to the student. To dispense with this is to allow pluralism to become a philosophical system instead of a variety of philosophical methods. The end result then would be only skepticism and confusion.

While affirming that every living philosophy must be constantly open to philosophical insights from any source, the philosophy departments of Jesuit colleges and universities are committed to the following positions as basic to the *Philosophia Perennis* and normative for unity. It is not intended, however, that this statement of commitments should be the only factor in determining the number of required courses, the specific courses required, or the approach to any particular commitment.

1. A realistic metaphysics as possible and necessary for the adequate constitution of a philosophy of created being.
2. The dualistic constitution and social nature of man, spirituality

of the human soul, freedom of the will, moral responsibility based on a realistic metaphysics.
3. The existence of a personal and transcendent God known by reason.[3]

Along with the communication of such basic philosophical truth, it also seems necessary to make the student aware of certain contemporary problems and their effect on present-day philosophy. One such problem is the relationship of philosophy to the methodologies of the various knowledges. There is much concern at the present time with the philosophy of science, of art, of history. In addition, Phenomenology and Existentialism have made the subject and subjectivity a primary interest of philosophy. Linguistic philosophy has made ordinary language its fundamental concern. To ignore these issues or to treat them as of no consequence would certainly leave the student unprepared to enter into any sort of dialogue with the intelligent graduate of other colleges and universities. To this list of important ideas we should also add an awareness of the tension that exists between freedom and authority, the philosophy of communism, and the contemporary investigations into the societal nature of man.

It is, of course, true that not everything can be done in two or three years of college. But it should be possible to acquaint the student with these movements in contemporary thinking, and put more emphasis, where possible, on the relationship between philosophy and the student's major field of interest. Participants in the workshop suggested that for history majors a course be offered in the philosophy of history, for science majors a course in the philosophy of science, etc. All of this should be aimed at giving the student as deep an insight as he is capable of into the basic truths of the *philosophia perennis* and simultaneously an awareness of problems and approaches current in present-day philosophical thinking. However superficial this may be on the undergraduate level, it seems to be absolutely necessary, if the philosophy taught in Jesuit colleges and universities is to be kept vital.

III. THE CONTRIBUTION OF
PHILOSOPHY AS AN ACADEMIC
DISCIPLINE TO THE MORAL,
RELIGIOUS, AND SPIRITUAL
FORMATION OF THE COLLEGE
STUDENT

Since philosophy holds the position it does in the present historical order—an intermediate discipline standing between other human knowledges and theology—part of its influence on the moral, religious, and spiritual formation of the student is indirect. Philosophy prepares and disposes the student for theology and reinforces this theology. In so far as philosophy establishes the existence of God and the universal providence of God, it at least negatively disposes the student for the revelation of that God and the possibility of a providence that directs all men to a supernatural end.

But philosophy also has a direct influence on the development of the human person. Certain dispositions are the natural result of the proper study of philosophy. And many of the truths with which philosophy is concerned have a direct relation to human conduct and action. Among the dispositions which philosophy tends to inculcate are the following:

1. In the quest for ultimates, which is really the nature of philosophy, philosophy conditions the student to become more and more wisely critical, to look for finality in things, to be impatient with accidentals and to seek for essentials. Philosophy tends to impart those qualities which are implied in the virtue of wisdom. Particularly important here is the fact that philosophy leads the mind to transcend the merely material and experiential and provides an insight into the possibility and necessity of some understanding of this transcendent realm.

2. Properly taught, philosophy provides this understanding in a balanced and harmonious way. Hence it avoids the extremes of rationalism and empiricism and is able to co-ordinate experience, intelligibility, and explanation. Along with the disposition to ac-

cept the spiritual dimension of being goes an openness of mind and a willingness to accept truth, however it may appear. There is a recognition both of certitude, which has been achieved, and of mystery, which shrouds the infinitude of being and accompanies it at every turn. The disposition engendered here is intellectual humility and charity.

3. The insights into being, man, and God which philosophy provides make the student aware of the possibility of an intellectualism within faith itself and of the confirmation by reason of at least some of the truths proposed for his belief. Thus philosophy makes possible for the student a real assent as opposed to a notional assent to many moral and religious propositions.[4] It provides the background for an integration of knowledge and action based on the realization that the speculative truths of which the student has become aware demand from him action in accord with these truths.

4. Among truths which demand a personal commitment and which orientate his life toward a reasoned choice for God are certainly the following: freedom of choice and the personal responsibility resulting from it; the spiritual and contingent nature of man; the fact of God as Creator and End; and "intersubjectivity" with all its implications of interpersonal relationships.

The teacher, of course, can and must play an important role in the development of these dispositions in the student of philosophy. Thus, in the treatise on habits, the teacher can call attention to the infused habits as well as to those which can be developed naturally. He can speak of Christian perfection as well as of natural perfection. In much the same way he can link up the whole notion of vocation with the philosophical truth of God's providence. Philosophy and theology are distinct disciplines, but there is no reason for the professor of philosophy to pretend that a revelation has not been given. On the contrary, he should recognize the incompleteness of philosophy and point out the necessity of a revelation as the only way in which man can achieve his true identity.

No student should ever be left with the impression that ethics is the final word on the development of his moral life.

IV. THE FUNCTION OF
PHILOSOPHY IN RELATION
TO THEOLOGY AND OTHER
DEPARTMENTS

A. *The Function of Philosophy*
   in Relation to Theology

There is no need to repeat here what has already been said about the nature of philosophy and theology. It is recognized, at least by scholastic philosophers, that they are distinct disciplines, each with its own methodology and proper object. Nor need we enter here upon the controversy about the possibility or impossibility of a Christian philosophy. All Christian philosophers admit the incompleteness of a purely rationalistic approach to being, man, and God. They recognize, too, the need of a theology based on a revelation and operating under the light of faith. What is not always so clear is the relationship which should obtain between these disciplines in a Jesuit college or university.

If rightly co-ordinated, both philosophy and theology will contribute their share to the development of the mature college graduate that every Jesuit institution of higher learning aims to produce. However, the difficulties here are many. In almost every Jesuit college there is a disproportion between the hours devoted to these two disciplines. One of the main reasons for this, of course, is the need of at least several courses in philosophy as a preparation for any sort of speculative theology. This is not meant to imply that college theology should be merely a watered-down version of seminary theology. The list of topics suggested elsewhere in this book indicates just the opposite.[5]

B. The Function of Philosophy in Relation to Other Departments

Much of what I have to say here is equally relevant to the department of theology. And both departments could function as a unit in bringing their aims and methods before other departments of the college or university. There is need, certainly, for an integration of the various knowledges; and philosophy because of its search for ultimates can accomplish this, at least on one level. Workshop participants recommended that the philosophy department take upon itself the responsibility of engaging the rest of the faculty in a dialogue that clarifies our values and their relevance for other disciplines. This could be accomplished in various ways. A survey course could be given to new teachers in the aims and objectives of Jesuit education. One-day institutes, panel discussions with members from various departments, visiting lecturers, faculty discussion groups—all these could help create dialogue between departments. A real service in this direction would be for the philosophy department to publish its reading lists and even to enter into discussion with other departments in compiling such lists.

Communication with other departments has at times been lacking, and this has hurt the philosophy department as much as the others. Along with the insights philosophy can provide for the members of other departments go the insights which these other departments can provide for members of the philosophy department. Only in some sort of interchange and dialogue can faculty members become aware of the aims, methods, and problems of other disciplines. Philosophy, in so far as it attempts to be an integrating discipline, should be keenly aware of such aims.

Conclusion

It can be said in general that philosophy in Jesuit higher education is regarded as a vital part of what is called a Christian wisdom. In itself it is distinct from theology and from other areas of knowledge. Yet, it is also closely related to all other areas of knowledge. It gives support and clarity to the science of theology, and it serves to integrate other knowledges on the purely rational level.[6] It continually refers the student to what transcends the merely material and brings him face to face with what is ultimately real and meaningful. Nor does philosophy stop with speculative exploration. The explanations given by philosophy are of such a nature that some of them, at least, bring the student into direct contact with truths that demand a commitment in the practical order. It is precisely here that philosophy becomes lived as well as meaningful. Where this living takes place under grace, it is also true that such living becomes meaningful in terms of a higher destiny than philosophy itself is capable of holding out to man.

Neither is it of minor importance that philosophy can provide a natural wisdom which is coherent with and to some extent explicative of that higher wisdom given by the Triune God. To the extent that it can do this, philosophy not only provides an intellectually satisfying response to the basic human questions, but it makes clear that an intellectualism in the best sense of the word is possible within a revelation grasped by faith. "For there is necessarily one ultimate end of the universe which is a good of intellect. This is truth."[7]

On its own level of being philosophy introduces the student to a depth of thought and inquiry which is essential to his intellectual formation. In doing this it forms within the student the habit of philosophizing, of looking at problems in terms of ultimates. Carl Burlage puts it well when he distinguishes between philosophy taught on the graduate level and on the undergraduate level. In the former instance the object is to make scholars in the field of philosophy. In the latter, it is to make philosophers.[8] It is precisely this training in philosophizing that initiates the student into a new depth in thinking and thereby introduces him to a new and necessary maturity of mind.

In relation to the above-mentioned points, the stable, unchanging truths of the *philosophia perennis* are essential to the teaching of philosophy. We possess insights into the nature of reality, of man, and of God; and these insights can be communicated to the student. To the extent that he himself can acquire these insights, to that extent he can formulate for himself a truly rational foundation for the life he must live among the things that are. Nor does this imply that philosophy is nothing more than a series of already discovered truths handed down from generation to generation with no need for any further development. In a sense each man begins philosophy anew and brings to it not only his own character and background but the contributions of his own age. In the process by which he rethinks the wisdom of the past from his own particular vantage point there is always the possibility for new insights, deeper understanding, and more fruitful application.

Furthermore, philosophy is not meant to exist in splendid isolation from contemporary thought. The variety of approaches in contemporary philosophy is evident enough. Very few would deny that such pluralism can contribute much that is worthwhile to the student's quest for truth. It can emphasize neglected aspects of the reality which philosophy investigates, as well as provide new methods of procedure and bring into focus areas hitherto bypassed or taken for granted. And, what is perhaps most important of all, it can give the student the capacity to enter into living dialogue with those trained in the philosophical systems of today. There is, therefore, such a thing as a healthy pluralism in the methods of teaching philosophy; and there is no need to exile such pluralism from our departments of philosophy.

Another aspect of this openness of philosophy to further progress is the necessity it has to devote itself to questions that are of contemporary interest. Some of these questions have been mentioned above, and to ignore them would be to do the student a real injustice. Very few are capable of applying principles to a different set of circumstances, or of relating them to problems raised in areas with which they are not familiar. Hence, there is real need in the teaching of philosophy to introduce the student to current problems, to have him face the objections raised by contemporary thinking, and to have him realize that there are answers to the objections and objections to many of the answers. This does not mean that contemporary thought should be studied simply for the sake of increasing the list of "adversaries." It is quite possible that such study will deepen in the student his own awareness of the philosophical endeavor.

Finally, a word of caution should be added. What has been set down here is as much an ideal to be achieved as a recognition of the nature and function of philosophy in Jesuit colleges and universities. Not all students are capable of real philosophical insight. In many cases the habit of wisdom will remain pretty much in the inchoative stage. But they will have achieved an immense amount of intellectual maturity by being submitted to the philosophical process and by facing not a few of the problems with which philosophy deals. This is not unimportant. Nor is the realization that within the faith a real intellectualism is possible, and that there is good reason for the commitment to God and the life of virtue. For those who can see more deeply—and they are not just a handful—philosophy can contribute an integral and important part of that wisdom and integrated character which is the goal of Jesuit higher education.

Notes

1. See Carl Burlage, S.J., *supra*, pp. 181–183.
2. W. Norris Clarke, S.J., *supra*, pp. 141–163.
3. Jesuit Educational Workshop Report, V, 419.
4. See George P. Klubertanz, S.J., *supra*, pp. 38–68.
5. *Infra*, p. 285.
6. For a discussion of philosophy as an integrating factor on the level of undergraduate courses see George P. Klubertanz, S.J., *College Newsletter of the College and University Division of the N.C.E.A.*, XX (1956), 1, 10–13, 18.
7. Thomas Aquinas, *Summa Contra Gentiles*, Bk. I, c. 1.
8. Carl Burlage, S.J., *supra*, p. 181.

Part IV

MORAL, RELIGIOUS,
AND SPIRITUAL FORMATION

12

JESUIT STUDENT SPIRITUALITY FOR TODAY

Bernard J. Cooke, S.J.

As we begin to discuss the spirituality which we want developed in our students, it is obvious that there are many different points according to which the material could be divided; but perhaps three points are rather focal and can give us hinges for our discussion. The first of these is that the spirituality to be developed in our students must be Christian. Secondly, it must be maturely supernatural. And thirdly, it must be intellectually apostolic.

It is clear that any genuine spirituality which students have should be Christian. Obvious as that may seem, I think there is danger at times that we tend to form a spirituality which is based upon Stoic categories of thought rather than upon the figure of Christ. Perhaps it is because we tend to formalize our analysis of man and of man's spirituality that the precisely Christian aspect of the spiritual life has somewhat vanished from the point of view of our students. I think an indication of this fact is that very few of our college students think of themselves as Christian—as Catholic, yes, but not precisely as Christian.

Christian Decisiveness

Christian spirituality is spirituality which not only is like that of Christ, but actually, in the mystery of the Church, continues Christ's own religious experience. For this reason, at the very

215

heart of any genuine spirituality that calls itself Christian, there must be situated decisive use of freedom. Our students cannot have a spirituality which consists merely in a passive going through life without doing harm, a spirituality which is one of mediocre good example. It must be a spirituality which is one of decisiveness. To be a Christian involves an honest confrontation of oneself and of the world. If our students are to be effective in their own lives and are to contribute to the advance of the Kingdom of Christ in the world, they must not only be capable of honesty and courage; they must be educated to appraise objectively and without fear their own capacities and their own role in the world in which they live with its advantages, its potential, and its problems. Only if they possess such a capacity for open-minded, forthright living, will they be able to call themselves Christian. Only then will they be able to say that the spirituality which they possess is a continuation of the mind of Christ, Christ who Himself looked at the world which was His, looked at the role that He was meant to play, and without deviating, went straight forth to the task which was His. Our students, then, must be schooled to a type of Christian spirituality which is grounded in the use of their freedom.

Immediately, however, a certain tension arises if we are honest with ourselves and with the situation in which we and our students are placed. Freedom cannot be an unlimited thing. It must be governed by law, because without law the individual's life and the life of society are chaotic. For this reason, our students must be educated to understand and to accept freely and without reluctance the fact of authority. This authority applies both to the natural society in which man finds himself situated and to the supernatural society which is the Church.

As we know, the roots and exercise of authority in these two societies are quite distinct and different. Because of the fact that civil societies are grounded in nature, the demands of such societies can be studied and comprehended by natural understanding, and a greater measure of man's own free commitment of himself can come into the picture; whereas, with regard to the supernatural society, both the origin and the exercise of the authority are in a supernatural order commensurate with the supernatural destiny of man. For that reason there is a certain given aspect about the dominion which is meant to be exercised in the Church. This is not to say that in either natural or supernatural spheres, our students are to proceed with a blind, childish acceptance of authority— acceptance which never questions, which never appraises, wherein personal decisiveness and freedom and honesty are somewhat depressed and submerged. If a correct understanding of authority prevails, our students can be led and must be led to an understanding and an acceptance of authority which befits their human dignity and their human freedom.

Authority thus understood and accepted is not a burdensome thing. It is seen rather as an intrinsic need of life, as the requirement for any orderly and profitable social existence. An honest explanation of authority, both natural and supernatural, can be somewhat embarrassing in the light of the fact that authority is not infrequently misused in both orders of society. Yet, there is no profit in trying to hide such facts from our students; and we must face the danger that comes in explaining to them what authority should be—the danger that they will then turn this understanding to a judgment of the exercise of authority as they find it even in our own institutions. It may well be that it is only this honest confrontation of the problem which will save us from an outbreak of that anti-clericalism which has so plagued the Church in Europe for the past two or three centuries.

Sometimes, a supposed opposition is suggested between education for acceptance of authority and education for initiative. Actually no such opposition need arise if both aspects of the education are genuine and deep. If we are to turn out of our schools graduates who will be not just a credit to us, but pioneers in the formation of a Christian world, then we must educate our students for initiative. We must bring them according to their differing talents to the point where they can apply the academic instruction we have given them to the living of life and do so according to a pattern somewhat different from that in which they have already been formed. We must lead them to the point where they have both the courage and the insight required to take up the life which is theirs with decision, without reluctance, and make it a better life. Or, to put it another way, what we really should be turning out of our schools are students who will not simply wait to see how the world is going to develop and wonder whether that world will prove friendly or inimical to Christianity; we should be turning out of our schools men who look forward to building a world so that it can become Christian.

I think that it is difficult to find, among our graduates at present, men and women who really feel that the world is theirs to build, that the future is something that they are meant to construct; and I think that this reflects the mentality of many people in the faculties of our schools who think exactly the same way—who think that those who are going to form the economic, social, and political patterns of the future are graduates of schools other than our own. In many respects, what is needed both in faculty and students is a deeper measure of hope, trust that the Christian initiative, if exercised with prudence and with professional depth, can really shape a future according to the pattern of Christ.

Finally, under this topic of training our students for free decision, we might mention that what we wish to form in our students is a mature balance of judgment, that we wish them to be able to go out into any sort of situation and there come up with a judgment which is balanced, fearless, and mature. We want our students to be able to apply the understandings and the motivations of Christianity to these moments of decision. We do not wish them to be people dominated by every whim of imagination and every flurry of emotion. Moreover, we do not want them to succumb to the suggestions given them by a propagandistic and advertising-conscious world. We want them not to submit their freedom, not to capitulate, but rather to be masters of the environment in which they live. Yet we do not want this to be a question of a cold, haughty superiority towards the situation of life. We want

our students to live a full life, to have a richness of imaginative
and emotional experience; yet we wish them in the midst of this
to be deeply personal, intellectual, and profoundly Christian. In
short, we would like to have the students who graduate from our
schools go out into life and, in the midst of all the circumstances
that arise, choose with a prudence and a freedom somewhat like
that exercised by Christ Himself in His public life.

Following of Christ

However, it is not just a question of our students living their
lives as Christ would. The much deeper mystery is that they live
their lives with Christ; that in a very genuine sense Christ continues in them (or at least is meant to continue in them) the
mysteries which He began two thousand years ago. The graduates
of our schools are, in the mystery of Christianity, a rather privileged group in whom Christ is meant to continue the work of His
redemptive Incarnation. We should have as our ambition to produce students conscious of this fact and willing to live it in full
awareness and dedication. That means that the students whom we
educate must have a deep sense of their Christian dignity and
responsibility. They must know what it means to be a member of
the Church, a member of the Body of Christ, know what it means
when one says that (because of the sacramental character of Baptism
and Confirmation) they share in the priesthood of Christ and that
Christ utilizes them in His work of redemption and His supreme
function of worship of the Heavenly Father.

With this sense of dignity and responsibility, our students will
then go out to live with Christ the task of transmitting divine
revelation to the world of this twentieth century. This transmission
of revelation is obviously not just a verbal thing. It is the more
profound task of translating into the emergent mentalities and
institutions of human living the values and the insights which come
from faith. In turning out such students, we must never forget
that if they be genuinely Christian, their attitude of responsibility is

not one of heaviness, not one of a duty for duty's sake, but rather one of a profound happiness, a happiness which comes with the discovery of the genuine meaning of life. If the spirituality of our students is to be genuinely Christian, then it will be most essentially a spirit of gratitude. For the theology of the Mass itself tells us that the most basic spiritual attitude of a Christian, as of Christ Himself, should be one of *eucharistia,* of a giving of thanks.

Living out the mystery of Christ's redemptive Incarnation does not mean that one can perform all the same external actions which Christ Himself performed. Rather, it is a much more personal process, in which, with a deep consciousness of the meaning of what Christ did, with a grasp of those principles which were and are those of Christ, a man goes to translate these into the most contemporary forms. To put it another way, in the decisions of life and in the actions which flow from them, the true Christian lives according to the values of Christianity. That standard of judgment by which he chooses the goods of life is a standard not of the world about him, but of Christ. The motivations which guide him as he chooses a way of life, as he associates with certain groups of friends, as he works to construct a world about him, are the orientations coming from a deep understanding of the mystery of Christ and of the mystery of the Church. Truly Christian conduct of life means that one must act in constant union with Christ, aware of the fact that Christ does live in one, and that one is to live out the thinking and the love of Christ Himself. This involves necessarily an awareness of the true reality of life. It means seeing those deeper meanings which are hidden from those who do not have faith. It means that, conscious of the depth and the greatness of Christianity and knowing that toward which human history is being moved, one sees the great areas still unrealized in the Christian dream. In terms of this, without bitterness or anger, one can and must be positively critical of oneself, critical of the Church and the culture in which one lives. For one sees the inadequacies which still exist, sees them to some extent as Christ Himself sees them, and so strives with courage and with optimism to lead himself and the Church and human society a step further in the development of the new man in Christ.

Spirituality of the Spiritual
Exercises of St. Ignatius

Perhaps one can restate what we have been saying in the last few paragraphs in terms of the spirituality that should flow from a deep grasp of the *Spiritual Exercises:* the Christian that we wish to produce in our schools is a man who would be able to situate himself in the context of sacred history. Knowing the sweep of God's action over the centuries, and seeing the finality and the implications of this divine action, one would be able to see the present moment as the latest stage in this divinely guided process. Without pretending to have a vision of the future, the Christian should still, from an analysis of the eschatological orientations of both Old and New Testaments, see the general direction in which the future should develop. One would be able to see working in the history of the present moment the force of the kingdom of Christ, and seeing it one would feel impelled to offer himself to Christ for service in this Kingdom. This seems to be the import of the meditation on the Kingdom of Christ.

Again, such a mature Christian, having grasped the implications and the importance of Christianity, and having seen the century-long opposition to the work of God operative in human life because of false attraction of these earthly goods, would be able to discern false values in life. Such a person would have almost an instinct that would guide him in the practical judgments of daily life, whether it be in professional, business, or political circles. Such an ability to appraise the currents of thought in judgment, oftentimes a subtle and difficult matter, was the purpose of St. Ignatius in the training which he provided for his own men in the Society of Jesus and for all who make the *Spiritual Exercises.* One of the most basic meditations in the *Exercises* is that of the Two

Standards, and closely linked with it is the all-important matter of Discernment of Spirits.

Thirdly, the truly mature Christian not only is conscious of the process of sacred history in which he is a part and is able to discern the false attractions which would lead him away from participation in the work of the Kingdom, but he is able to translate this in terms of his own vocational choice, according to his own circumstances and skills and capacities and interests. He is able to discern the contribution which he can make, by means of which the work of the Church will be furthered and the Kingdom of Christ more deeply achieved in the contemporary world.

Sacramental Living .

Theological analysis tells us quite definitely there can be no genuine Christian spirituality which is not a living out of the sacraments, for the sacraments are the proper actions of the Church. They are the supreme occasions of grace, and they are the very purpose for which a Christian is called into the mystery of the Church. Moreover, there can be little doubt but that the Holy Spirit, working in the Church at the present moment, is drawing Christians to a form of spirituality which is much more profoundly sacramental. Perhaps we are at one of the great turning points in the spiritual life of the Church, when we are moving away from a medieval concentration on devotional Christianity and from a post-Reformation concentration on adherence to the externals of the Church and are instead moving into a much more profound living of the mystery of the Church itself—this means in its sacramental actions. For this reason, the students who graduate from our schools should be already immersed in a deep sacramental life and be prepared to live this life yet more profoundly in the years which lie before them.

Such a sacramental spirituality involves all that we have said already about free decisiveness as the kernel of Christian life for the simple reason that it is in the sacraments that the Christian most deeply opts for the Christian way of living; and this option is joined, above all in the Sacrifice of the Mass, with Christ's free acceptance of His destiny. Again, such a spirituality in no way pulls a Christian away from involvement in the practical obligations and needs of life, for the simple reason that the whole process of mediation of divine truth and divine grace to human beings in the world in which they live finds its focus in the sacramental actions. This process of which we sometimes speak—"living out the Mass"—is in no way an artificial thing but something which, if understood, is a most natural and a mature expression of Christian faith and life.

For the most part, the students whom we have in our classes in Jesuit colleges and universities are born Catholics, baptized before they themselves were able to express the choice which that sacrament indicates. Unfortunately, comparatively few of them have ever been led in the course of their earlier education to make that baptismal choice their own, consciously and deeply to reiterate it and express it. We cannot absolve ourselves of the obligation of seeing to it that by the time they leave our doors, our graduates have thought through the implications of this baptismal choice and have begun to live more deeply the commitment which it involves. An examination of Baptism or of any of the sacraments which follow it makes us conscious of the depths of spirituality which these sacred actions involve; for at root they all commit the Christian to a sharing in, a living out, of Christ's death and resurrection. It is in and around these sacramental actions—above all the supreme sacrament of the Eucharist—that our students should express their faith and lead their lives.

One could build a whole theology, as a matter of fact, a whole explanation of life, around the action of the Mass. But suffice it to say here that this action is without question the most important and the most focal in the lives and experience of our students, both while they are with us and when they go forth into mature life. Into this action of the Mass must flow all their decisions, all their hopes and dreams, all their thinking, all the academic preparation we have given them. It is only here, in this act, that they can become truly conscious of their dignity as Christians at the very moment when they are expressing their dignity and responsibility most by joining in Christ's sacrificial worship of the Father. Unless the thought-life and love-life of our students have been oriented towards this greatest of all human actions, we cannot tell ourselves that we have formed in our students a genuine spirituality; nor have we been faithful to our own Jesuit traditions. We must never forget that it was in large part due to the influence of the early centuries of Jesuit preaching and teaching that a more widespread and deeper use of the sacraments came into being.

Missionary Outlook

So far, then, we have seen that a genuine Christian spirituality is one that is grounded in mature use of free decisiveness, that it consists in conscious cooperation with Christ in the continuing mystery of the Redemption, and that it involves a clear living out of the sacramental actions. The final point we would like to take under this notion of spirituality is that it must be international and missionary.

One of the things that is most noticeable as one studies the Old Testament is the way in which revelation constantly works to move the people of Israel away from a nationalistic or racist interpretation of their destiny. In the high prophetic movement this impulse of revelation finds magnificent expression, but a certain reversal occurs within the strictly Judaic period which was consequent upon the Babylonian Exile. Development of a nationalistic mentality perverted the nation of the people's election to the choice of themselves as a nation opposed to other nations, instead of a mediator chosen for the sake of others.

Christ Himself comes, quite obviously, to inaugurate a dispensation of salvation which applies to all men; and while there was a certain reluctance on the part of Judaizing tendencies in the primitive Church to accept the full implications of this teaching of Christ, by the end of the Apostolic period the point had been successfully established. In successive waves of endeavor, the apostolic life of the Church has flourished over the centuries, indicating the essentially missionary orientation of the work of Christ.

Yet this advance has not been without its problems and its misunderstandings. One of the most basic misunderstandings, and one which we have not completely worked out yet, is the confusion which existed between the notion of mission and the notion of crusade. Mistakenly, not a few Christians have thought that the mystery of Christ could be imposed upon people and upon cultures. If we have seen the foolishness of this in the past, the evils which often accompanied such an application of the Christian mystery (all too tragically we have reaped the fruit of this sad misunderstanding), the orientation of our students for genuine missionary effort, whether it be at home or abroad, will become one that is consonant with the deeper missionary principles of Christian revelation and Christian redemption.

It is important that we instill in our students an international point of view, an interest in countries and cultures other than their own, and an awareness that the mystery of Christianity is in no way limited to its American, or even its occidental, expressions. They do know to some extent that ours is not the only form of Christianity, and we ourselves teach them that. But it is important, I think, to recognize that ours is not even the most perfect form; at least, that is a very definite possibility. We must prepare our students to go into another culture, to make it their own, to be willing to adopt the mentality and the customs and the points of view of other people with sympathy and with deep understanding and with love, in order that they can participate with those peoples in the building of Christianity which is truly Catholic.

Such has always been the nature of Christianity, and at no time in the history of the Church has this been so important as now when an unprecedented cultural interchange confronts us. If one looks objectively at the world situation as we find it today and at

the blessings which have been given to the American Church, it is
very difficult to see how we can avoid the conclusion that a tremendous obligation rests upon us of providing genuine Christian
leadership in the larger world picture. The rest of the Catholic
world can with justification look for us to send forth, not just
a sizable group of missionaries, but a group beyond comparison
with that provided by other portions of the Church. Since our
schools have a large proportion of the Catholic leadership in this
country, it would seem that upon our schools rests a very special
responsibility for the missionary apostolate throughout the world.

In many parts of the world it seems that the thing needed, in
order that people and cultures be brought to Christ, is the formation of lay leadership. Such formation of South American lay
leaders or African lay leaders or Asian lay leaders must in large
part be accomplished by lay leadership from other countries.
Again, such formation of lay leadership, if it be done, will have to
be done in large part by well-educated and missionary-minded
Americans. Certainly, our schools should share a large part of the
responsibility for producing lay leaders of this kind. If such students are to emerge from our institutions, then the spirituality
which we instill into our students must involve a deep grasp of
those Christian principles which can be operative at any point in
history and in any of the many cultures of mankind. It must be a
spirituality which sees the more profound meanings of the catho-
licity of the faith and the life which are ours.

Supernatural Maturity

The second basic point around which we can group our discussion of the spirituality of our students is: such spirituality must
be maturely supernatural. It is obvious that the ontological reality
of their spirituality which is sanctifying grace is a supernatural
reality. What we have in mind in this portion of our paper is the
fact that in conformity with this ontological reality, the living out
of grace should be a mature process in which our students are

conscious of the supernaturality of the life which is theirs. There are many ways of approaching this subject. Perhaps a simple and rather logical way of organizing the material might be to discuss it in terms of the three supernatural areas of activity—faith, hope, and charity.

To begin, then, with faith. It is clear that the students who leave our colleges and universities should leave with a much deeper grasp of what it means to be a Catholic than they had when they entered our schools. Somehow or other, during these years there should have occurred a change of that attitude which characterizes a child's acceptance of faith into that of the adult who knows why and what he believes. The faith possessed by our graduates should be a clear acceptance of Christianity with all its implications on the supernatural basis of the revelation given by God. It should be, moreover, an accurate faith, in which the assent given to revelation is directed toward those truths which are really part of revelation and not toward those peripheral issues which so often border on superstition and magic. Not only that, but the faith should be something which involves an understanding that is accurate and meaningful to the students and to those with whom they will come into contact.

Perhaps we could express the point by saying that our students, when they leave us, should possess a culturally and theologically educated faith. By this we would mean that both aspects of the theological process would have been provided them during their college years. The first aspect, that of clarifying for them the factual elements relative to what they believe and why they believe it, should rest upon a clear perception of the historical realities of the revelational process, both in the Old Testament and during the period of the Church, a rather accurate understanding of the sources of revelation, and an objective appraisal of the contemporary reality of the Church itself. The second or more analytic aspect of theology would then deepen for them an understanding of what the revelation really means and what its implications are for man's life on this earth. However, such deepening of faith would not be something which employed only abstract knowledges or analytic types of understandings; it should involve the whole of human culture past and present. In the theologizing process, if it be integral, one must utilize in the "minor of the syllogism" not just philosophical understandings, but any understanding of God, man, or his world drawn from history, literature, art, science, any discipline of knowledge which man develops in his educated life.

The faith of our students should be thus scientifically deepened; yet it must remain throughout realistic and personal. There is no opposition between a very deeply personal and operative faith and an academic and scientific deepening of this faith. Sometimes the opposition is raised—and much fruitless discussion has sometimes resulted—between an intellectual approach and a volitional approach. Actually, this opposition vanishes, at least in the area of theology, if one realizes that what is to be communicated is a *concrete and realistic understanding*. Between this and the scientific there is no opposition, nor is there any opposition between this and the volitional impact and emotional conditioning which should result. Opposition can arise between an excessively abstract presentation of the faith and the emotional and volitional carry-over. But such an abstract presentation of the faith is neither adequate nor genuinely and deeply theological. One can see that if theology be correctly taught our students, then it can function as a most important synthesizing principle, not just in their whole academic formation, but in the entirety of their conscious living. Such should be the type of faith that we would want our students to have as they leave our schools to begin their life in the world, a faith deepened and clarified by everything else which they have learned in the educational process.

When they leave our doors in graduation, we would hope that our students would have developed a genuine personal relatedness to the three Divine Persons, a relatedness which they would have learned to express in their own prayer. To put it another way, we would want them to have a genuine supernatural life, a conscious and affective response to the revelation which they have encountered in Sacred Scripture and in the sacraments of the

Church. Such a personal orientation toward God would be the product of our classroom instruction, as well as of the liturgical life which we would have encouraged, the special direction that they would have received through personal contact, and spiritual deepening in organizations such as the Sodality. Such development of faith would lead to genuine maturity and would fit them for the actual context of life in which they would live out the years which lie ahead of them. Such a faith would prepare them to be genuine apostles, people capable of spreading an intelligent insight into revelation among those who are their intellectual and professional peers. Their faith would possess deep human warmth, a sense of happiness, and clarity derived from their entire college education, but above all a scientific approach to theology.

Patient Hope

Let us pass on to the need of supernatural hope in our students and graduates. Obviously, there is no question here of a naive trust that everything will somehow work itself out, but rather a question of that deep hope which many perceptive thinkers of our day have claimed is the greatest spiritual need of contemporary man. Our students, too, as they go out to face the task of Christianizing the world, are going to need a very profound trust in the supernatural power of the mystery of Christianity. They should leave us thoroughly realistic about life, its problems and its potentials, about the Church—a divine mystery expressing itself in human form. We must not leave them with naive, mistaken notions about the difficulty of the task which faces them if they will live truly as Christians. However, in orientating them toward a realistic appraisal of life, we should also be very careful that we do not destroy the idealism that is characteristic of youth and that all too many of our apostolically-minded Catholics lose long before middle age. We must teach them that the idealism to be preserved is one grounded, not in their own human capacities, but in the power of the Holy Spirit working in the midst of the Church.

When we send them forth to participate in the active life of Christianity, they must be prepared by mature patience with life; not that they will have acquired this completely, but at least they should be pointed in this direction. They must be prepared to be deeply patient with human society and its frail attempts to achieve a better situation for mankind. More importantly, they must be patient with themselves, ready to accept the fact that they have a deep need for redemption and that the process of supernatural transformation may take much longer than they anticipate and be achieved by means they do not expect. Again, they must be prepared to be patient with the mystery of the Church, to accept the fact that many elements in the Church may be in need of betterment, even rather deep reformation; the fact that within the Church the very people who should encourage the projects in which they will be interested may seem to be opposed to all that is good and noble. Even more profoundly, they must learn to be patient with God, that is to say, to accept the mystery which is enunciated already in the Old Testament when God says "My ways are not your ways."

However, in saying that our students must be patient, we must be sure that we understand what we mean; we do not mean that they should be passive. The truly patient person is not the one who just stands by waiting for things to happen, willing to accept them with an attitude of long-suffering. Rather, the truly patient man is one who works continuously and energetically to better the situation in which he finds himself, to help establish the Kingdom of God on this earth, and will continue with this effort even when things do not go according to his preconceived plans. The truly patient man continues as long as possible to achieve the things which he thinks should draw a good, either the one he intends or one whose ultimate worth is beyond the project which he himself had intended. Such hope is grounded in a deep and realistic appreciation of the mystery of the Church, to whose organic development the individual efforts of each one of us make some small but ultimately worthwhile contribution.

Christian Love

Thirdly, we can discuss Christian charity. Here our ideal should be to form graduates who have the hallmark of genuine maturity: they are men unafraid of love, faced with the prospect and the need to commit themselves to a life in which love must be exerted on every hand. Our graduates should be fitted to meet this challenge. Our classroom instruction and the other aspects of our college and university life should motivate them to express their human personalities in love of themselves, of their fellow-man, and above all, of almighty God. Love will demand that they make some courageous decisions, decisions which perhaps will not exactly coincide with their own personal selfishness, their own pleasure, or their own individual secular benefit. That they love this way, however, is a dictate of their Christian vocation. It remains as true in our day as in all previous periods of Christianity that the first law of a Christian is a law of love. It is by their love of others, a love which is deep and affective, that they will enter most profoundly into their destiny on earth, redemptive co-working with Christ.

That means that our students should be taught what love really means, what are its dynamics. Not only that, they must be presented, in the various academic disciplines which they study, with the insights and the motivations which will lead them to commit themselves to life in generous and responsible love. In the experience of communal life shared in college society, they must be led to discover the love of other people and to respond to this love by their own giving of themselves to the betterment of men's life together. They must be orientated to an apostolic expression of this love, being conscious of the fact that, as Christian, their love knows no bounds, but must extend to all mankind. They must be instructed—for it does require instruction—as to the way in which love, be it of self or of other men or of God, can grow; and they must be encouraged by some of the most basic orientations and atmosphere of the college to look on life as a process of growing even deeper in true Christian charity. It is here, of course, that an intelligent and active liturgical life can be an invaluable help.

One area of expressing love is particularly important for our students because of the specific society in which they live. Our students must leave us with the ability to live sympathetically and yet apostolically in a pluralistic society. Sympathetically, because it is not really easy to accept as something of genuine value the opinions of others who differ from us in matters as fundamental as religious belief. Yet our students must go out prepared to accept the deep sincerity as well as the open intelligence of these others who for the moment are separated from us in faith. While they must remain deeply appreciative of the dignity and freedom and sincerity of their fellow Americans, they must never abandon an apostolic outlook, an outlook which wishes to share with others a treasure which, for some strange reason, has been given to us, in God's providence. Such an apostolic point of view, if it be grounded in genuine love, will lead our students to go ever more deeply into the understanding of their faith in order that, confronting honestly the real questions of our fellow Americans in matters of religion, they can then give them an understanding of the Catholic position commensurate with their education and intellectual depth. Genuine charity will dictate also that in this pluralistic situation our Catholic college graduates will not pull themselves apart from others as a group without civic responsibility, but that they will cooperate to the fullness of their power in the betterment of the profane aspects of the world in which they find themselves, so that men may be better equipped to discover the deeper supernatural aspects of life.

Intellectually Apostolic

The third major area with regard to the spirituality of our students is: their spirituality should be intellectually apostolic. Because of the background, academic and cultural, which is theirs, there is a very special role in the apostolic life of the Church which should be filled by the graduates of our Jesuit institutions. The number of things to be done in the apostolate is without number, and there are many things which can be done by people who have not had the opportunities for intellectual formation which the graduates of our institutions have had. But there is an area, and a most important area, of the apostolate, one which in a sense is at the root of practically everything else, which can only be handled by those who have had training such as that which we wish to give our graduates. The thought-life of the Church, its advance, its deepening, and its spread into the intellectual currents of our times is of the utmost importance and must be the basis of all external development of Christianity. The furthering of those aspects of other apostolic endeavors which require deep and practical thinking is central in the whole development of the Church. It is in this area that our Jesuit college graduates have a most important function to fill; and if they have an important function to fill, the spirituality which we develop in them should prepare them for this function. Under this notion of the spirituality of our students being one which is intellectually apostolic, one should first begin with the point that they should be deeply formed in their faith. Not only must they believe, but that understanding must be in categories of thought and life experience which are meaningful to the people of our times. Our students must understand their faith, must be theologically formed in it in such a fashion that they are then able to translate the significance of their faith and its practical applications in a way which can be understood by those who do not enjoy the Faith.

We must insist, however, that the theological formation given them in their faith be one which is not couched in abstract categories of thought or in abstract terminology. Rather, it should be deeply rooted in the culture which is theirs. This culture is not one flowing from Rome and Greece, not even one flowing from Rome, Greece, and Israel; but is a culture which also has deep roots in the Anglo-Saxon world. If the formation in faith does not take into account the total cultural picture, if our students are

not taught to relate to their cultural heritage of arts and literature
and history and law the deeper insights of their faith, then they will
not be able to exercise with intelligence and maturity that intellectual apostolate which is proper to them.

In this area of a deep and practical vision of what Christianity
really is, one insight seems to be of key importance; that is the
vision of the reality of the Church. If our students are to exercise
that role which is theirs, a role which is genuine and important,
a role contributing to the development of the intellectuality of
Christianity, then they must really understand the reality of the
Church. They must see the Church for what it is and that it is
truly this. Moreover, they must grasp the reality of their own role
within the Church in order to understand exactly what it is they
are meant to contribute, what this thought-life of the Church really
means, and how they can play a role in its deepening and expansion. Too few of our students have any notion of the life of the
Church itself as a developing process. Too few of them are really
aware of the way in which the faith-life of the Church is meant
to be a leaven in the midst of the intellectual life of our times.

Lacking this insight, they can have little grasp of the way in
which they themselves, as educated, mature Catholics are meant
to contribute to this process, so that the thinking of the decades
ahead may be drastically different. Given such an insight into
the reality of the situation, it may well be that many of our students
will be attracted to genuine Catholic apostolic action. Students at
present are somewhat repulsed because they think of Catholic
action only in terms of somewhat artificial projects which Catholic
action groups think up to keep themselves busy. Not only that,
but if this deeper realization of the true apostolate which is theirs
comes home to them, then they will see that this apostolate is in
no sense something which will take them away from either professional achievement or true personal growth. As a matter of fact,
they will begin to realize that only if they are professionally profi-
cient, only if they are genuinely personal, will they be able to be
effective in this area of intellectual apostolate.

Another approach to this question which covers somewhat the same ground but perhaps in a different fashion is this: we wish to turn out from our Catholic institutions, particularly from our Jesuit colleges and universities, graduates who are able to size up new situations in a developing world, who are able to evaluate these situations and guide them according to a Christian pattern. To do this, which is a most difficult task, to express the basic realities of Christianity in new forms, to appraise according to Christian principles situations which have never existed before in history, and to find solutions which will fit the Christian vision of life, is something which requires a deep formation on the part of our students. Verbal knowledge of the principles of Christianity and a formulistic explanation of the mysteries of faith will not suffice. In the formation which we give them, they must be led beneath the surface of things to the point where they see the real dynamic forces of Christianity which are at work in every period of history and in every culture and civilization, so that, understanding these deeper realities of the faith, they will be able to make them operative in a future situation.

If the Catholic apostolate in the years to come is to be effective, there must be some place in the Church a hard-core group of intelligent people who are able to see the genuine developing needs of the Church. Our Catholic action groups are filled with people who can carry out projects, people who can keep active. What is lacking is genuine intellectual leadership so that the action is going some place, so that the projects are accomplishing what needs to be done. Apostolic Catholics with insight necessary for intelligent planning must come from our schools. Our function must be to train at least a certain portion of our student body to fulfill this absolutely vital role in the Church's life. More and more, if the Church follows its present trends, decisions and planning and the implementation of these decisions and plans are going to be left to lay people within the Church. Many of the lay people who will logically fall into this situation will be the graduates of our institutions. We must prepare for the situation by training them so that they can intellectually approach the responsibilities and potentials which will be theirs, so that they can fill the function which the Church will expect of them.

All of this would seem to add up to the fact that we must find some way of developing within our students a spirituality which is thoroughly integrated with their intellectual development, a spirituality which takes into account what is happening to them as they study literature and art and history and philosophy and science, a spirituality which builds upon rather than opposes the academic formation which they are receiving in the rest of their education. We must be careful that some of the subtle anti-intellectual strains which have been found at times in the spiritual writers in the Church do not seep into our presentation of Christian spirituality, and that our students feel no opposition between their intellectual life and what we call their spiritual life. Rather, the development of their cultural life should be totally absorbed into and transformed by the deeper vision of faith and the orientations of hope and charity.

Not only that; their spirituality must be built upon and exploit the apostolic activity which will be theirs in the midst of a professional or business life. An apostolate must be given them as something which is in itself sanctifying. Above all, if this apostolate is an intellectual one, we should find it possible to explain to them how, being intellectually aware of the reality of the Church and its developing thought-life, they can live in a constant consciousness of this reality and so be developing a spirituality of contemplation in the midst of activity. There are activities which are distracting in a way which is destructive of genuine supernatural life. Yet, if the activities which people are engaged in are those which are really personal and intellectual, there should be no real opposition between these and the development of a truly contemplative mentality. It seems to me that in thinking through this problem for ourselves, and in training our students in a spirituality which will be at the same time apostolic and intellectual, we will be returning to some of the deepest insights of St. Ignatius and understanding more profoundly those things which are characteristic of our Ignatian heritage. The spirituality which is ours is described by Nadal—and he is following Ignatius—as being one of contemplation in action. Our graduates—like ourselves—are called to a key role in the development of the Church's intellectual life in the course of Christian history. In the midst of consciously living the thought-life of the Church in an ever more profound fashion, we will be quite naturally, and almost necessarily, deepening our contemplative spirituality.

These, then, are the three points, the three salient areas, which seem to suggest some of the things we must keep in mind in our Jesuit colleges and universities, in our teaching of philosophy and theology and the other disciplines as well as in those co-curricular or extra-curricular aspects which also contribute to the development of the total personal growth of our students. How these objectives can be obtained is a much more complicated and more difficult question.

Selected Bibliography

Braso, Gabriel. *Liturgy and Spirituality*. Translated by Leonard Doyle. Collegeville, Minn.: The Liturgical Press, 1960.

Cooke, Bernard, S.J. "Faith and Human Personality," *Catholic Mind,* LVII (1958), 450–458.

Danielson, J. "The Ignatian Vision of the Universe and of Man," *Cross Currents,* IV (1954), 357–366.

Lavelle, Louis. "In the Presence of Being," *Modern Catholic Thinkers,* edited by A. R. Caponigri. London: Burns & Oates, 1958.

Mouroux, Jean. *The Christian Experience*. New York: Sheed & Ward, 1954.

Oraison, Marc. *Love or Constraint*. New York: P. J. Kenedy & Sons, 1959.

Teilhard de Chardin, Pierre, S.J. *The Divine Milieu*. New York: Harper, 1960.

Young, William, S.J. (ed.). *Finding God in All Things*. Chicago: H. Regnery Co., 1958.

13

THE PLACE OF
RELIGIOUS ACTIVITIES ON
THE CATHOLIC COLLEGE CAMPUS

Vincent J. O'Flaherty, S.J.

The term "religious activities" is used here to describe certain features of the Christian life: the Sacrifice of the Mass, retreats and missions, spiritual direction, organizations intended either for a select number of people within a given environment or for the faithful at large. The point at issue is whether such activities ought to take place on the Catholic college campus, whether they should be actively promoted by the institution itself.

The point of view may be taken that any attempt by a college to make of such activities an integral part of student life constitutes a prostitution of the very notion of education. Indeed, even an educator or teacher who is a good Catholic may be found (though he would be distinctly in the minority) who would say that the promotion of the moral, religious, and spiritual formation of its students is simply not the business of the Catholic college, except insofar as a well-integrated curriculum excellently taught gives glory to God. Let other, proper agencies provide religious activities, this man would say. To do so is not a college's affair and can only jeopardize its tending well that portion of the Lord's vineyard which it is supposed to be tending.

However, since the school is a thing of the Church, any judgment on the function of a Catholic college must take into account the nature of the Church's life. The whole of the Church's life, of which Catholic colleges are a part, is centered on that

VINCENT J. O'FLAHERTY, S.J. 239

unique act by which the Father wills to be worshipped, the celebration of the memorial of the Lord.

This does not mean that a chemistry course should include liturgical overtones or moral exhortations or anything except chemistry, any more than it means that a Catholic college should be satisfied with anything less than academic excellence. But a Catholic college cannot be satisfied even if it is achieving academic excellence, even if its student body is responding wholeheartedly to a well-integrated curriculum composed of intellectually challenging courses taught by dedicated and competent teachers working under optimum conditions. To the extent that the object on which the effort of the Catholic college is focused, the student (and we have in mind throughout this chapter the Catholic undergraduate), does not worship God in spirit and truth, the effort is, in the final analysis, to no avail. Such a concept of education, seeming to be an attack on human values and on the whole institution of education, may bring on outraged cries from those who do not hold it. Then Catholic educators have to resign themselves to being the cause of outraged cries. Catholic education, like everything else, finds its meaning in the Mass.

There is, then, one moment above all to which the Catholic college in its work with the student looks. It is not the moment when the student achieves, or at least begins the earnest pursuit of, academic excellence. It is that moment when, in union with the risen victim-priest, Jesus Christ, the student who is pursuing academic excellence places at the disposal and service of the Divine Majesty his life and his efforts to become "a workman who does not need to be ashamed of his work, one who knows how to handle the claims of truth like a master."[1] This means that if his search for truth is to be truly relevant, the student must bring it to the altar and offer it there, and it must be taken up into the offering of Himself to the Father being renewed in the Mass by Truth Incarnate. And the student's offering of his search for truth has meaning only if it is the offering of a human being who seeks to know and desires to accomplish what the Father wills him to do with his life in the service of Jesus Christ, who is still about His work of redemption today in His body, the Church.

Now one may agree heartily that the whole institutional effort of the Catholic college finds its meaning in the Church's supreme act, the Mass. One may further agree that the Catholic college has to consider all efforts expended on the student abortive unless the student relates what he learns to the worship of God in spirit and truth. Yet one may, nevertheless, still contend that the Catholic college ought to promote the Christian life among its students in a manner proper to a college, that is, in the teaching situation. This would seem to be especially true in an era when theology is gradually assuming once again the pre-eminent position which belongs to it by right in the Catholic college curriculum.

Certainly no one can deny that the growth in the student of the Christian life requires the competent presentation and serious study of the history of salvation, of God's Word about Himself become flesh in Jesus Christ, of the risen Christ's body, His Church, and those carriers to men of trinitarian life, her sacraments. Not only the study of theology (and this would include the study of Christian morality and spirituality), but also the study of philosophy, the humanities, and other subjects can be a positive factor in the student's progress as a Christian. This can happen without the nature of the discipline suffering the least violence or manipulation. And this will happen, especially, if the various courses are taught by priests, religious, or lay people who, by the witness they bear to Christ in their own lives, exert a considerable Christianizing influence on their students simply by being good teachers in the classroom.

Why then do we find religious activities within the Catholic college structure? Are they elements foreign to the college? Have they been introduced onto the campus because their promoters have misunderstood the proper function of educational institutions in the Church? Or have they been introduced because other agents which should properly have been providing for the students' spiritual needs were, in fact, not doing so? Do religious activities on the Catholic college campus play an essential role in the formation of the student?

In coping with this question it is important to realize that there is one element which must find a place in the formation of the Catholic college student if he is to reach Christian maturity. Normally the school must provide this element; no other agent can do it satisfactorily. It cannot, however, be handled adequately in the classroom. This element is the integration of the student's academic pursuits and of the preparation he is making for his future career with his Christian vocation. It is because of the role they play in the effecting of this integration that spiritual activities on the campus are normally indispensable.

It is remarked frequently enough that Catholic colleges have not been notably successful in developing this singleness of vision and purpose in their students. Catholic college alumni are known in their parishes as good Catholics who raise model families, are often seen at the Communion rail, and tithe generously. They are also, often enough, respected within their professional or business milieu for their integrity and competence. But relatively seldom do they seem to realize, or do their acquaintances perceive, any effective unification of these two theaters of their lives. The sense of vision and of purpose is missing which could transform them, within their professional and business lives, into apostles. One often hears the charge made that the impact of our Catholic college graduates on American society has been on the whole insignificant. More often than not, the reason given for this is the lack of Catholic intellectuals. But an even more compelling reason may be advanced: the lack of vision of these Catholics, their failure really to have grasped, during their formative years, the connection between their education and their Christian vocation, between scholarship and their Christian vocation, between culture and their Christian vocation, between the career for which they were preparing and their Christian vocation.

It is not enough for the college student to have the example before him of teachers who have achieved this integration in their own lives. The fact is that students all too often simply miss the point. Neither is it enough for the student to be told of the need for this integration or even to be given the doctrinal basis for it in theology or religion class. Among the other things to be learned at college, the student must learn, there where the problem presents itself, to live, to act out, this integration. St. Ignatius Loyola wrote once that members of his order engaged in teaching in colleges were to see to the students' "good education in life and doctrine"[2]; therefore, not only in doctrine, but in life too. Indispensable lessons concerning life, the living of the Christian life, can only be learned within the family or the parish. But there are other equally indispensable lessons in the living of the Christian life which only the college can teach. Only the Catholic college can supply the atmosphere in which the student can begin to effect this integration within himself. And the college does this precisely by means of religious activities.

This is certainly true of the student Mass. When a group of college students participate in a mass celebrated in a college chapel, they worship together as members of a particular sort of community, one made up of college students. They may have come originally from different parts of a city or even a nation and may represent a number of different diocesan or social or economic or ethnic backgrounds. Two facts concerning them account for their being together now at this altar, their community of faith and that of their educational involvement.

The psychological helps this situation affords to the individual for bringing unity into his life as Catholic and as student are based on the simple fact that here at this altar a group of people dedicated to academic and professional pursuits are worshipping together. The integration is being enacted to an extent that would not be possible were the student to attend Mass in another setting and with another group of people. It need hardly be added that the sort of celebration of Mass had in mind here is not that in which the priest goes silently about his business while a shuffling and coughing but otherwise mute assembly of young people marks time behind him.

The efficacy of the Mass in the individual Christian's life depends to a large extent on the disposition in which that individual comes to the Mass. Because of this fact, the wonderful sacramental and liturgical renewal in the Church in our time could degenerate into a deordination, were the need for contemplation in the life of the Christian, and therefore of the young American Catholic college student also, ever to be forgotten. Hans Urs von Balthasar, in his modern spiritual classic, *Prayer,* has remarked that "a liturgical movement unaccompanied by a contemplative movement is a kind of romanticism, an escape from time, and inevitably calls up, by opposition, the counter-romanticism of a false conception of the sacred character of secular activity."[3] And, concerning the intimate relationship between contemplation and the liturgy, he has said, "The individual contemplating in his room is not separated from the choir of the Church at prayer, but . . . celebrates her liturgy in a different form, no less real and effective."[4]

Contemplation is vital to the Catholic college student if he is to grow to Christian maturity. And, again, he must be taught that it is not simply as a member of a family or a parish but, in an especial way at this stage of his life, as a student that he should come to contemplation. Otherwise contemplation itself may become an escape from reality, instead of what it must be, a listening to God's word directed to the core of a man's being and a learning how to answer to that word.

Student retreats offered by Catholic colleges (the word "retreat" is far from appropriate for the thing signified), are not always conducive to contemplation. In fact, it is possible for retreat schedules to be so cluttered with over-long conferences, various devotions, group projects, and question-box periods as to render contemplation all but impossible. Yet the retreat can and should be a holy time when the student who is disposed to do so can give himself wholly to the contemplation of the mysteries of the life of the Word and the meaning these mysteries have for his own life. God, indeed, never confronts a man in prayer but that this confrontation takes the form of an injunction, a call. It is in time of retreat especially that the individual receives not only clarity concerning the demands of love God has on his life but also courage to respond in obedience to those demands.

Even prescinding from practical considerations, the student derives a special advantage from making a retreat geared to students and made available to them by the college they attend. The student has come to the college to prepare himself for a future in which as a mature person he will place what, by virtue of his education, he has become and knows and can do at the disposal of the human family's common good. In so preparing himself it is essential that his eye be single. His life as a member of human society and his Christian life must not be allowed to develop at different levels. This readying of himself for responsible, productive adulthood must be fused with the student's even more basic task of ascertaining God's Will for himself, of striving to hear from what direction Christ is calling to him personally, "Follow me." It is pre-eminently within the atmosphere of a well-directed student retreat that the young person can integrate his concentration on preparing himself for the future with his responsibility to follow Jesus Christ's call to him wherever it leads.

In these matters of learning to contemplate and of integrating one's life as student with one's life as Christian, one's task of preparing for adulthood with one's task of finding God's Will, spiritual direction can play a crucial role. By spiritual direction is meant here neither the solving of moral problems nor psychological counseling nor the passing on of the director's own personal experience, although all of these may play their parts. Above all, spiritual direction should be for the student an experience of opening himself to someone who can help him to see what in his life here and now constitutes a response to, and what a turning away from, God's call to him. It is a fact of experience that when they seek such spiritual guidance, young people turn to teachers whom they admire and trust. In turn, teachers who are qualified to give spiritual direction are in an especially favorable position to help their students integrate present preoccupations and plans for the future with their Christian vocation.

There are students on every Catholic college campus who need and deserve to have true spiritual direction, who have the dispositions necessary for contemplation, who feel the weight of Christ's call to be understood and followed, who turn up at Mass and Communion with some regularity. Among these some may be natural leaders or intellectually gifted; others may tend to merge into the crowd. In any case, such students would seem to deserve special attention. Certainly they ought not be left to try to go it alone in their efforts to live full Christian lives during difficult years. That could lead only to discouragement, to the growth of an individualistic notion of their faith, or to the failure to realize their full spiritual potential. When banded together into groups for the living of the Christian life, such students not only give each other mutual support in the hard business of going from good to better; they also become a true leaven within the college community.

The sort of group envisioned here is not the informal, casually organized study or inquiry club, but rather an organization with a rule of life to which the members formally commit themselves. Some, faculty members as well as students, may be reluctant to admit the value of such relatively well-organized groups or suspicious that a way of life proper to religious is being foisted upon these young lay people. The reluctance and suspicion may come of a certain discomfort at the thought of these young people committing themselves at all formally to anything which will make demands on them in the name of fidelity or responsibility. But normally some degree of commitment and organization constitutes the price one must pay for spiritual formation and apostolic effectiveness, especially in an age when Christ's adversaries are exceedingly well-organized.

It is important that there be such groups on Catholic college campuses, involving students as such and geared to students' needs and problems and schedules. Too, the college campus affords an excellent training ground for the sort of apostolate their members will exercise later on in the professional and business world. Moreover, the college itself benefits from the presence of this leaven. These groups need not develop into exclusive clubs on the periphery of the college's life. If they develop as they should, they can serve as the heart of the student body, injecting Christian life and spirit everywhere on the campus.

Thus far the case for on-campus religious activities has been that such activities are needed if the student is to integrate his academic efforts into his Christian vocation. These same religious activities can, however, contribute to the academic process itself. The student who engages in these activities with an understanding of what he is about and why he is about it, becomes, precisely because of this experience, a better student. The human being who has broken loose from his own self-centeredness and put himself actively at the service of the Son of Man and his cause approaches the arts and sciences with an openness and with a sense of purpose which can only enhance his potential as a student. Again, the student, precisely because of his engagement in spiritual activities, comes to an experiential Christian understanding of man and the world which both challenges and completes the understanding of man and the world that is to be had from the study of literature, history, philosophy, and theology.

The religious activities described thus far presume the presence within Catholic college student bodies of young people capable of responding generously and enthusiastically to the demands of the Christian vocation; and there are such. The hard fact is, however, that many of the hundreds of young people one sees milling about the campus between classes lead less than outstanding Christian lives. Many have only a very notional grasp of the good news of Christianity. Much more real to them are noise and excitement and the claims of their bodies and money. Their spiritual aspirations reach often not much higher than a desire to save their souls; some give only occasional thought even to that.

If it is true that the Catholic college, as an *alma mater,* must have a deep concern for the spiritual welfare of all her students, she must show a special solicitude for these. Promoting a meaningful, attractive, and accessible sacramental and liturgical life on campus is an essential means of reaching these students. This, however, is not an all-sufficient solution. Expending time and energy on the formation of the spiritually sensitive and apostolically-minded students is itself an effective way of reaching those who steer clear of chapel and priests.

The college can attempt to draw these students closer to the life of the Church by providing priests who understand them as their confessors, by scheduling missions (the expression "open retreat" is being deliberately avoided here as unfortunate) conducted by priests who know the mentality and problems of these students. The college can promote an organization, membership in which commits the student to the faithful carrying out of some basic practices of Christian life, the daily offering of oneself to Jesus Christ, attendance at Mass and reception of Communion on some days besides Sunday, some form of devotion to the Mother of God—all of these done with apostolic intent.

An implication underlying this entire treatment of spiritual activities on the Catholic college campus has been that the teachers whom the student encounters in the classroom and the administrators with whom he deals in the college offices are, when these have the power or the qualifications, precisely those who should offer the Masses the students attend and direct the retreats and missions the students make and counsel the students in spiritual matters and hear their confessions and moderate their spiritual organizations. In this way the students will avoid constructing a dichotomy between the spiritual and the academic. More positively, they will, through this twofold relationship with people whose influence on their formation is considerable, learn to effect that integration of doctrine with life which is so essential to Christian maturity.

This places heavy demands on the time, energies, and apostolic zeal of the teachers and administrators concerned. However, although in particular instances the playing of these two roles may be impossible, they are not at all incompatible. This has been amply demonstrated by authentic scholars, fine teachers, and efficient administrators who have at the same time given themselves devotedly and effectively to the spiritual formation of students.

As the laity assume an increasingly active role in the life and mission of the Church, their need for spiritual as well as intellectual formation will increase, a spiritual formation suited to their calling and their responsibilities. The burden on the priests, religious, and laity concerned with this formation will increase correspondingly. But if God wills that our Catholic colleges provide an atmosphere conducive to the full flowering of the Christian life, he will provide the men and the means.

Notes

1. II Tim. 2:15 (Knox translation).
2. *Monumenta Historica Societatis Iesu: Monumenta Ignatiana*, Series I, IV, 311. Letter to Father Anthony Araoz, December 1, 1551.
3. Hans Urs von Balthasar, *Prayer* (New York: Sheed & Ward, 1961), p. 98.
4. *Ibid.*, p. 83.

14

NON-RELIGIOUS ACTIVITIES
AND SPIRITUAL DEVELOPMENT
P. H. Ratterman, S.J.

In explaining the relation of non-religious activities to the moral, religious, and spiritual formation of the college student, I include as non-religious activities everything that occurs in student life which is clearly non-instructional and is not traditionally understood as religious.

First I shall discuss a particular facet of spiritual formation which is especially important to this whole consideration. Second, I shall outline briefly four areas of non-religious campus activities and demonstrate how each is of particular significance to spiritual development. And third, I shall discuss four problems, currently very much alive in the non-religious activities area, the resolution of which is very important to the spiritual formation of students on our campuses.

I. SHIFT OF EMPHASIS
IN LAY SPIRITUALITY

There has been a significant development in the spiritual formation of students on our campuses, a consideration of which will help to bring into focus the importance of non-religious activities to the spiritual formation of Jesuit students.

It shall be a basic presumption of this paper that the full spiritual development of the students involves a great deal more than what has been traditionally referred to as "the interior life." Until recent years the predominant emphasis of lay spirituality, and therefore of student spirituality, seemed to be placed on "the interior life" or personal salvation. Love of neighbor was not forgotten but was largely limited to carrying out corporal works of mercy by an individual or by a pious society, and this was frequently explained as an overflow from the development of the interior life.

Of late years there has been a gradual but quite radical change of emphasis whereby the basic concept of the spiritual life, more and more being proposed to the Catholic layman, is precisely our Jesuit ideal of "seeing God in all things" and "service" to Christ's Kingdom, the Church. There is today an ever increasing realization of the full meaning of "the Kingdom" to the total mission of the Church. The relationship between political and economic justice and the salvation of souls is coming more into focus. The full religious implications of such basic social concepts as human dignity, freedom, rights, and responsibilities are being forced upon us by revolutionary social developments. The spiritual formation of students must, as a result, concern itself with many matters which are not explicitly religious, and the non-religious activities program must assume a greater responsibility for the spiritual formation of our students.

II. CATEGORIES OF NON-RELIGIOUS
ACTIVITIES AND THEIR RELATION
TO THE SPIRITUAL DEVELOPMENT
OF OUR STUDENTS

Non-religious campus activities do not group easily because of their tremendous variety in purpose, form, and content. However, for the purposes of our discussion campus activities may be divided into the following four categories: (1) those which develop an appreciation for the true, the good, and the beautiful, which I shall refer to as "liberal arts activities"; (2) those which develop the natural moral virtues; (3) those which develop respect for law and authority; and (4) those which develop social-mindedness.

In order to demonstrate the importance of non-religious activities to the spiritual development of students, let me say a word about the activities in each of these categories and point out briefly their relationship to student spiritual development.

A. Liberal Arts Activities

There is a whole category of non-religious activities the goal and purpose of which is identical with that of the liberal arts. Dramatic societies, glee clubs and choral groups, debating societies, science clubs, language clubs, literary societies—this whole myriad of student organizations—perform in the co-curricular activities area the function of the liberal arts in the classroom, exposing students to the true, the good, and the beautiful in the material and human universe. These non-religious activities familiarize a student with the natural beauty, wonder, and order of the created universe, making him receptive to the eternal truth, beauty, and goodness that is God. Properly directed, they can lead a student to "see God in all things."

In our modern era of specialization, where there is such intense pressure in the classroom to complete degree requirements through the attainment of specific knowledge, these activities fulfill a definite "liberal arts need" on our campuses. Very frequently it is only in the out-of-class liberal arts activity that the student finds time to wonder about the larger implications of what he studies in the classroom.

B. Activities Which Develop
Natural Moral Virtues

Second, there is a category of non-religious activities which are very important to the spiritual development of students since, either as their principal aim or as a by-product, they develop the natural moral virtues and a consequent appreciation of basic moral truth and goodness. In a sense, of course, all activities rightly pursued develop natural virtues; but there are, I submit, certain non-religious activities having to do with social propriety and etiquette which more directly than others develop the natural moral virtues.

Learning to be cooperative, considerate, and thoughtful of others in dormitory life is such an activity. Sportsmanship and fair play on the field and in the stands; respect for faculty, clerical and lay; refinement and respectability at proms and weekend dances; clean language in the locker room and student lounge; proper dress and good manners—these are all non-religious refinements which are characteristic of a gentleman in the natural order. They are all natural virtues and they are conspicuously present or absent on individual campuses depending on whether or not there are non-religious programs and "activities" by which such qualities are developed and made the expected and accepted thing.

The development of natural virtues is obviously an objective of the religious program on any campus. To achieve this goal, however, religious ideals and the effects of religious organizations must be supplemented by strong non-religious programs.

C. Activities Which Develop
Respect for Law
and Authority

The third category of non-religious campus activities which I consider important to the spiritual development of students is made up of those which develop respect for law and authority. The most effective of these activities are those which involve students themselves in the responsibilities which accompany the making of laws and the exercise of authority. I have in mind that complex of activities popularly referred to as "Student Government," but more accurately described as "Student Participation in University Government."

It must be kept in mind that young men of college age are rebellious of authority almost by psychological necessity. It is part of growing up, to resent and challenge authority at every turn. Reasonable involvement in the exercise of university authority with respect to their own activities helps students to overcome this rebellious challenge by exposing them to the difficulties and frequent frustrations which are incident to the administration of a university society. College students who learn to administer wisely the functions of group self-government develop necessarily a deep respect for law and authority.

Any program which serves to develop respect for law and authority in college students is important to spiritual development for the following reasons. First, respect for law and authority is not just a civic virtue but a religious virtue as well. Second, respect for university law and authority cannot but lead to a more ready acceptance of civic and ecclesiastical authority. Third, participation in the law-making and authority functions of the university teaches students through actual experience the universal purpose of law and authority, the ordering of society to ideals and goals. Fourth, such programs develop mature social responsibility. And fifth, such programs forestall the frustration which more mature students understandably develop, with a possible attendant anti-clericalism, if kept too long under an authoritarian discipline they have long outgrown.

D. Activities Which Develop
Social-Mindedness

Another group of campus activities which are important for spiritual development is comprised of those which develop social-mindedness. We find on our campuses today a proliferation of student groups representing political stands of every hue and supporting all manner of social causes. We find our students (even priests and nuns) walking in picket lines and participating in public demonstrations—all in the name of social justice.

Explain or criticize the modern student concern for social causes as one will, it must be recognized as a phenomenon to be considered in modern education and, I suggest, a phenomenon to be turned to the spiritual advantage of our students. The greatest enemy of both education and religion on a college campus is student apathy. There is little apathy on today's university campus unless it is one imposed from above.

Is it not possible that some relationship exists between this sudden concern for social problems and the new emphasis on social salvation which we find today in the spirituality of the layman? Cannot all of this campus interest, enthusiasm and energy somehow be turned to "seeing God in all things" and "serving" Christ's Kingdom?

Apropos of this discussion are the remarks of Pope John XXIII in paragraphs 231–32 of *Mater et Magistra:*

Education to act in a Christian manner in economic and social matters will hardly succeed unless those being educated play an active role in their own formation, and unless education is also carried on through action.

Just as one cannot acquire the right use of liberty except by using liberty correctly, so one learns Christian behavior in social and economic matters by actual Christian action in those fields.

III. NON-RELIGIOUS ACTIVITY
PROBLEMS IMPORTANT TO
STUDENT SPIRITUAL
DEVELOPMENT

There are many problems in the non-religious activities area the resolution of which is very important to the spiritual formation of students on our campuses. Practically all of these problems are modern manifestations of the tension which exists between freedom and authority, or between freedom and order, on the university campus. Four of these problems are particularly germane to any consideration of student spiritual formation.

A. The Problem of Student Rights

The issue of student rights is very much alive today in university communities and is likely to become more so in the years ahead. It finds its most radical expression on secular campuses, but other colleges are by no means exempt from its influence.

Any number of forces seem to be contributing to an exaggerated and educationally unsound demand for certain student rights. First, secular universities have abandoned in varying degree any responsibility to teach and require traditionally accepted Christian moral standards. Along with this an increasing number of parents seem to consider their responsibility for moral and educational guidance as terminating with the completion of high school. "He is old enough to decide for himself now," parents will say. It is but one further step for college students to judge that religion and morals are one's private affair and that neither university nor even family may interfere with what students consider their personal rights in these matters. The ultimate appeal is to "sincerity" or to the right for freedom of conscience. The obligation to develop an informed conscience, or an "informed sincerity," is either overlooked or considered an additional student right.

There is also the tendency on the part of students in secular schools to consider the university an appendage of the state and to apply civil concepts to the administration of all university affairs. For instance, students argue that since freedom of assembly, speech, and press are guaranteed by the constitution in civil society, these same freedoms should be respected without restriction in the university society. Or, applying civil norms to disciplinary situations, students demand a right to have recourse to all the legal formalities provided for criminal court proceedings.

Last and perhaps most significant, the concept of student rights appears to complement the ideal of education in a pluralistic society which will not allow state university commitments to any particular truths. The ultimate value in such a society is the right to seek truth. Any interference with free inquiry, open discussion, and free expression on the part of the university is interpreted as a denial of the student right to seek truth.

The promotion of student rights will, I feel, become stronger on the secular university campuses with corresponding repercussions on our own. An exaggerated concept of student rights ultimately challenges the very right and responsibility of a university to spiritual formation.

B. In Loco Parentis

In the summer of 1961 the United States National Student Association Congress, as a logical consequence of previous stands on student rights, adopted a policy statement denying the traditionally accepted in loco parentis relationship between student and university administration. Throughout the following two years Catholic administrators and, by and large, the students of Catholic colleges rallied to the defense of the in loco parentis doctrine with a great deal of support from seriously concerned administrators of secular schools.

The discussion of in loco parentis provokes, at least in my mind, a great deal of perplexity. I find I can accept in loco parentis as a basis of university responsibility and authority only with serious reservations. I cannot but wonder about my own position, for example, with respect to undergraduate married students who are self-supporting and independent of all parental authority. I ask myself questions about the graduate school student, the evening division student, the part-time undergraduate student—and then about students of college age in other educational situations: in military academies, in trade schools, in commercial art schools. The precise responsibility of the school to the total educational welfare of the student seems to differ in each case. Further, it seems always to be something tacitly agreed to and mutually understood when a student matriculates at a particular institution.

In defense of in loco parentis it could be supposed, possibly, that different schools, or the same school in different circumstances, assume a parental responsibility for education in differing degrees. But this does not solve the problem. Even more basic difficulties remain.

Parental authority is by its very nature an authority to be transcended. The mature man is self-responsible and therefore ultimately self-directed. Parental authority must be regarded as a substitutional authority which by its very nature ought to be phased out as the adolescent approaches and achieves maturity. Anyone exercising authority *in loco parentis* would be bound by this same obligation. If the authority exercised by a university is, therefore, exclusively *in loco parentis,* its authority necessarily must be phased out as students reach maturity. Does a university then have no authority over mature students?

I do not question that some schools exercise some authority over immature students *in loco parentis.* I do not question that in very many colleges we assume a great deal of responsibility for younger students *in loco parentis* when we advertise that we educate "the whole man" and encourage high school graduates to find on our campuses "a home away from home." Insofar, however, as a number of our students, it is to be hoped a high percentage, do reach maturity during their undergraduate years, an exclusive reliance on *in loco parentis* as a basis for authority and educational responsibility is, to my mind, indefensible. Many colleges have, I suspect, long since ceased to rely on *in loco parentis* as an exclusive or even extensive basis for authority. In actual practice we seem to have developed as the basis of our authority and responsibility an implicit, mutually understood contract which takes into account the fact that the total university community comprises a society which is not only distinct from all other societies, but is quite unique both in its goals and in the means it must use to achieve these goals.

When a student matriculates, either directly on his own authority or indirectly through his parents, he freely affiliates himself with a particular university society. There is a definite agreement according to which each party assumes certain obligations. The university assumes the obligation to educate. The student assumes the obligation to become educated. The specifics of the contract—the precise educational goal, the means to be used, the nature and extent of authority, etc.—are all determined by the matriculation contract. This, I submit, is the actual form of the student-college relationship which exists on a very large number of campuses today.

There are a number of reasons for explicitly recognizing that the student-university relationship is dependent on an educational contract. First, if university authority is based on contract it is not phased out as students mature. Parental responsibility for the contract is gradually replaced by self-responsibility as the student approaches and achieves maturity. The obligations of the contract for both university and student remain constant. The primary source of our educational responsibility and authority is a matriculation contract which is in good part structured by the very nature of Christian education.

Second, on a contract basis a university can make provision for situations where the exercise of authority is only remotely similar to that exercised by parents. After all, what parent has one thousand or ten thousand children? How is authority *in loco parentis* to be applied to the varied student population of a large university community? The college administrator had best conceive his job as exercising authority in a separate and distinct society which is united to achieve specific educational goals by what must necessarily at times be unique and distinctive means. The role of the college administrator is only analogous to that of the parent.

Third, a contract provides a basis of authority which is understandable and acceptable to students. Students can appreciate and identify themselves with goals. They can understand that a university has a right to adopt as policies and rules all the means which are proper and necessary to achieve accepted goals. There may be argument, and there always will be argument, about a specific policy or rule; but the authority structure is clear and accepted if it is determined by contract.

Fourth, the issue of student rights with upper-class undergraduates can be discussed and resolved with a great deal more understanding if the basis of university responsibility is considered to be contractual rather than transferred parental authority. The situation is much less confused if extension of parental authority is not a part of the argument.

In summary, I feel that if we are to fulfill our educational responsibilities as we conceive them, to form students in Christian wisdom, we must assume a greater responsibility for the total educational welfare of our students than the exercise of authority *in loco parentis* seems to provide.

C. Freedom with Responsibility

Agreement to educate the whole man involves the responsibility to develop in students a mature capacity for the right use of freedom. The obligation to develop this particular capacity is shared by the faculty, the director of spiritual activities, and the administrator of the co-curricular program. Difficulties which arise in educating students to a responsible use of freedom in the co-curricular area can result in whole "winters of discontent" and bring such frustration that administrators may seriously be tempted to deny that such an obligation really exists. "Students come to college to learn and not to teach," we may find ourselves saying. "Let students concentrate on academic excellence and the deepening of their spiritual lives. If the university leads students to attain these objectives—by rule and ukase if need be—it has fulfilled its responsibilities. Outside the classroom let students be seen and not heard. There is no problem in reconciling student freedom with university authority. Student freedom in the co-curricular area has no place on the university campus."

I personally find it difficult to reconcile such thinking—which I admittedly have exaggerated and caricatured—with the responsibility a university assumes to educate the "whole man." Surely such a commitment involves a responsibility to assist students in developing maturity; and maturity implies, if nothing else, an ability to exercise freedom with responsibility in live campus (and off-campus) situations. How is the mature capacity to exercise freedom with responsibility to be developed on a campus where students are allowed no freedom and given no responsibility outside the classroom?

Moreover, it would seem that the university ideal requires that free inquiry, open discussion, and free expression of views be encouraged in matters of educational importance. To what extent does the educational welfare of undergraduate students entitle them to inquire, discuss, and express their views? How, when, where, and under what circumstances is the expression of student views allowed? These are not easy questions to answer. On one hand there certainly exists a temptation in every college administrator's heart to restrict and censor student expression in order to assure a calm and objective campus atmosphere. But is it possible and always to the best educational interest of students to study in such an atmosphere? John Courtney Murray tells us that argument is a characteristic of truly civil society. There must be argument on the university campus, and the nature of the college student is such that he will not allow the argument to be confined to the classroom. He will at times be brash, irreverent, and disrespectful. These tendencies must be curbed, but the argument must be allowed.

There is a final reason why student life cannot be handled extensively by administrative rule and ukase. A significant number of students will rebel against such administration and as a consequence frustrate the entire educational mission of the university. There will always be a number of students, ironically well-represented in the high intelligence group we make every effort to attract, who will bring to campus, or soon acquire, some rather extreme and exaggerated ideas regarding student freedom and student rights. These leaders will consider it their obligation to arouse the general student body to an active support of their ideas. A student vs. administration mentality spreads as a logical sequence.

It is no answer to say—and I have heard this said—that such a student should be expelled. Others will only come to take his place. It is no answer to deny that students have any rights in the university community—and I have heard this too. If the university has obligations, the students have rights. The only answer seems to be that of developing policies of university administration which take into account our responsibility to develop in students a mature capacity for exercising freedom with responsibility. We must teach these principles by repeated explanation and consistent application to all pertinent campus situations.

This is not for the fainthearted but is, as I see it, the challenge to a university which assumes responsibility for educating the whole man. One wonders whether we have the courage to apply to student freedom the norm enunciated by Pope John XXIII, "Constraint where necessary; freedom where there is doubt."

D. Student Status in the University Community

A fourth student problem which is important to their spiritual formation is the increasing voice our students are demanding in university affairs.

Students have always found ways to make themselves heard when they have objected to a university policy or regulation (or athletic coach). We are faced today, however, with what I believe is a totally different type of student expression. Students today want to express their ideas on all manner of subjects, if not in the name of the university, at least in their own name as an important segment of the university. This expression may be positive or negative. It may take the form of endorsement or condemnation of something the university, a public figure, an organization, or a government agency has or has not done. It may be a protest by individual students, a petition signed by a group of students, a resolution adopted by a student organization, or a public demonstration. A great deal of this will be emotional and immature. However, we must take cognizance of the fact that students are not only exercising their right to express their views as private citizens in the civic community but are also seeking an increasing voice in university affairs as members of the university community.

A first reaction to such efforts on the part of students is that they be put in "their place." But this only brings the true problem into focus. What is "the place" of students in a university? What status do students have on the university campus?

Let me present the extreme student position in this matter. A university, so the argument runs, is basically a society of scholars united to pursue truth freely. Students and faculty are the essential elements of this society; administration is accidental to the true purpose of the university. Student government, according to this way of thinking, is necessarily anti-administration, its principal function being to protect against encroachments by administration on student rights and freedom. Student and faculty should speak for the university. Both "the place" and the voice of students are very important in a university society so conceived.

Our Jesuit idea of a university—by and large the traditional idea of all university education in our country—is something quite different. Administration plays a central role. Administration determines the original commitment of our universities, to educate youth in Christian wisdom. The administration must see to the fulfillment of this commitment in all phases of university life. Although the administration seeks and must have student cooperation in pursuing this fulfillment, the administration alone speaks with the official university voice. The official status and the voice of students in American universities have historically not been of significance or importance.

We are inclined to consider the position we have traditionally afforded students on our campuses as essential to the form of government established in our schools. And it may well be argued further that any sharing with, or delegation to students of, time-consuming and highly specialized administrative responsibilities may not only seriously jeopardize the welfare of our universities but would be inconsistent with the scholarship expected of the students.

However, having particularly in mind the type of active social apostolate for which we are preparing our students, we do well to give careful consideration to the matter of student status on our campuses and student voice in university affairs. Even though it is essential to our educational integrity that we reserve the right of final decision in all matters vital to our university commitment, I feel we ought more and more *to involve* students in matters which are immediately their concern in the university society. May I present my reasons?

First, I again return to our educational responsibility to develop maturity in our students. Would it not be strange if we encouraged our students to interest themselves in social problems of the larger society in which they live but discouraged any interest they might show in the university society of which they are members? Perhaps this is a place where the analogy between university and family society is applicable. Maturity is developed in children by involving them in the solution of family problems and encouraging them to assume family responsibilities. To develop maturity in students it seems essential that we involve them in seeking solutions to university problems and encourage them to assume responsibilities in the university society. We can hardly expect such involvement without allowing students increased status and voice.

Second, I timidly suggest that administrators might well arrive at wiser decisions with regard to many of the student problems we will face in the years ahead if we work with students in seeking solutions. The application of principles to practical campus situations demands a type of wisdom and insight into student views and attitudes which students frequently possess in greater measure than we do.

Third, we have a serious obligation to avoid any campus situation which may well frustrate our total educational mission. Specifically we must make every effort to avoid the student vs. administration mentality which, however undeserved, leads inevitably to carping student criticism and a consequent cynicism toward everything a university is and stands for. Mutual involvement in the common university enterprise with proportionate and shared responsibility, presupposing a mutual understanding and a deep mutual respect, seems essential to avoiding the student vs. administration mentality on the modern university campus.

It is important, both to our total educational mission and specifically to the spiritual welfare of our students, that we develop a student role which allows them a respected voice and status in the university community. This may take the form of improved communications, more frequent consultation, or granting older students a place on university committees—whatever is necessary to provide that students be truly involved in university affairs.

One must reasonably ask, can students be educated to the responsibilities which such status and voice presuppose in our university communities? I believe that they can. It is precisely my point that we cannot today educate students to the maturity required of the lay apostolate unless we significantly involve them in the affairs of the university society of which they are members.

15

MORAL FORMATION, HIGHER EDUCATION, AND DEMOCRATIC SOCIETY
Victor R. Yanitelli, S.J.

I. Understanding the Terms

The phrase "moral, religious, and spiritual formation" seems to breed a sense of unease in academic circles. Apart from the occasional Catholic educator who takes its import for granted—and for whom any examination of conceptual content would only be redundant—there are those who perceive in it an implied limitation of freedom, a climate of confinement. To them, the phrase tastes of dogma, which has no place in the academic scene as they see it. To escape semantic traps, it is well, then, to define terms—all but one of them. The definition of "formation" is reserved to a later part of the chapter since its proper understanding presupposes a whole range of prior relationships.[1]

Basically, "moral" describes the ethical dimension of a student's development, his habitual attitudes on justice, integrity, and respect for his neighbor's rights. "Religious" refers to the life of sanctifying grace at its minimal level, for instance, that of the Ten Commandments and the Precepts of the Church and all that this level implies by way of various devotions, the sacraments, and prayer. "Spiritual" would relate more to the ascetical life, the development of an inner core of spirituality on the higher level of the Counsels. All three include that whole area of student development which is other than intellectual or physical. All three interpenetrate one another and embrace the substance of both the natural virtues of prudence, justice, temperance, and fortitude, and the supernatural virtues of faith, hope, and charity.

These moral, religious, and spiritual elements of the student's formation are distinguishable in the abstract from the intellectual elements—but distinguishable only in the abstract. In the concrete, existential situation of the student here and now, they are inseparable. More than that, they need each other. Moral, religious, and spiritual formation is intrinsic and essential to the achievement of the college objective, the perfecting of the total human being. Yet, the whole process would become educationally meaningless if it did not take place right at the heart of intellectual formation.

What it comes down to, then, is that moral, religious, and spiritual formation is an over-all and pervasive part of the intrinsic work of the college. It is essential to the total educational process even though it is not its only end. The excellence of the Catholic college's intellectual formation, its development of the creative powers of imagination and of critical judgment, cannot in any way be compromised or subordinated. But this involves also concern for the emotional growth and stability of the student, the acquisition of self-discipline, the habit of judgment based on objective evidence. Neither process can be desultory or casual. They are the first steps in the perfecting of the human being.

II. Formation in Catholic Education

The Catholic college's efforts in the intellectual and the psychological areas of student development do not differ very much in principle from those of the rest of American education. They aim at bringing forth whatever excellence is possible to the intellect and to the psyche of the student. What Catholic education adds above and beyond the rest is a view of life wherein the student shapes his spirit according to the revelation of God given to man in the world and in the Word made flesh. This is the Incarnational view of life in which all things are sanctified.[2] By it, all knowledge is made sacred. Matter partakes of holiness because the Second Person of the Trinity testified to its goodness by assuming unto Himself a material body. The Incarnational view is the unifying trinitarian view of matter, man, and God. It alone gives ultimate significance to the questions of man's destiny and man's history, to the problems of life and the world, of love and society.

The Incarnational view of life is the great commitment of Catholic education. As such, it is not of itself in violation of the academic purposes. One or other mistakenly zealous Catholic educator may in his ardor subordinate intellectual aims to moral, religious, and spiritual formation. However, the formation itself as described above does not in principle contradict the free pursuit of the mind after truth. All the intellectual and human freedoms are open to the inquiring Catholic mind because all the truths of science, arts, letters, and philosophy are contained within the Incarnational view of life. In its highest and noblest sense the Incarnational commitment of Catholic education fosters full freedom in the pursuit of truth, because all truth is summed up in the Incarnation.

When the students work from a frame of reference which answers the why of life ultimately and therefore intelligibly, freedom paradoxically flowers rather than fades, whereas freedom without goals issues in an act of wandering uncertainty. Freedom for the sake of freedom, freedom without any limit, becomes chaotic rather than purposeful. This is the dilemma of Sartre and of the atheistic existentialists, for whom the greatest expression of freedom is the purely gratuitous act, i.e., the irrational act. It follows, then, that the moral, religious, and spiritual formation of the student is of the very essence of Catholic education, its *sine qua non*.

Moral, religious, and spiritual formation as it culminates in the Incarnational view of life does not and cannot end within the student himself. There is an overflow which must go beyond the student's personal and private development. In the thinking of the Church today and from the declarations of the recent Popes, part of one's personal salvation seems necessarily to demand some positive concern for the salvation of one's neighbor.

Because of the Incarnation, the student has become part of salvation history, part of the mission of Christ to the world, the involvement of love between God and man. Through the action of the Holy Spirit, he has become united with all the members of the Mystical Body and thus to Christ as its head. As a consequence, his moral, religious, and spiritual formation takes place within the life of the Church, Christ's Mystical Body on earth. It follows that the purpose of all Catholic education inevitably includes a preparation for service within the life of the Church.

The Church is in the world, and the formation of the Catholic graduate prepares him to live in that world. True, his service within the life of the Church is a kind of apostleship. But it must first and foremost be an apostleship of competence. The competent professional man, the competent accountant, the competent chemist, the thinker, writer, worker with his hands, all render service to society in this world. When that competence is imbued, permeated, motivated, and vitalized by the Incarnational view of life, then the competence itself (and therefore the total life of the graduate) becomes both service to society and service within the life of the Church.

This is precisely what the non-Catholic American college hopes will happen when it states that its goal is "the education of the whole man" and then goes on to add "for citizenship in a democratic and free society." The college expects to make a direct contribution to consistent excellence in character by a properly balanced emphasis on learning. Edward D. Eddy, Jr., in his study on *The College Influence on Student Character* concludes: "We hold, therefore, that excellence of character in the educated man depends upon a more searching, more challenging, more strenuous collegiate experience in totality. The principles which call forth allegiance in the academic community are those which may also serve to guide the man of character in the world community."[3] Briefly, then, in Eddy's view the college influence on student character may be conceived as a program of character formation through devotion to the ascetical tasks of study.

It is fitting here to give a well-deserved word of acknowledgment to the body of other denominational colleges that are also committed to moral, religious, and spiritual formation, each in its own particular way. Their presence is needed now on the American educational scene even as the presence of the Catholic college is needed. For the problem of American education which is specifically enunciated as the problem of "educating *for* democracy" grows daily more complex, more confusing, and more deeply rooted. Nor does it seem to yield to Eddy's solution of character formation through hard work.

III. Formation in American Education

Plato probably uncovered the sources of the problem best when he said that "republics must live by virtue." The young person's democratic world has built-in hazards to integrity, to honor, and to justice. When he or she sees a parent spend hours of labor falsifying tax reports; when the group accepts cheating in examinations as honorable so long as one "gets away with it"; when public servants use the public office for private gain, and, what is more, are expected by society to make a surreptitious personal profit, not only is this a challenge to our young men and women, it is most of all a challenge to the educator.

It is not the existence of immorality that gives one pause. This has been and will be in every society made up of men. What is truly frightening is the democratic student's acceptance of fraud as a legitimate way of life. This is the real cancer, a multiparous evolution of what Frank Gibney calls the Genial Society, that species of "live and let live" relationship with each other and with the government of free society, in which honor and integrity are broadly compromised and the only sin is to get caught. "Getting away with it" has become "part and parcel of a half-conscious dissociation of civil or white-collar crime from an individual's public morality. The more important the person is who gets away with it, the less people want to believe in his guilt."[4]

It would seem that American education could provide the preventive medicine necessary to counteract the carcinogens in the body of American society. And yet, it is the dilemma of the American college that its concept of "education *for* democracy" seemingly cannot properly be taught without contradicting the *Lehrfreiheit* and the *Lernfreiheit* of academic freedom. Consequently, the question of moral education remains unanswered, its need neglected. Ralph Barton Perry, Harvard's Edgar Pierce Professor Emeritus of Philosophy, looked upon the contemporary situation as the "standing paradox of education," and his analysis makes plain the reason why:

Its [moral education's] importance is pointed up by the grave crises of modern civilization. The development of technology culminating in the applications of nuclear physics threatens to destroy mankind; and they can be converted to good, rather than destructive uses, only provided they are subject to moral control. Society is threatened at home by conflict between employment and labor, and the only possible solution of the problem is a moral solution. Mankind lives under the horrid threat of a war in which all may go down together, and the only escape lies in implanting in the minds of men good will and the spirit of justice. Political democracy is profoundly corrupted by the development of the mass mind, and the only salvation of democracy is to instill in the people at large the virtue of integrity. Civil rights are perpetually jeopardized and often destroyed because the people neither understand them nor respect them. The favoritism and venality of public officials is notorious.[5]

Unfortunately, the concern of the serious educators for a moral education that would produce the virtue by which the republic must live has had no greater effect than perhaps an increased attention to "Religious Activities," "Religious Emphasis Week," Newman Centers, YMCA, and Hillel. On the plane of social studies, the Hazen Foundation made possible the work of Professor Philip E. Jacob on *Changing Values in College,*[6] which preceded the

Eddy work by two years. "Values" became the cynosure for a while, but the attention is beginning to fade. Perhaps it may be because the teaching of values has stumbled over the same obstacles that tripped moral education and have banished all moral, religious, and spiritual formation from the classroom. Thus the problem continues; and so does the spectacle of education committed at least in principle to some sort of democratic formation for citizenship, finding itself self-forced to conduct its processes as if it were uncommitted. In fact, modern American education seems to be dominated more and more by the secularist philosophy which is committed to noncommitment and absolutely rejects the absolute.[7]

IV. Pervasive Significance of Moral, Religious, and Spiritual Formation

Our intention here has been to expose in terms of the American educational dilemma the overriding relevance of moral, religious, and spiritual formation to the student in his world. And for him college is indeed a world. Richard Hughes described it well in *The Fox in the Attic:* "After all, it is only grown men ever who think of school as a microcosm, a preparation for adult life: to most boys at any time school *is* life, is itself the cosmos: a rope in the air you will climb, higher and higher and—then quite vanish into somewhere uncomprehensible anyhow."[8]

The prevailing majority of students arrive at college not only uninformed but also psychologically unformed. College may be the last and most crucial step in nature's preparation for a mature adulthood, but rare is the student who realizes it. He is still growing physically; and, if he is fortunate, college will one day suddenly awaken him to the fact that he can think. This last step, which consists in the development of his powers of abstract reasoning, frequently enough overwhelms him. With it comes the fierce striving for identity as an individual, what Rudolph Allers has termed "the formation of self."[9] And since self-realization must be accompanied by an independence which reacts at times violently against all restraint, the student usually begins at this moment to look upon all authority as evil. His parents, his faith, his conscience, the college administration, the police, sometimes even the ushers in the local movie, all take on the abhorrent aura of restrictive symbols, the authorities that keep him from doing what he wants to do and from being what he wants to be.

His own college world is not and cannot be terminal but is a preparation for something else. Its orientation is totally beyond itself. And yet, when those who have been through it try to explain the student's feelings about things in terms of their experience, the communication is at best superficial. Necessarily so, because the student cannot be expected to understand that which can only be learned by an experience he is yet to have. As one Harvard graduate reflected on this fact: "Someone could advise you from now to doomsday, unless you learn these things on your own you would not take his advice."[10]

In addition to the more personal awareness of his own growth in these matters, the coming to terms with the fact of sex, his own talents and propensities, the college student also is part of that collection of his equals in age, occupation, and interest known as the peer-group. The struggle for the esteem of the group often conflicts with the individual student's drive toward self-realization. Because the group whose respect he cherishes and hungers after is composed of individuals in exactly the same phase of life, who are undergoing the same growing pains of becoming adults, he sometimes suffers a spiritual blindness, a strange inability to evaluate. At this point and in this context, he no longer thinks for himself. All unawares he becomes a member of the class identified by David Riesman as "other-directed."[11] He becomes the non-conforming conformist, non-conforming to the authorities of the stodgy adult world, conformist even down to the minutiae of dress, hair-do, tastes, pleasures, and attitudes to the likes and dislikes of the peer-group. Students form a large segment of *The Lonely Crowd*.

All too frequently the college permits a wall of separation to be built between the academic life of the student on the one hand and his life outside the classroom on the other. The preceding chapters by Vincent O'Flaherty and P. H. Ratterman have highlighted the significance of moral, religious, and spiritual formation vis-à-vis the various student activities, religious and non-religious, that go to make up the extracurriculum. In them, one can perceive the extracurriculum as a natural extension of the curriculum, and in both curriculum and extracurriculum, the continuum of both intellectual formation and moral, religious, and spiritual formation. They are all four inseparable. They meet in the one student. Together with the home and certain other off-campus factors, they constitute the entirety of his inner and outer environment. At this stage of life, they are the shapers of the man. Leibnitz's dictum: *"Le présent est gros de l'avenir"* applies most aptly to the student's college life in its entirety.

The history of the extracurriculum in this respect makes fascinating reading. It shows, for instance, how student activity outside the classroom actually changed the character of the American college. Frederick Rudolph's history of the American college and university makes the forthright statement that "the first effective agency of intellect to make itself felt in the American college was the debating club or literary society. . . ."[12] Because the post-colonial college concentrated so vigorously on discipline and the molding of character, the students reacted by bringing reason into debates, disputations, and literary exercises. Because piety held sway in the curriculum, students reacted by enshrining intellect in their extracurricular clubs.

Students changed the college library from a collection of pious tracts to a storehouse of all knowledge simply by building up their own libraries in the literary society and later in the fraternity quarters. "In 1835 the literary societies at the University of North Carolina contained 6000 volumes, the best collection in the state. By 1840 the literary societies at Bowdoin boasted between 5000 and 6000 volumes; at Brown 3000; and at Williams 10,000. In every case, these libraries were superior to the college libraries. Works of fiction, history, politics and science were available to students because their literary societies purchased them."[13]

The literary societies enshrined intellect in opposition to piety and brought the library to the college. Their successors, the fraternities, enthroned good manners and success in this world as a reaction to the sombre other-worldliness of the pietists. Students also discovered muscle as a part of the whole man and immediately created organizations for it. This led to the rise of football and the multi-million-dollar gate receipts that have made football a kind of public possession. "Make your classes as interesting as football," was the great Knute Rockne's retort to the professors who complained of apathetic students.[14]

Contemporary college administrators have witnessed the rise of student discussion on their rights as citizens in the academic community. They are now involved in the question of student freedoms, student participation in politics and in civil rights demonstrations on behalf of the American negro—social action of every variety. Now if the moral, religious, and spiritual formation of these students is to be truly meaningful, the phenomena that accompany their activities must first be understood, and understood in the context of student life. No other avenue exists through which they can be channeled toward purposeful academic and human goals. It is a process and one that cannot be legislated, as some disciplinarians may have discovered to their regret. Rather must it be developed out of the institution's commitment to the whole man. To echo P. H. Ratterman: "How is the mature capacity to exercise freedom with responsibility to be developed on a campus where outside the classroom students are allowed no freedom and given no responsibility?"[15]

There is no facet of college student life where moral, religious, and spiritual formation is not applicable, no area in which it is not needed. And it cannot be said often enough that moral, religious, and spiritual formation must be an integral part of and flow from the intellectual formation, the ascetics of study, and the devotion of the pursuit of truth. When the Los Angeles Workshop declared: "To this formation—that is the moral, religious and spiritual formation—all the activities and all the personnel of the college must contribute according to their own natures and functions within the institution," it did in effect bestow upon all college personnel a responsibility and a share in the total educational enterprise.[16] As such, it made them all, in one way or another, directly or indirectly, educators.

It is the educator's task and his greatest challenge to reach the student, to break open new horizons for his mind and spirit, to enlarge and broaden his scope, to provide ever new and more exciting opportunities for the expansion of his intellect and the crystallization of his ideals. It is to be fondly hoped that all this will eventually be done *with* the student rather than *to* him or *at* him. For it is in this manner that he will learn the art of determining the choice of the good freely for himself. This is in the end the only valuable, lasting kind of choice, the only intelligent use of freedom.

"Formation," then, will come to mean not legislation but rather self-directed maturity, not indoctrination, brainwashing, or conformism. Formation consists rather in the internal free growth of the student founded on his nature as a student and grounded in his personal grasp of reality. Moral, religious, and spiritual formation understood in these terms brings meaning to Catholic education both as Catholic and as education. It brings a sense of deep significance to all the disciplines of classroom work and to all the activities related to student life. It communicates the necessary sense of social awareness and, among other things, guarantees the expected outcomes of professional integrity and democratic citizenship in a free, pluralistic society. In terms of his own person, it lays the foundations for the student's growth, bringing reason to his emotional life and passion to his involvement in society and to his service for Christ's Church in this world.

At its best, moral, religious, and spiritual formation produces a man formed in Christian wisdom, a man possessed of the Incarnational view of life, in a word, the fulfillment of the Los Angeles Workshop's "Profile of the Jesuit College Graduate":

The ideal Jesuit college graduate (man or woman) should have achieved a level of academic maturity consistent with certain intellectual qualities. He must have the ability to analyze, synthesize, and evaluate evidence in pursuit of truth; he must also be able to distinguish various types of evidence associated with different kinds of methodologies in the humanistic and scientific disciplines. He should have a special competence in one of these disciplines in order to give depth to his learning in one area of investigation. When in possession of evidence, he should be able to communicate it effectively. He should also have an understanding of and be able to evaluate his own culture (its literature, art, and philosophy) both in its historical development and in its present structure; he should also have some acquaintance with and appreciation of other cultures. Finally, he should have a deep understanding of his Faith that will give him a unified view of life, an awareness of the Church as continuing Christ's redemptive action; and a clear perception of his proper role as a member of the Church.

Moreover, he should be marked in the matter of personal maturity (moral, religious, spiritual development) by the following: He should be decisive in confronting life, courageous and hopeful in exercising initiative, yet loyal to legitimate authority. This will demand a positive-minded patience that is neither passivity nor abandonment of ideals. In response to the Christian vocation revealed in Scripture and Sacrament and specified by the contemporary needs and potential of the Church, he will be personally dedicated to Christ and generously committed to creative involvement and leadership in the intellectual, social, political, cultural, religious life of his world. He must also have a balanced appraisal of reality, especially of the material and the bodily, a recognition of the power and danger of evil, yet a reverence for the goodness of creation and of human achievement.

As a person he should be open in love to God and men of every race and creed; this will enable him to live sympathetically yet apostolically in a pluralistic world. He should have a developing familiarity in prayer with the three divine Persons. This will lead to liberality of mind, awareness of his Christian dignity, and freedom of spirit. Along with this he should have a balance of intellectual humility and independence whereby he respects the traditions and accomplishments of the past but is open to new ideas and developments.[17]

Notes

1. Robert J. Henle, S.J., Chairman of the Planning Committee for the Los Angeles Workshop, has already defined these terms in "A Comment on the Meaning of 'Moral, Religious and Spiritual Formation,'" *Jesuit Educational Quarterly*, XXVI (1963), 5–14. The substance of these paragraphs draws heavily from what he has said there.
2. For many of the thoughts on the Incarnational view of life, a debt of gratitude is due to Joseph F. MacFarlane, S.J., whose paper "Profile of a Jesuit College Graduate" was read at the Rockhurst College Workshop, August 25–29, 1963. The workshop was the result of a combined effort on the part of the Missouri and Wisconsin Provinces of the Society of Jesus. Its purpose was to follow up and to expand in the practical order the results of the Los Angeles Workshop.
3. Edward D. Eddy, Jr., *The College Influence on Student Character* (Washington, D.C.: American Council on Education, 1959), p. 176.
4. This is all quite heavily documented in Frank Gibney, *The Operators* (New York: Harper, 1960).
5. Ralph Barton Perry, *Realms of Value* (Cambridge: Harvard, 1954), p. 428.
6. Philip E. Jacob, *Changing Values in College* (New York: Harper, 1957).
7. Charles Donahue, "Freedom and Education," *Thought*, XXVIII (1953), 217.
8. Richard Hughes, *The Fox in the Attic* (New York: Harper, 1961), p. 110.
9. Rudolph Allers, *Character Education in Adolescence* (New York: Wagner, 1940), pp. 20–37.
10. Dean K. Whitla, "Guidance in a University Setting," *Harvard Educational Review*, XXXII (1962), 454.
11. David Riesman, *The Lonely Crowd* (New Haven: Yale, 1961), p. 76, n. 1, p. 77.
12. Frederick Rudolph, *The American College and University, A History* (New York: Knopf, 1962), p. 137.
13. *Ibid.*, p. 143. See also pp. 136–155, 373–393.
14. *Ibid.*, p. 287.
15. P. H. Ratterman, *supra*, p. 260.
16. "Statement of Positions," *Jesuit Educational Quarterly*, XXV (1963), 243.
17. *Ibid.*, pp. 244–245.

Selected Bibliography

Murray, John Courtney, S.J. "The Christian Idea of Education," in Edmund Fuller (ed.), *The Christian Idea of Education, A Seminar at Kent School* (New Haven: Yale, 1957), pp. 152–163.

Riesman, David. *The Lonely Crowd.* New Haven: Yale, 1961.

Rudolph, Frederick. *The American College and University; A History.* New York: Knopf, 1962.

Sanford, Nevitt (ed.). *The American College; A Psychological and Social Interpretation of the Higher Learning.* New York: Wiley, 1962.

Williamson, E. G. *Student Personnel Services in Colleges and Universities.* New York: McGraw-Hill, 1961.

APPENDIX

STATEMENT OF POSITIONS[1]

I. GENERAL PRINCIPLES

The Jesuit university is set within the Church, of whose mission it is a part. The mission of the Church is to produce the Christian person; the mission of the Jesuit university is to produce the educated Christian person. The university as distinct from other agencies in the Church forms students in Christian wisdom.

In the Jesuit view, education includes the development and perfecting of the total human being. Hence no education is complete unless it includes the intellectual, moral, religious, and spiritual formation of the student. Thus, the moral, religious, and spiritual formation, which is of particular importance at the collegiate level, is an over-all and essential objective of every Jesuit college. To this formation all the activities and all the personnel of the college must contribute, according to their own natures and functions within the institution.

This cardinal principle of Jesuit educational philosophy is one of the assumptions upon which the discussions of this workshop rest. The academic disciplines of philosophy and theology, which are the core of Christian wisdom, must foster the intellectual formation of the student and, in harmony with this goal and with the academic nature of these disciplines, contribute to the moral, religious, and spiritual growth of the student into personal Christian maturity.

279

II. PROFILE OF THE JESUIT
COLLEGE GRADUATE[2]

The ideal Jesuit college graduate (man or woman) should have achieved a level of academic maturity consistent with certain intellectual qualities. He must have the ability to analyze, synthesize, and evaluate evidence in pursuit of truth; he must also be able to distinguish various types of evidence associated with different kinds of methodologies in the humanistic and scientific disciplines. He should have a special competence in one of these disciplines in order to give depth to his learning in one area of investigation. When in possession of evidence, he should be able to communicate it effectively. He should also have an understanding of and be able to evaluate his own culture (its literature, art, and philosophy) both in its historical development and in its present structure; he should also have some acquaintance with and appreciation of other cultures. Finally, he should have a deep understanding of his Faith that will give him a unified view of life, an awareness of the Church as continuing Christ's redemptive action; and a clear perception of his proper role as a member of the Church.

Moreover, he should be marked in the matter of personal maturity (moral, religious, spiritual development) by the following: He should be decisive in confronting life, courageous and hopeful in exercising initiative, yet loyal to legitimate authority. This will demand a positive-minded patience that is neither passivity nor abandonment of ideals. In response to the Christian vocation revealed in Scripture and Sacrament and specified by the contemporary needs and potential of the Church, he will be personally dedicated to Christ and generously committed to creative involvement and leadership in the intellectual, social, cultural, political, religious life of his world. He must also have a balanced appraisal of reality, especially of the material and the bodily, a recognition of the power and danger of evil, yet a reverence for the goodness of creation and of human achievement.

As a person he should be open in love to God and men of every race and creed; this will enable him to live sympathetically yet apostolically in a pluralistic world. He should have a developing familiarity in prayer with the three divine Persons. This will lead to liberality of mind, awareness of his Christian dignity, and freedom of spirit. Along with this he should have a balance of intellectual humility and independence whereby he respects the traditions and accomplishments of the past but is open to new ideas and developments.

III. THE DEPARTMENT OF
THEOLOGY AND THE TEACHING
OF THEOLOGY IN COLLEGE

A. *The Department of Theology
and Its Discipline*

The theology department is an organic part of the project in learning which is the college or university. In general, therefore, it has the same basic academic responsibility towards its exacting discipline and its students as any university department, that is, it engages in teaching, in research and in the communication of knowledge and understanding.

But since theology deals with a knowledge and understanding of God's Revelation, its subject matter has unique educational implications. Revelation is not just a series of propositions directed to the intellect alone, but rather God's self-communication demanding the total human response of supernatural faith. Theology's task, therefore, is not to construct a faith; supernatural faith is necessarily presupposed in any theologizing, properly so called. Theology rather aims at a presentation and understanding of this faith-accepted communication made by God, our Salvation.

Further, since what God has revealed of Himself through Christ is not only true but good, the very understanding of this revelation carries with it an appeal to the whole person, intellect and will, already oriented through faith toward God who so reveals Himself as our final supernatural end.

The department of theology, then, best contributes to the total development of the student, including his moral, religious, and spiritual development, in the following ways:

1. by teaching theology according to its own exacting academic demands, that is, by teaching theology as an effort toward further understanding. In this way this unique subject matter can, by an in-built dynamism, release its own religious impact inasmuch as the properly academic aim of theology is to bring one to whom God has communicated Himself into more fully realized contact with this revealing God of salvation;
2. by carefully selecting themes, emphases, teaching methodology, reading assignments, etc., which are most calculated to build up the knowledge component and intelligent motivation of virtuous action, with particular reference to the needs of the American college student and the American layman in today's world.

In this context, then, we understand why the theology department's first and immediate concern is not the good Christian conduct and habits of the student. To propose its discipline in such a way would be to negate theology as an academic effort, to confuse it with ascetical exercise, and to erase the distinction between library, seminar and classroom on the one hand, the chaplain's office, confessional and chapel on the other. But most pertinently (and somewhat paradoxically), to deny theology its properly academic methodology is to militate against theology's necessary and wholly substantial contribution to the moral, religious, and spiritual development of the student.

B. *The Starting Point for the Teaching of Theology in College*

Pre-notes: (1) The starting point referred to here envisages ideally a curriculum extending through four years of undergraduate study.

(2) By starting point is meant the point at which college theology may begin, not the point at which the treatment of individual mysteries or particular courses may begin. Thus, we are not asking where to start the treatise on the Trinity; whether, for example, with the New Testament or with the Councils.

Determining the starting point for teaching theology demands the consideration of two things: the concrete situation of the student and the nature of theology.

Concerning the student, we must determine what, in view of his cultural, psychological, religious, moral, and credal situation, are his most genuine and profound needs and pre-existing problems. Then we must determine, in view of these needs and problems, the area of theology and the theological approach with which he can most profitably begin his study. In view of the psychology of learning, the student ought to begin with what is more immediate and familiar in his experience.

The nature of theology requires that theology begin within faith in the Christian mystery. Granting this faith, various approaches to the understanding of the mystery are possible, provided analysis and synthesis proceed on a basis of sufficient familiarity with the data of revelation in its historical context.

For the college student today the following are possible starting points:

1. Salvation history in Scripture. The reasons for beginning here are the following: (a) salvation history introduces the student to the privileged source of Christian teaching; (b) it need not suppose previous philosophical training; (c) it has a humanizing effect by introducing the student to the perennial concerns of the people of God in the Old Testament and in the New Testament; (d) it corresponds with the psychology of learning by beginning with the historically concrete and with familiar human experience; (e) it affords the student a knowl-

edge of the data of Christian revelation in its historical context.

2. The Church. An ecclesiological approach which begins with the study of the Church today in her existence, life, worship, and teaching, and then proceeds to an understanding of this mystery through a study of the Church's origin and development in history. The reasons for beginning here are the following: (a) the Church is the home not only in which the student lives but from which he must continually draw his Christian life and its growth, and whose life he reflects in all that he does; (b) the Church is the student's immediate point of contact with Christ as the revelation of God; (c) the Church is the immediate context in which the student will come to Christian maturity; (d) this starting point corresponds with the demands of the psychology of learning by beginning with what is more immediate in the student's experience.

Both starting points mentioned above—Salvation history in Scripture and the Church—are kerygmatic and humanistic in character.

3. The starting points of different theological syntheses; for example, the conception of the Trinity as unifying all theology (as in the *Summa Theologiae* of St. Thomas); or the conception of Christ, or the conception of the Mystical Body, or the conception of the Mass—each considered as a unifying principle of God's self-communication in history.

It would seem that the psychology of learning does not recommend the starting points of these different syntheses, at least in their present state of development, in that they begin with what is more remote in the student's experience and because an understanding of the different conceptions supposes a previous study of the history of revelation and an analysis of its content.

4. The possibility of other starting points is admitted, such as the history or sociology or phenomenology or philosophy or psychology of religion, provided these areas are undertaken as starting points within the context of Christian faith.

C. *Some Basic Themes for the*
   Teaching of Theology in College

It is believed that any program of college theology should include a treatment of the following basic themes. The list is not intended to be exclusive or complete, much less to name courses or determine the order or division of teaching:

1. The theology of the layman: treating the lay state of the Christian vocation as implying social and individual responsibilities in the world.

2. The theology of society: with particular reference to the function and limitation of authority and the full exercise of responsible freedom.

3. The theology of the Incarnation and its extension in space and time as the Church.

4. The theology of culture: the fulfillment of person through the creative use of the created universe.

5. The theology of the primacy of charity in Christian moral life so as to avoid Christian moralism.

6. The theology of the Trinitarian character of Catholic spirituality.

7. The location in history of God's Self-Revelation.

8. The liturgy as recital and re-enactment of the saving event; sacraments as mystery and encounter.

9. A theology of the faith as assent and commitment and the method of theologizing within the Faith.

IV. PHILOSOPHY

A. *Approaches and Patterns for the*
   Teaching of Philosophy in College

We approve and recommend the admissibility and the desirability of a variety of methods and approaches to achieving the basic insights and commitments proper to the *philosophia perennis*. Such a pluralism of approach recognizes the need of making philosophy relevant to our students today and makes possible the best use of the varied backgrounds of all the teachers in the Jesuit colleges and universities. This can also insure that the philosophy courses provide a strong intellectualism in the climate of flexibility and tolerance.

Besides the variety of approach in the development of a particular subject, this pluralism may also be implemented in a diversity of curricular patterns, e.g. the historical, systematic, or a combination of these, always keeping in mind the basic insights, the continuity of teaching and the necessary unity noted above. Again, with a view to relevance for our students, provision should be made within this curriculum for acquaintance of the student with contemporary philosophical views.

Without violating this admissible pluralism in approach, care should be exercised in staffing departments to select teachers who are philosophically commited to the basic insights of the *philosophia perennis,* as set forth below (in 4b).

To foster understanding and progress, the publication of papers and texts which make use of various philosophical approaches should be encouraged.

B. *Some Basic Philosophical
    Commitments*

While affirming that every living philosophy must be constantly open to philosophical insights from any source, the philosophy departments of Jesuit colleges and universities are committed to the following positions as basic to the *philosophia perennis* and normative for unity. It is not intended, however, that this statement of commitments should be the only factor in determining the number of required courses, the specific courses required, the sequence of the courses, or the approach to any particular commitment.

1. A realistic metaphysics as possible and necessary for the adequate constitution of a philosophy of created being.

2. The dualistic constitution and social nature of man, spirituality of the human soul, freedom of the will, moral responsibility based on a realistic metaphysics.

3. The existence of a personal and transcendent God known by reason.

C. Some Philosophical Problems of Particular Importance Today

In order to achieve maximum vitality for philosophy and to develop students able to contribute to the understanding of contemporary issues, it is recommended that Jesuit philosophy departments introduce students especially to the philosophical problems arising from:

1. The methodologies of the various knowledges and interests of man, e.g. science, art, anthropology, history.

2. The tension between freedom and authority.

3. The contemporary investigations of the societal nature of man.

D. The Contribution of Philosophy as an Academic Discipline to the Moral, Religious and Spiritual Development of the College Student

This statement is more of a deduction from the nature of the philosophical process as experienced in the life of the student than an empirical one. Although there is much testimony from Jesuit graduates about the good philosophy has done them, this testimony is hard to assay. Those effects of philosophy on the personal lives of students here listed are what it seems philosophy is geared to achieve, naturally tends to achieve, should most readily achieve. The statement is, as a matter of fact, as much a list of ideals to be pursued by philosophy teachers as a statement of achievement.

Inasmuch as in the present historical order philosophy by its very nature stands in an intermediate position between the other human knowledges and theology, part of its influence on the moral, spiritual, and religious formation of the student is *indirect:* that is, it derives from the fact that philosophy prepares and disposes the student for theology, and reinforces this theology. This indirect influence is not the least important value of philosophy.

Secondly, philosophy has some *direct* influence on the development of the human person. Thus: (a) certain dispositions are a natural result of the proper study of philosophy; (b) many of the truths with which philosophy is concerned have a direct relation to human conduct and action.

Among the dispositions which philosophy tends to inculcate are the following:

1. In its quest for ultimates, which is the nature of philosophy, philosophy conditions the student to become more and more wisely critical, to look for finality in things, to take the "long view," to be impatient with accidentals, to seek for essentials: i.e. philosophy tends to impart whatever qualities are implied in the virtue of wisdom.

2. Since philosophy seeks to understand all things, it tends to raise the mind to familiarity with and acceptance of the spiritual dimensions of being. This is a strong antidote to modern materialism.

3. Owing to the nature of philosophical activity, the student has the opportunity to achieve a measure of confidence in the employment of his cognitive and appetitive powers—a necessary ingredient of maturity.

4. Philosophy properly taught avoids the fixed extremes of rationalism and empiricism, and inculcates an openness of mind to truth in whatever guise it may appear. Without this disposition our graduates lose their potential effectiveness as a ferment in society. The disposition here is intellectual humility and charity.

The effective graduate will have a balance of firm convictions and of openness to further knowledge and understanding.

5. Since the introduction to philosophical thinking occurs in college at the same time as the awakening of the student's powers of higher reason, philosophy has the natural function of guiding his reason to an understanding of himself in history, so that he can make a reasoned choice for God and give a fundamental orientation to his life.

Moreover, philosophy is concerned with certain truths which of their nature pose the question of personal commitment and thus are operative in the life of the student.

Such truths, to mention a few, are: (a) his freedom of choice and personal responsibility; (b) his spiritual nature; (c) his contingency; (d) the fact of God; (e) "intersubjectivity" with all its implications of interpersonal relationships.

There may be topics now generally slighted in our philosophical teaching which merit fuller and deeper treatment than they have received in the past. For example: the nature and implications of human love, the relationship of a personal God in personal dialogue and encounter with man, morals and the politician, morals and business, the unity (international) of man, etc.

It is believed, also, that certain activities and attitudes on the part of the teacher will increase the effectiveness of philosophy in the life of the student.

a. The philosophy teacher should not only not be embarrassed to point out to the student the relationship of truths in philosophy with those of other disciplines, including theology, and with the realities of his own life, but he should actively and constantly strive to do so.

b. The philosophy teacher has the double task of developing firm convictions in his students and leaving problematic what is problematic, inviting the students to further probings.

c. Philosophy teachers should be given the opportunity and urged to teach an occasional course in the history of philosophy:

this for the teacher's own development, to cure any lingering dogmatism, etc.

d. In the sequence of the curriculum, theology and philosophy should be so arranged that theology complements, according to its nature, the incompleteness of philosophy. The students should not be left, for example, with the impression that ethics is the final orientation of his moral life.

e. For effectiveness of philosophy courses in student formation, it is essential that the teacher be deeply conscious of the moral, religious, and spiritual implications of his field.

V. THE FUNCTION OF PHILOSOPHY AND THEOLOGY IN RELATION TO OTHER DEPARTMENTS

In every college and university there can be found many reasons for improving communications between the various disciplines. But nowhere is this more evident than in Jesuit colleges and universities where the objectives include not only the intellectual development, but also the moral, religious, and spiritual formation of our students. Especially now is this integrated view needed because of the challenge of our times. It is believed, therefore, that the philosophy and theology faculties through various interdisciplinary approaches should assume the added responsibility of engaging the rest of the faculty in a dialogue that clarifies ideas and values and their relevance for other disciplines. Furthermore, if philosophy and theology are to serve as vital integrating factors in the Jesuit system of education, there is a strong need for these departments to acquaint the rest of the faculty with their programs, methods, and objectives.

In some instances, a survey course by the philosophy and theology departments, particularly for new teachers, may be given. In-service institutes or one-day workshops or panel discussions, or invited distinguished lecturers are other ways of effecting a closer relationship between these departments and other areas of the university. Continued informal interchange at a person-to-person level may be still another way.

A continuing exchange of information between the members of the philosophy and theology departments as to what each is trying to do, and exploration of ways and means of cooperation would seem essential because of the very close relationship of the two disciplines and the adjustment required by the renovation of methodology in the theology department. A program of joint departmental meetings might help to this end.

Just as philosophy and theology should make a contribution to other disciplines, so other disciplines should make a contribution to philosophy and theology. Continuing dialogue with other disciplines will also lead to a more satisfactory solution of common problems.

One way for the departments of philosophy and theology to complement the undergraduate major programs offered in other departments would be to offer courses in the philosophy of science, the philosophy of history, the theology of art, etc. Also comprehensive review courses and seminars in the senior year could include some lectures by professors of philosophy and theology who are conversant with the major field.

VI. RELIGIOUS AND OTHER
NON-INSTRUCTIONAL ACTIVITIES

A. *The Relationship of the Teaching of*
   Philosophy and Theology to the
   Effectiveness of Religious Activities

While a great deal has already been said on this point from the general standpoint of the departments of theology and philosophy, it is further felt that emphasis on certain aspects of theology and philosophy would directly increase the effectiveness of religious activities.

In the teaching of the theology of faith more emphasis could be put upon the act of faith as one of personal commitment and less emphasis upon the formal element of intellectual assent in that act. This second, less desirable emphasis tends at best to impoverish the original and biblical notion of faith, and at worst to have the student considering the act of faith as nothing more than the conclusion of a syllogistic process. The understanding of faith as personal commitment can directly render more effective the conventional spiritual activities. To take one example, for the generality of students assistance at Mass can be recognized as an especially meaningful instance of this personal commitment. Or again, for those engaged in Sodality activities, their projects can be recognized for what they are: instances, now upon the purely human level, of personal commitment. Or, finally, to take the Apostleship of Prayer, its characteristic procedures can be seen for what they are, personal commitment to a way of life that has its basis in the commitment of faith to God and God's life.

God in theology should be presented also by different and more relevant analogies than has been the custom. Here a clue could be obtained from the progressive revelation of the Godhead as recorded in Scripture, always in images meaningful to the particular cultures. Again, the psychological implications of God's revelation of Himself, especially as triune, should be brought more to the fore. The God that generates the word in the unity of love is the God students should know. Did they know that, such an activity, again, as the Apostleship of Prayer, with its inevitable emphasis on redemptive love, would gain in substance. As one participant puts it, "What is needed is the realization and not the mere knowledge of God. This should be, under God's grace, a personal conviction of each student, and the emphasis should be placed upon the fact of personal commitment. Furthermore, the implications of God's existence should be pointed out to the students when the proofs of God's existence are being studied, for example that since there is a God, who created, then there is necessarily an eternal and natural law. A practical implication of creation and conservation of each individual is the timely explanation of the true sense of vocation."

More emphasis should be placed upon the Church as an organism, and less upon its organizational characteristics. Proceeding in this way a mature and religious understanding of authority could be achieved. Similarly the ecclesial dimensions of the Sacraments should be brought to the fore, that the Sacraments are a way fitting the life of the Church, and that they all have their specific social implications; e.g., the Sacrament of Penance, in which one confesses to having offended against the co-members of this body which is the Church, that the soul in sin is a displaced member who through the ministrations of the Sacrament's grace is restored to his former position. Again the two aspects of the priesthood of the faithful, the sacrificial coming from Baptism and the prophetic function coming from Confirmation should be stressed. Here too, in the context of the theology of the Church, the Liturgy should be discussed.

The incompleteness of philosophy should be recognized: otherwise there results a rigid rationalism and a distortion of morality through the acceptance of ethics as an ultimate norm. Moreover philosophy should inculcate an awareness that there are absolutes.[3]

B. *The Contribution of Religious*
   Activities to Moral, Religious, and
   Spiritual Formation

By religious activities we mean any and all of those means provided by our colleges and universities for the specific purpose of promoting the Christian life and holiness of our students.

By formation we mean the interior results of the operation of three agencies: God, giving Himself and His grace; the administration and faculty who provide the opportunities mentioned above and guidance of the same; and the students themselves who understand them, accept and actively participate in them in such a way that they achieve their own Christian maturity by the cultivation of a vital love of God and their fellow men in personal response to Christ the King living and operating in the Church today.

Four major activities provided by the Jesuit college or university are the following:

1. *The Liturgical and Sacramental Life,* in so far as, in the words of Pope Pius X, the primary and indispensable source of the true Christian spirit is to be found in the active and intelligent participation on the part of the laity in the public and solemn prayer of the Church. In practice on campus this refers to: the Holy Sacrifice of the Mass, the Sacrament of Penance (and for the married, the Sacrament of Matrimony). It is in the Sacraments that the Christian meets the living Christ of today.

Care should be taken that the students have an opportunity to participate in the splendor of the liturgy properly celebrated.

2. *The Apostleship of Prayer.* This is a Jesuit means of developing the liturgical and sacramental life in the generality of our students. This is particularly true in the light of recent developments. Of late years the Apostleship has been given a definitely theological and liturgical cast that it lacked before. It is now centralized in the Holy Sacrifice and devotion to the Sacred Heart as explained in the *Haurietis aquas.* It is now emphasized as a way of life rather than a "devotion."

3. *Retreats.* These are the *Spiritual Exercises* which engage the student annually in a brief but intense communication with God in an atmosphere of silence and recollection. They are the means that are most conducive to aid the student to seek and know and follow the will of God in his regard.

The closed retreat should be employed wherever possible.

Directors for these retreats should be chosen for their interest and competence in communicating the kind of spirituality described in the papers of the Workshop.

4. *The Sodality.* The precise purpose of this organization on Jesuit campuses is to give to any and all who are both willing and capable of membership guidance in deeper spirituality by

means of a rule of life that leads through consecration to the obligation of striving for the greatest possible holiness and to life-long apostolic action according to one's state of life.

The Sodalities on our campuses will be effective in so far as they accept the apostolic challenge of their own environment which is that of collegiate life and all that that implies.

C. Relation of Theology and Philosophy to Non-Instructional Activities Other Than Religion

Non-religious non-instructional activities are here considered to include all aspects of student life outside the classroom which are not traditionally regarded as religious.

It should be the purpose of the non-religious activities program, as part of the total effort of the institution, to develop students who may well be trusted to conduct themselves among their peers with adequate Christian wisdom not only as students but also throughout life as citizens in a free society.

It is not to be assumed that philosophical and theological principles taught in the classroom will automatically be adopted by students outside the classroom. There is "a gnawing body of evidence which indicates that students are as likely to set the ethos of a campus as to adopt an institution-sponsored ethos, and that they are more apt to take their values from each other than from their professors and the administration."

There must be, therefore, a strong, concerted directive influence which sees to the implementation of philosophical and theological principles in student life outside the classroom. Such direction presupposes that the principles of Christian living are convincingly presented in the classroom. It is important that administration and faculty be aware of the educational significance of non-religious activities.

A well-directed program of non-religious activities should provide a proving ground where the principles learned or to be learned in the classroom are made meaningful and vital. Most important are those activities which involve students themselves in the responsibilities which accompany the making of laws and the exercise of delegated authority.

The full benefit of the non-religious activities program can only be achieved if it is structured to encourage the growth of personal and group responsibility. The atmosphere should be such as to provide opportunity for the development of leadership qualities in the student.

It is very important that students be given clear concepts with respect to the necessity, nature and limits of authority. Since a student's understanding of authority derives in large part from his experience of its exercise, it is most important that responsible agencies within the institution which exercise authority do so with full respect for the dignity, rights, freedoms and degree of maturity which individual students possess.

D. *Administration of Religious Activities*

It is clear that there should be some central authority in our colleges and universities specifically responsible for spiritual and religious life and having a stature and status consonant with the high place this life has among the goals of the institution. However, it is also clear that the description of the functions and the location of such responsibility within the structure of the institution has not been satisfactorily and adequately worked out. It is believed, therefore, that a study should be made to produce such a description of the functions and the location of this responsible authority within the structure of the college.

The Chaplain or Director of Religious Activities should also be the chairman of a special committee established to aid and advise him in his work, particularly in planning an over-all religious program for the entire year.

The administration of the college or university should encourage religious activities on campus by making provision for budget, staff, necessary facilities, attendance at conventions, etc.

Those in charge of religious activities should realize the importance of public relations and communication. This would be facilitated if discussion of both the purposes and problems of religious activities on campus were given a place in Faculty Meetings.

Notes

1. Editor's Note: Out of the papers and discussions of the workshop described in Chapter I, there developed a consensus with regard to certain basic issues and problems. Workshop participants thought many of these issues were sufficiently important to warrant the issuance of a formal statement of positions. These positions were hammered out in committee meetings and plenary sessions and finally reviewed and approved by the group as a whole. While there was general agreement on these statements, it should not be assumed that every participant subscribed to every position. There was general consensus, not absolute unanimity. In the case of most of the statements, however, the consensus was overwhelmingly in favor of the positions adopted. This Appendix omits those portions of the statement concerned with the training of philosophy and theology faculty and with the development of student personnel officers because these portions were directed to Jesuit administrators and did not have wide applicability to those in different circumstances. It should be noted, though, that the problem of manpower, both training of faculty and appropriate allocation, was recognized as one of the most important problems discussed at the workshop. Finally, it should be observed that this statement of positions is selective and is not meant to be either a complete theoretical essay or a complete and detailed blueprint for action. The full text may be found in "Statement of Positions," *Jesuit Educational Quarterly*, XXV (1963), 243–264.
2. This statement refers primarily to the Catholic undergraduate student.
3. Cf. Burlage, *supra*, pp. 181–182.

BIBLIOGRAPHY

Editor's Note: This is a severely selective bibliography intended merely to assist the interested reader in beginning a wider reading program. Most of these books contain extensive bibliographies.

Workshop Proceedings

McGannon, J. Barry, S.J. (ed.). *The Role of Philosophy and Theology in American Jesuit Colleges and Universities.* Volume II of the Proceedings of the 1962 Jesuit Educational Association Workshop. New York: Jesuit Educational Association, 1962.

McGannon, J. Barry, S.J. *Patterns in the Teaching of Philosophy and Theology in American Jesuit Colleges and Universities, 1960–61.* Volume III of the Proceedings of the 1962 Jesuit Educational Association Workshop. New York: Jesuit Educational Association, 1962.

Yanitelli, Victor R., S.J. (ed.). *Report of All Pastoral and Disciplinary ("Non-Instructional") Personnel in the Jesuit Colleges and Universities of the United States.* Volume IV of the Proceedings of the 1962 Jesuit Educational Association Workshop. New York: Jesuit Educational Association, 1962.

Henle, R. J., S.J. (ed.). *Final Report of the Workshop on the Role of Philosophy and Theology as Academic Disciplines and Their Integration with the Moral, Religious and Spiritual Life of the Jesuit College Student.* Volume V of the Proceedings of the 1962 Jesuit Educational Association Workshop. New York: Jesuit Educational Association, 1962.

Note: Volume I was a temporary book. Its contents were incorporated in Volume V.

Other Works

Deferrari, Roy J. (ed.). *The Curriculum of the Catholic College: Integration and Concentration.* Washington: The Catholic University of America Press, 1952.

Deferrari, Roy J. (ed.). *Theology, Philosophy, and History as Integrating Disciplines in the Catholic College of Liberal Arts.* Washington: The Catholic University of America Press, 1953.

298

Donohue, John W., S.J. *Jesuit Education: An Essay on the Foundations of Its Idea.* New York: Fordham University Press, 1963.

Farrell, Allan P., S.J. *The Jesuit Code of Liberal Education.* Milwaukee: Bruce Publishing Company, 1938.

Ganss, George E., S.J. *St. Ignatius' Idea of a Jesuit University.* Milwaukee: Marquette University Press, 1954.

Masterson, Reginald, O.P. *Theology in the Catholic College.* Dubuque, Iowa: Priory Press, 1961.

McLean, G. F. *Philosophy and the Integration of Contemporary Catholic Education.* Washington: The Catholic University of America Press, 1962.

The Role of Philosophy in the Catholic College: Proceedings of the American Catholic Philosophical Association, XXX (1956).

INDEX